TAX HAVENS AND THEIR USE BY UNITED STATES TAXPAYERS

by

Richard A. Gordon

With an Introduction by

Adam Starchild

Books for Business
New York-Hong Kong

Tax Havens and their Use by
United States Taxpayers
-An Overview

by
Richard A. Gordon

ISBN: 0-89499-137-X

Reprinted from the 1981 edition

Books for Business
New York - Hong Kong
http://www.BusinessBooksInternational.com

Tax Havens: Of Morality and Patriotism

Tax Havens and Their Use by United States
Tax Payers -- An Overview

Capital Preservation Through Global Investing

Offshore Asset Protection and Tax Deferral
with Portfolio Bonds

TAX HAVENS AND THEIR USE BY UNITED STATES TAXPAYERS - AN OVERVIEW

Table of Contents

TAX HAVENS: OF MORALITY AND PATRIOTISM

by

Adam Starchild

In considering the effects of a work of the scope and purpose of <u>Tax Havens and Their Uses by American Taxpayers -- An Overview</u>, it is imperative that we establish exactly what purposes tax havens are created for, and the political implications. The report examines a number of highly effective methods of tax reduction. But who really wants to reduce his tax burden?

The question may seem stupidly naive. Who doesn't want to keep more of what's his? But this sort of answer, derived from the cynical "everyone is selfish" notion is not what we are looking for.

Tax reduction as outlined in this report requires considerable initiative, alertness, determination, and dedication. Not that it doesn't pay. Sad to say, the net gain from each hour dedicated to developing a tax reduction strategy is almost certain to be higher than the net gain from an hour of productive employment. Thanks to "progressive" taxation, this goes double for someone in a relatively high tax bracket.

There is also a psychological dimension to tax reduction that must not be neglected. Most people derive a "clean" feeling from making a living through their work, but feel that there is something "dirty" about "scheming" to reduce their taxes.

Heavy taxes, whether used to provide luxury for a ruling elite or to support welfare schemes, always have the effect of penalizing individual initiative and productivity, reducing investment capital and thus the resources required for economic growth, reducing the standard of living, and forcing individuals to hide things, both activities and incomes, from the government and from one another. Heavy taxation is, therefore, a danger to the future of the high-tax countries.

Organizing a tax haven operation assumes at the outset that the underlying operation is productive (or has the potential to become so) or that assets are available for investment. It also assumes that a viable business-investment format exists in the contemporary scheme of world business; and iddeally, a plan exists that includes short - and long-range business-investment goals. In other words, a tax haven operation is not the magic formula through which something is created from nothing.

Tax lawyers and accountants usually like to stress the distinction between two seemingly similar methods of tax reduction: tax avoidance and tax evasion. It is important to understand this distinction, as well as to realize the limitations of its applicability to the ideas and information present in this book. At first glance, the distinction seems quite obvious. Tax avoidance is using whatever legal means are available to minimize a tax burden; tax evasion is the use of illegal means to the same end.

Using the services of an accountant, classifying certain verifiable expenses as "business expenses" with an acceptable, or seemingly acceptable, justification to reduce the taxable net income from one's business or profession is legal. Even if the tax authorities do not accept the validity of these deductions, and even, if worse comes to worse, all compromise attempts fail, the businessman doesn't have to fear being indicted for a criminal offense. The worst that can happen is that he will have to pay the tax he believed he didn't have to pay. This is tax avoidance.

On the other hand, willfully failing to report part of his income on his tax return or failing to comply with other reporting requirements is acting illegally. This is tax evasion.

Lawyers and accountants will explain, most sternly, that while they can help one to the best of their abilities to avoid taxes legally, by using all possible accounting tricks and legal loopholes, they will have nothing to do with tax evasion schemes. They cannot be accomplices to a crime; it could destroy them professionally, and anyway, they are law-abiding citizens. Thus, it would seem that the distinction between avoidance and evasion is important.

However, once one looks into the matter, he will discover that the distinction is far from clearcut. Vagueness, ambiguity, and holes in the law make it unclear just what and how one is legally obliged to report. For instance, a U. S. investor is legally required to report any involvement he may have as a founder, shareholder, director, or officer of a new foreign-based involvement he may have as a founder, shareholder, director, or officer of a new foreign-based corporation; or as a trustee, founder, or beneficiary of a foreign trust. Once he makes such a report, the Internal Revenue Service takes care to demand from him an annual report of profits made by the foreign legal entity, even if these profits are not distributed to him and other shareholders as income. On the basis of this report, and if the foreign corporation satisfies certain extremely complex provisions of Subpart F of the U. S. Tax Code, the investor may be taxed on that part of the profits that corresponds to his proportion of ownership of or beneficial interest in the foreign entity, even though nothing was paid to him in the United States. If he does not report involvement in the new company or trust, or doesn't report its business in a manner detailed enough to permit the IRS to infer whether he has Subpart F liabilities, or fails to pay taxes if he does have such liabilities, he is a criminal tax evader.

So what now? A lot depends on his lawyer. Still more important will be the judge's interpretation of the relevant tax code sections: complex, vague and ambiguous as they are, and his application of this interpretation to the complex facts of the case. What the judge does will depend on his legal erudition, familiarity with precedent, and political sympathies. (Is he a secret conservative with a secret dislike of the IRS? Is he a welfare statist? Is he a civil rights pioneer who believes one should pay income tax but that the IRS shouldn't violate individual privacy?) Even his daily mood can affect the outcome.

If a defendant loses the first round, he can appeal, introducing still more complexities.

The law, one's strategy, and a host of other factors may entail so much uncertainty that a harsh legal decision against the tax avoider could become unlikely. The defendant's lawyer may be convinced that his client is a genuine tax avoider, albeit a slightly clumsy one, the IRS lawyer may claim that he is an evader; the judge may reach an in-between verdict; the appeals court may reverse the trial judge; and so on. Thus, the IRS may decide that the whole matter will cost more than what the government stands to gain and try to compromise out of court, or even drop the whole thing. On the other hand, it might try to make an example of the avoider/evader, going all out to force a new precedent and thus cow potential tax dodgers, and so on. In such a case as our example, anything can happen given America's crazy tax laws, bureaucratic and political imperatives, and the imponderables of human nature. But even a clearcut, legal tax avoidance could be fought in court by the IRS and become, Wonderland-like, tax evasion.

Let us take an all too familiar example. A salesman claims as a business expense the cost of a dinner with a representative of another company in a very classy restaurant. The IRS, which has bugged the table, produces a recording of the dinner conversation to prove that the meeting was social rather than business; 95 percent of the talk was about the relative sexual merits of certain secretaries; only 5 percent was business. Did the salesman try to deceive the IRS and thereby evade taxes?

"No," he says, "it is well known in business circles that the guy I was dealing with does not sign any contract unless he is well drunk and has had an opportunity to brag about his sexual exploits. The sex talk was a necessary ingredient of business negotiations." But can he prove it? Can the IRS disprove it? Can the salesman sue the IRS for bugging the table -- a violation of his privacy -- and have the recording thrown out as evidence, voiding the case against him?

As you can see, there is no simple yes or no "criminal evasion" or "legal avoidance" answer in such situations. It all depends on the judge, the attorneys, the defendant's determination and resources, the IRS's determination and (vast) resources, the specific facts involved, the political context, and so on. Again, legal avoidance can all too easily be 1984ishly transformed into harshly penalized evasion. It can also work the other way round.

What must be borne in mind is that in practice there is a continuum between easy-to-discover tax avoidance, provable tax avoidance, and punishable tax avoidance. What one is faced with is a set of probabilities. His fate does not depend on hard and fast rules and facts, but on circumstantially determined chance. Some things he might do have very unclear legal status, and he may play for time, using complexity and good professional advice to guarantee himself almost complete safety.

Thus the most important distinction to bear in mind is that between tax reduction methods that can lead one to court and prison and those that protect one from such consequences as well as protecting the money from the taxman. The legal distinction between avoidance and evasion is the key here. If pushed, one may admit that he is involved in tax planning for tax avoidance purposes -- strictly within the letter of the law -- and that he abhors tax evasion as much as the next guy. There is no simple legal classification applicable to most approaches. Our dinner example illustrates this point. Indeed, in this typical case, would you be able to decide for certain that the classification of the dinner as business-related is or is not legally correct? Presumably, the salesman wouldn't have held the dinner for other purposes. Presumably, he would have eaten something anyway. Presumably, he did so because the other guy invited his wife at the salesman's expense, indicating he does not do business with anyone who eats out without his wife. (We are changing the story to overillustrate the point.) Who could tell? Even the salesman cannot be entirely sure about it.

To consider the question of the morality of tax avoidance, we must first set forth a working definition of the word morality. In the context of taxation, morality is not considered an absolute, but a concept which, like the tax laws themselves, is subject to interpretation. One person might argue quite convincingly that it is morally wrong to tax a working widow with children to help provide the day-to-day support for a war veteran who is able to work but prefers not to; and still another person can argue just as convincingly on behalf of the veteran. Others would argue the libertarian position that all taxation is theft.

The morality of taxation changes with the times. Prior to World War I, when taxes were comparatively low, though certainly not popular, most workers and small businessmen were exempt from the controversy by virtue of low incomes. During times of national emergency, particularly during and directly following World War II, tax avoidance was frowned upon even by those who were looking at larger tax liabilities each year. But as progressive tax rates brought taxes higher and higher each year in highly industrialized and populated nations, the attitudes of taxpayers underwent a gradual, but definitive change.

Today, even the individual worker for which the tax system is supposedly designed, can see that a tax system in which higher income brackets produce progressively higher tax rates is stulifying to individual initiative and productivity. Businessmen and corporation executives feel not only duty-bound but morally obligated to use the legal tax avoidance measures available to them. Thus, whether the loss of revenue to the nation is through the use of tax advantages internal to the nation's tax structure, or through the establishment of a tax haven company in a foreign country, the tax avoidance principle is exactly the same. From a purely pragmatic viewpoint, legal tax avoidance by a company may not be the road to wealth, but simply a means of economic survival in a time when industrially emerging nations are becoming major competiors in the world marketplace.

The "losers" in the business of tax havenry are presumed to be the heavily industrialized, heavily populated, and heavily taxed countries of the world. If two nations could personify this description, they would be the United States and Great Britain (communist-controlled nations are excluded from a discussion of tax havenry). Yet the attitudes of these governments toward tax havenry is ambivalent to say the least. The United States, for example, actually established itself as a tax haven for foreigners by not imposing a withholding tax on interest paid to foreigners on their U. S. bank deposits, and allowing foreigners to buy, hold, and sell U. S. securities without incurring a capital gains liability. There are, of course, economic reasons to justify these tax rulings (a reversal of the ruling on interest paid on bank deposits would remove billions of dollars from U. S. banks.)

As another illustration, we can consider the attitude of the U. S. toward Puerto Rico, a commonwealth in association with the United States, which has gained a reputation as a tax haven for certain U. S. industries. Nearby lies the British Virgin Islands, a British-controlled group, which has deliberately passed legislation to attract American as well as other foreign investment money. If we stand on the premise that the governments of industrialized nations are dedicated to stopping tax havenry wherever they find it, we would nevertheless have to acknowledge that an intrusion of the U. S. into the affairs of the British Virgin Islands could conceivably cause a weakening of relations between the United States and Britain; however, there would be no such restraints on the U. S. as regards Puerto Rico. And the same could be said of Great Britain: Can we believe that the British Virgin Islands, with a population of about 12,000, could establish itself as a tax-haven country without the implied consent of Great Britain?

If tax havenry takes needed revenue from industrialized nations, why then do they not only tolerate it, but seem to sanction it?

Superficially, in the case of Puerto Rico, tax havenry gives the Puerto Rican economy a boost. In the case of the British Virgin Islands (and other British territories or ex-colonies), Great Britain believes that it is best for all concerned to give the islands an autonomy in decisions concerning their internal economic development. Further, the British Virgin Islanders hope that tax havenry will provide enough external income to make the Islands independent of British grants-in-aid within the next few years. Somewhat the same situation exists with the Dutch-controlled islands that have established tax havenry to attract foreign money. This being the case, we can say that there is no external threat to tax havenry from free world nations.

Nevertheless, the ambivalence of governments of industrialized nations regarding tax havens is present. The United States, for example, finds it beneficial to spend inordinately large amounts to investigate tax fraud and evasion within the nation, and also sends agents abroad to uncover illegal tax schemes set up by Americans.

That ambivalence shows throughout this report, and by the very fact that the government commissioned such a report to begin with.

The report, by creating an impression of widespread abuse, deals with cases of fraud so prominently and frequently that it unfairly contaminates the overwhelming majority of transactions that are legitimate in all respects and are undertaken by taxpayers seeking nothing more than to exploit foreign markets for their goods and services at the the lowest cost, including the lowest tax cost. The report also distorts the effect of substantive tax rules, for example by saying the the 10% Subpart F exclusionary rule shelters "enormous" amounts of income from taxation, when in fact, that rule almost always serves only to shield relatively insignificant amounts of passive income generated from the investment of profits that are not Subpart F income. To illustrate this statement the report states that foreign subsidiaries of an unnamed domestic corporation earned gross income of "more than $1.0 billion" that was shielded from U. S. taxation. This illustration fails to state whether that level of income was earned by the subsidiaries in one year or over a number of years, and does not explain in any way why the situation was abusive. There are very few domestic corporations that have foreign subsidiaries capable of generating over $1 billion of gross sales income in a single year (or even over a number of years), so the situation must be viewed as atypical.

Similarly the report states that foreign base company sales income category of Subpart F income can be avoided merely by "structuring (the CFC) as an assembly operation rather than as a sales company," without making it clear that the regulations, supported by a decided case, make it clear that "minor" assembly operations will not avoid such categorization.

It is fair to state that the situation is not as dire as the report would have its readers believe and that the proper response to the real problems presented in the report should be a calm and well-reasoned one not influenced by an undue sense of urgency or impending calamity. Unfortunately, the congressmen to whom this report is addressed are unlikely to take it that way.

TAX HAVENS AND THEIR USE BY UNITED STATES TAXPAYERS -
AN OVERVIEW

Introduction

This study was undertaken at the request of the Commissioner
of Internal Revenue, the Assistant Attorney General (Tax
Division), and the Assistant Secretary of the Treasury (Tax
Policy).

The purpose of the study was to develop an overview of
tax havens and the use of tax havens by United States taxpayers.
The study sought to determine the frequency and nature of
tax haven transactions, identify specific types of tax haven
transactions, obtain a description of the United States and
foreign legal and regulatory environment in which tax haven
transactions are conducted, describe Internal Revenue Service
and Justice Department efforts to deal with tax haven related
transactions, and to identify interagency coordination
problems.

Our findings are based on a review of judicial decisions
and published literature in the field of international tax
planning, research into internal IRS documents concerning
taxpayer activities, interviews with IRS personnel, personnel
who deal with tax haven issues for other Federal government
agencies, and lawyers and certified public accountants who
specialize in international taxation. Our findings are
also based on a statistical analysis of available data
concerning international banking, United States direct
investment abroad, and foreign investment in the United
States. While we cannot claim that we uncovered all of the
methods employed to use tax havens, we believe that our
inquiry was extensive enough to give us an understanding of
the situation and to enable us to develop options which
might be useful in improving the administration of the tax
laws as they apply to tax havens.

The findings and recommendations of this report are
directed to six main areas:

First, identifying tax havens, the policy issues raised
by them, and the concerns of other countries;

Second, describing the patterns of use by United States
and foreign persons and presenting options for curbing that
use should that be desired;

Third, describing patterns of use to evade United
States taxes;

Fourth, describing the impact of United States income
tax treaties on tax haven use;

Fifth, describing the United States information gathering
capability, the problems caused by limitations on our information
gathering ability, and presenting options for improving
United States information gathering;

Sixth, an analysis of the administration of the tax
laws and presenting options for improving that administration.

A number of government professionals contributed substantial
time and effort to the study. These include, George Bagley,
Clyde Donald, Vince Gambino, Ross Summers, and Bill Wells of
the IRS, Jack Feldman, Kenneth Klein, Mike Patton, and
Alban Salaman of the Office of the Chief Counsel IRS, and
Ron Cimino and Richard Owens of the Tax Division of the
Department of Justice. Roy Richards served as the research
assistant. H. David Rosenbloom, Thomas Horst, and Joel Rabinovitz
of the Office of the Assistant Secretary of the Treasury
(Tax Policy) provided useful comment and criticism of the
report. One of the most important parts of the study was
the effort to quantify the use of tax havens. The effort
was directed by Berdj Kenadjian with the help and assistance
of the IRS Unreported Income Research Group and the IRS
Statistics Division. The special efforts of Marie Yauss who
typed and retyped numerous drafts of this report are gratefully
acknowledged.

The study could not have been completed without the
support of former Commissioner of Internal Revenue,
Jerome Kurtz.

The statements of positions on legal issues in this
report are the positions of the Special Counsel for International
Taxation and are not necessarily those of the IRS or any
other agency of the Federal government.

I. Overview of Findings and Options

International tax avoidance and evasion, including the use of tax havens to avoid or evade United States taxes, have been of long-standing concern to the Congress and tax administrators. Numerous provisions have been added to the tax laws to limit such use, and to limit the erosion of the United States tax base. In 1921, the Congress focused on foreign subsidiary corporations that were used to "milk" United States parent corporations. In the 1930's the Congress focused on individuals creating incorporated pocketbooks in tax havens and transferring assets to tax havens to avoid paying United States tax on the appreciation. In 1962 the Congress focused on perceived abuses by multinational corporations. In 1970 the Bank Secrecy Act imposed reporting requirements on transactions which were believed to be particularly susceptible to abuse. In 1976 the Congress dealt with the use of foreign trusts.

The use of tax havens to evade United States tax has been of special concern to the Internal Revenue Service. Beginning in the mid-1950's and continuing through the 1970's the IRS conducted numerous special projects and investigations which sought to identify taxpayers using tax havens to avoid United States taxes. Today the IRS devotes substantial resources to international transactions through general civil and criminal programs and through special programs. The use of tax havens to aid in the commission of nontax crimes, including narcotics trafficking, has also been of special concern to other Federal agencies.

Foreign governments have also been concerned with the use of tax havens to avoid or evade their taxes. Some countries have adopted legislative provisions intended to limit the use of tax havens by their nationals. Many of these provisions are based on United States law.

Nevertheless, legal and illegal use of tax havens appears to be on the increase. The available data and interviews with practitioners, IRS personnel, personnel from other agencies and representatives of foreign governments support the view that taxpayers ranging from large multinational companies to small individuals to criminals are making extensive use of tax havens.

The study was limited to transactions involving countries having (1) low rates of tax when compared with the United States, and (2) a high level of bank or commercial secrecy that the country refuses to breach even under an international agreement. Several additional characteristics of most tax havens include: (a) relative importance of banking and similar financial activities to its economy; (b) the availability of modern communication facilities; (c) lack of currency controls on foreign deposits of foreign currency; (d) self-promotion as an offshore financial center.

Today, many tax havens thrive largely because of the presence of foreign banks. The existence of this financial business brings an economic advantage to the tax haven in terms of jobs and revenue. The resulting highly developed and sophisticated banking and communications infrastructure in the tax havens also makes it possible to move illegally earned income swiftly and efficiently.

The decision of a country not to tax transactions or to attempt to attract offshore financial business is a legitimate policy decision. When local laws and practices deny information to countries whose tax base is being eroded or whose laws have been violated, a situation exists that attracts criminals and is abusive to other countries. Most tax havens have strict secrecy provisions and will not cooperate with other countries seeking to enforce their laws.

The data support the perception that activity through tax haven entities has increased, and that tax haven entities are increasingly diverting capital away from entities formed in economically advanced countries that have highly developed systems of taxation.

In 1968, according to IRS data, the total assets of foreign corporations controlled by United Stated corporations and formed in tax havens were $11.7 billion, representing 12.1 percent of the worldwide assets of United States controlled foreign corporations. By 1976 these amounts had risen to $55.4 billion and 17.6 percent.

Commerce Department data, while based on a different universe, confirm these trends. Those data show a steady growth in direct investment levels in United States-controlled tax haven businesses from $4.7 billion in 1968 to $23 billion in 1978, a five-fold increase. For the same period, direct investment levels in nontax haven business grew from $57.2 billion to $145.1 billion, an increase of two-and-a-half times.

Over the same period, Commerce Department data show earnings of tax haven entities increasing from $0.5 billion to $4.4 billion -- a nine-fold increase -- while earnings of nontax haven entities were increasing from $6.0 billion to $21.3 billion, or by three and a half times. Ownership by United States persons of tax haven subsidiaries has increased more than ownership of nontax haven subsidiaries.

The data tend to confirm that some industries use tax haven entities more than other industries. For example, in 1976 United States-controlled tax haven corporations engaged in the transportation business had assets of $9.0 billion, which represented 74.2 percent of the assets of United States controlled foreign corporations in the transportation business. The comparable figures for contract construction were $2.2 billion and 41.8 percent. Assets of United States-controlled tax haven companies engaged in finance, insurance, and real estate, including banking, were $20.9 billion, which represented 28.0 percent of the assets of United States controlled foreign corporations in that business. In 1976, $2.4 billion or 23 percent of the assets of United States-controlled foreign corporations engaged in providing services were held by tax haven corporations.

Banking activity in tax havens has also grown. Total deposits in banks in the tax havens surveyed were $385 billion in 1978; deposits by nonbanks were $89 billion of this amount. Comparable figures for year-end 1968 were $11 billion and $5 billion, respectively.

The extent to which tax havens are being used by narcotics traffickers and other tax evaders, including those earning legal income, could not be quantified reliably. Data concerning illegal use of tax havens are often soft or unavailable. The report does, however, refer to a methodology that might be a first step in making an estimate. Present currency flow projects may also help. The perception is that such use is large and is growing.

There is a wide range of use of tax havens by United States persons. While many attribute evil motives to any such use, this is not the case. Some use is for criminal purposes, but much is perfectly legal. In some cases the tax consequences of the tax haven transactions reflect clear congressional decisions as to the scope of United States taxing jurisdiction.

From a tax planning point of view, tax havens, in and of themselves, do not provide a United States tax advantage; the United States tax advantage is provided only in combination with both the United States system of deferral of taxation of earnings of foreign corporations and the United States system of consolidated worldwide foreign tax credits.

Often whether a transaction is tax avoidance or tax evasion is difficult to determine, in part because the terms are not well defined, and in part because the law governing the transactions is imprecise and the information incomplete. There also are many grey areas. Tax havens transactions can be loosely categorized as follows:

(1) Transactions that are not tax motivated and may have no United States income tax impact. Such use includes branch banking that may avoid United States reserve requirements but has little impact on United States income tax liability. A tax haven subsidiary may be used to avoid currency and other controls that may be imposed by countries in which the company is carrying on business. It may also be used to minimize the risk of expropriation of business assets. A foreign person may use a tax haven bank or nominee account to shield assets from political oppressors.

(2) Transactions that are tax motivated, but consistent with the letter and the spirit of the law. Examples are shipping, banking through subsidiaries, sales by tax haven subsidiaries not involving related parties as well as taking advantage of certain de minimis exceptions to anti-tax haven legislation. While some of these uses create anomalous situations, they are legal. For example, a United States taxpayer has sheltered over $100 million in passive income in a foreign company the income of which is not taxable under the anti-avoidance provisions of the Code.

One of the most common tax motivated but legal uses of a tax haven subsidiary is to shift United States source income to foreign source income to increase the amount of foreign taxes paid by a United States taxpayer that can be credited against, and thus reduce, United States taxes otherwise payable by the taxpayer.

(3) Aggressive tax planning that takes advantage of an unintended legal or administrative loophole. Examples are the use of captive insurance companies, the use of investment companies, some forms of service and construction businesses being conducted through tax haven entities, as well as a wide range of aggressive transfer pricing situations.

(4) Tax evasion--an action by which the taxpayer tries to escape legal obligations through fraudulent means. Fraudulent use includes marketing so-called "double trust" schemes involving attempts by United States persons to transfer United States assets to tax haven trusts. It also includes marketing tax shelters, including certain questionable commodity transactions, to United States persons through a tax haven in order to hide the fact that the transactions that are allegedly creating losses do not take place. One tax straddle shelter may have involved as many as 1500 investors and deductions of as much as $150 million.

Fraudulent use has also included forming sales companies that are structured to appear to deal only with unrelated parties but that in fact are dealing with related parties, forming corporations to appear to be banks, hiding the fact of ownership of tax haven corporations, the use of a Cayman Islands corporation by a United States person to hide corporate receipts and corporate slush funds.

Tax havens may be used to commit crimes that violate tax as well as other laws. The most serious fraudulent use of this kind is by narcotics traffickers to accumulate or launder large sums. Often phony shelter schemes violate securities as well as tax laws. Shell banks established in St. Vincent have been used to defraud United States banks and other businesses.

The provisions of the tax law that apply to international transactions in general and to tax haven transactions in particular are among the most complex in the Internal Revenue Code. The two most important provisions affecting tax haven transactions are subpart F, which taxes United States shareholders of a United States controlled foreign corporation on certain categories of income, and section 482, which authorizes the Commissioner to reallocate income among related entities to properly reflect their income. Both of these provisions are primarily transactional in nature, that is, each separate transaction must be analyzed to determine its tax effect. Also, the foreign personal holding company provisions and the foreign trust provisions may apply.

The proper administration of subpart F and §482 often requires IRS access to detailed books and records which are not always available. The complexity coupled with information gathering problems makes the law in this area extremely difficult to administer.

Income tax treaties with tax havens are often used by residents of nontreaty countries to achieve a reduction in United States tax. The United States has a large and growing network of income tax treaties mostly with other high tax countries, but about 16 treaties are with tax havens. Many of the tax haven treaties are the result of the extension of the old United States-United Kingdom treaty to former United Kingdom colonies. The treaty with the Netherlands Antilles is in force as a result of the extension of the United States-Netherlands income tax treaty. United States treaties with Luxembourg, the Netherlands and Switzerland were independently negoiated.

There is significant use of tax haven treaties for investment in the United States. In 1978, 43 percent of the gross income paid to all nonresidents of the United States was paid to claimed residents of tax havens. Forty-six

percent of the gross income paid to residents of all treaty
countries was paid to claimed residents of tax haven treaty
countries. Nearly 80 percent of all United States gross
income paid to residents of tax havens and reported to the
IRS was paid to corporations. All of this indicates significant
third-country use of tax haven treaties.

Third-country residents use tax haven treaties primarily
to minimize tax on income from United States investments by
a combination of reduced rates of tax on income paid from
the United States, the low rate of tax in the tax haven and
the low rate of tax on distributions to the investor from
the tax haven. The use of tax haven treaties includes
forming conduits in the tax haven to lend into the United
States, the use of holding companies engaging in back-to-
back licensing and lending transactions, real estate investment
and finance companies established by United States corporations
to borrow abroad free of the United States withholding tax.
There is some evidence of use of tax haven treaties to evade
United States tax.

In order to administer the tax laws and to prosecute
those who evade their tax obligations, the IRS and Federal
prosecutors must have access to relevant information. The
ability of the IRS to gather information is severely limited
where international transactions in general and tax haven
transactions in particular are involved. With respect to
legitimate business transactions, information-gathering
problems include the existence of multiple overlapping
forms, the sometimes inaccessability of adequate books and
records of overseas entities, the uncertainty of the extent
of the United States Government's powers to compel production
of books and records maintained in tax havens, the ability
of taxpayers to use the court system to delay the production
of records and some intentional procrastination and delaying
tactics by some taxpayers.

Reports of currency transactions with domestic financial
institutions have been helpful in developing some criminal
cases, but more work is needed to improve the quality of the
information and the dissemination of the information.
Reports of transportation of currency into and out of the
United States and reports of interests in foreign bank
accounts have not been particularly useful to date.

Substantive laws are not the direct impetus to illegal
activity, although complicated laws are more susceptible to
abuse. The problem is getting information to tie the
United States taxpayer to funds accumulated in or routed
through a tax haven so that a prosecution for tax evasion is

possible. Lack of meaningful exchange of information is the real problem and that lack encourages abuse. The IRS does not have available the process of the courts to command the production of records that are in the hands of third parties in the tax havens. Even if information is obtained, it is rarely in a form admissible in United States courts.

Exchange of information provisions in the existing tax treaties with tax havens are simply inadequate because they do not override local bank or commercial secrecy laws. In any event, the United States does not have treaties with most tax havens. The only mutual assistance treaty in force to which the United States is a party is with Switzerland, and it has not been useful for dealing with tax crimes.

There also are some administrative problems with the international enforcement of the tax laws, such as achieving effective coordination among international enforcement functions. Further, the volume of transactions with which the IRS must deal continues to grow, but the resources devoted to auditing international transactions have not kept pace with the growth in international trade, and many smaller cases, which can be the most abusive, do not receive expert attention. The international experts are not trained in the kinds of abusive transactions used by individuals such as partnerships and trusts. It is difficult for criminal and civil agents to get competent, expeditious, technical help in the field without going through a formal referral process.

The Chief Counsel's Office also has the problem of diffused technical expertise in the international area. Additionally it has no easily accessible central focus of international information gathering expertise.

It can be argued that the basic reason why there continues to be so much tax haven activity is the lack of effective administration by all nations, coupled with taxpayer awareness of that lack. The central issue then becomes whether the present legal structure is administerable or whether it should be changed regardless of other policy concerns because it is not administerable.

There exists the potential for a serious abuse of the United States tax system through tax havens. What is needed is a coordinated attack on the use of tax havens, including better coordination and funding of administrative efforts to deal with tax haven problems, and perhaps substantive changes in United States law and treaty policy. In order to deal with these problems, consideration of the options set forth is recommended. While some options can be accomplished administratively, others would require legislation or changes in existing income tax treaties. We recognize the existence of policy considerations in addition to tax considerations. The following options are presented purely from a tax administration point of view. Some of them would apply to international issues in general, because it does not make sense to limit them to tax havens.

The adoption of many of the options set forth in the report will require that more resources be devoted to international enforcement efforts. Today the IRS does not have the additional resources. If decisions are made to adopt options which require additional resources, the Congress will have to make the resources available.

The United States alone cannot deal with tax havens. The policy must be an international one by the countries that are not tax havens to isolate the abusive tax havens. The United States should take the lead in encouraging tax havens to provide information to enable other countries to enforce their laws. For example, the United States could terminate tax treaties with abusive tax havens, increase the withholding tax on United States source income paid to tax havens and take other steps to discourage United States business from using tax havens. However, such steps taken unilaterally would place United States business at a competitive disadvantage as against businesses based in other OECD countries. Accordingly, a multilateral approach to deal with tax havens is needed.

The more important options, summarized below, as well as others, are presented in more detail in the following chapters:

.Chapter VII - options for administrative and legislative changes to deal with technical problems;

.Chapter VIII - options for changes for tax haven treaties;

.Chapter IX - options for information gathering;

.Chapter X - options for administration of the tax system.

Options That Can Be Adopted Administratively. The following options could be accomplished administratively:

1. To make clear the obligation of taxpayers to produce the books and records of foreign subsidiaries, publish regulations requiring that books and records of foreign

corporations controlled by United States persons be maintained in the United States regardless of foreign laws, unless those books and records are made readily available to examining agents on demand.

2. To encourage agents to insist that taxpayers meet their burden of substantiating deductions, valuations, or pricing, give clear directions to the field as to actions to be taken by agents to deny deductions or reallocate income where a taxpayer has not met the burden of proving the tax consequences of a transaction.

3. To ease the administrative burdens of complicated and lengthy audits, study the §482 regulations to determine whether clearer more administerable rules are possible.

4. To address the problem of unauthorized use of treaties, change the present system of withholding of tax on payments of fixed and determinable income to foreign persons to a refund system.

5. To simplify reporting obligations of taxpayers, and to make the reporting more useful to the IRS, combine into one form the existing hodge-podge of international forms that a United States person investing overseas must file.

6. To improve coordination with respect to international issues in general, and tax haven issues specifically, the Assistant Commissioner (Compliance) could study ways of improving coordination among the various international functions and could consider creating a group to coordinate tax haven issues and collect and disseminate tax haven information.

7. To enable the IRS to provide expert coverage to tax haven cases outside the large case program, expand the IRS International Examination program and give the examiners additional training in partnerships, trusts, and tax treaties.

8. To provide better information gathering guidance to field agents and to District Counsel trial attorneys, designate a person in the National Office of the Chief Counsel as the international information gathering expert.

Legislative Options:

1. To relieve some of the administrative burdens and to give more certainty to transactions involving controlled foreign corporations formed in tax havens, expand subpart F to add a jurisdictional test that would tax United States shareholders of a controlled foreign corporation formed in a tax haven on all of its income.

2.   To enable the IRS to deal better with tax haven businesses that are in fact run in the United States, add a management and control test to the present jurisdictional tests for subjecting corporations to United States tax.

3.   To simplify and rationalize the taxation of tax haven income, eliminate some of the overlap among the provisions which deal with tax havens by combining the foreign personal holding company provisions with subpart F.

4.   To emphasize that the burden of proving the substance of tax haven transactions is squarely on the taxpayer, provide for the specific disallowance of a tax haven related deduction unless the taxpayer establishes by clear and convincing evidence that the underlying transactions took place, the substance of those transactions, and that the amount of the deduction is reasonable.

5.   To discourage taxpayers from taking overly aggressive positions on the chance that they will not be identified, provide for the imposition of a no-fault penalty of a fixed percentage of a large deficiency resulting from a tax haven transaction.

Treaty Options:

1.   To deal directly with United States tax treaties with tax havens, terminate the existing income tax treaties with the Netherlands Antilles and the United Kingdom extensions and consider terminating income tax treaties with other tax havens, with possible renegotiation.

2.   To prevent future abuse, be selective in negotiating income tax treaties with countries with which the United States does not have a significant trade or investment relationship, and do not enter into full scale income tax treaties with known tax havens. As an alternative, selectively enter into limited treaties with tax havens that would include a nondiscrimination provision and a competent authority mechanism and would contain an exchange of information provision overriding bank secrecy laws and practices.

3.   To ensure that information necessary to administer the tax laws is available, and to insure that information necessary to prosecute those who do not comply with those laws is available, insist upon a strong exchange of information provision in United States income tax treaties that would override foreign bank secrecy laws and practices.

4. To deal with changes in local laws and practices of
treaty partners, conduct periodic reviews of treaties to
determine whether they are being abused and whether they are
serving the function for which they were initially negotiated

5. To provide access to information to be used in
criminal prosecutions, vigorously pursue mutual assistance
treaties with the more important tax havens.

6. To encourage abusive tax havens to enter into
exchange of information agreements with the United States,
consideration may have to be given to adopting measures to
discouraging United States business from investing through
tax havens that do not give information, such as increasing
taxes on payments to those tax havens.

7. To limit the potential for abuse of treaties with
tax havens, and to limit the incentive for treaty partners
to adopt tax haven practices, incorporate strong provisions
to limit the use of treaties to residents of a treaty country

II. Tax Havens - In General

In this chapter, an attempt is made to set out the principal characteristics of tax havens, to explain some of the background, and to present some of the issues raised by tax havens from the perspective of the tax haven. The concern of countries other than the U.S. and some of the steps which they have taken to deal with tax havens is also described.

A. Characteristics

The term "tax haven" has been loosely defined to include any country having a low or zero rate of tax on all or certain categories of income, and offering a certain level of banking or commercial secrecy. Applied literally, however, this definition would sweep in many industrialized countries not generally considered tax havens, including the United States (the U.S. does not tax interest on bank deposits of foreigners).

The term "tax haven" may also be defined by a "smell" or reputation test: a country is a tax haven if it looks like one and if it is considered to be one by those who care. Many publications identify jurisdictions as tax havens, and the same jurisdictions generally appear on all of the lists.[1]

Most jurisdictions which are considered tax havens have at least some of the characteristics described below. All, however, offer low or no taxes on some category of income, as well as a high level of confidentiality to banking transactions.

Many countries having tax haven characteristics are often bases for minimizing taxation on various types of perfectly legal income and activities. These same countries provide anonymity sought by persons evading tax laws. Accordingly, there is a problem when looking at tax havens of combining legitimate and illegitimate activities and confusing the former with the latter. Care should be taken to avoid this.

1/ See, for example, M. Langer, Practical International Tax Planning, 278, 279 (2d ed. 1979); B. Spitz, Tax Haven Encyclopaedia (1975).

1. Low Tax

   Many of the jurisdictions that are considered tax
havens do impose taxes. All, however, either impose no
income tax on all or certain categories of income, or impose
a tax which is low when compared to the tax imposed by the
countries whose resident taxpayers use them.

   Some jurisdictions do not impose income taxes, or
impose very low rates of tax. In the Caribbean, the Bahamas,
Bermuda, the Cayman Islands, and the Turks and Caicos do not
impose any income or wealth taxes. In some cases the tax
situation may be part of a policy to attract banking, trust
or corporation business. In other cases it may exist because
the country never found the need to impose tax.

   Often, low tax rates are considered an evil. However,
many tax havens are small less-developed countries whose
residents are generally poor. In many cases, the small
population of the country makes an income tax system impractical
Instead, the country will establish a license or fee system
for generating revenue. Instead of imposing an income tax,
fees can be charged for bank licenses, commercial charters,
and the like. Administration costs of collecting those
revenues are kept to a minimum.

   Often jurisdictions, while imposing significant domestic
taxes, impose low rates on certain income from foreign
sources, a tax system used by a number of developed high tax
countries (such as France) as well as by some tax havens.
Panama is an example. Accordingly, a local corporation can
be formed and managed in the tax haven with no tax being
paid to the tax haven on its income from other jurisictions.

   Some tax havens impose low rates of tax on income from
specific types of business. Some jurisdictions, for example,
offer special tax regimes to holding companies, making them
especially useful as financial centers or situs for holding
companies.

   Some tax havens combine their tax system with a treaty
network. This combination can make them a desirable situs
for forming a holding company to invest in a treaty partner.

2. Secrecy

   By definition, all of the jurisdictions with which we
are concerned, afford some level of secrecy or confidentiality to persons transacting business, particularly with
banks. This secrecy has its origin in either the common law
or in statutory law.

Common law secrecy is found in those jurisdictions which were or still are British Colonies. It derives from the finding of an implied contract between a banker and his customer that the banker will treat all of his customer's affairs as confidential. If violated, an action for damages for breach of contract lies against the banker.

Many jurisdictions have confirmed or strengthed the common law rules by statute, and have added criminal sanctions for breaching secrecy. In many cases the law was strengthened to maintain or improve the particular jurisdiction's competitive position. For example, in 1976 the Cayman Islands, which had strict bank secrecy before, tightened its laws by adding more substantial sanctions against persons divulging most banking and commercial information.[2] This tightening was a reaction to <u>United States v. Field</u>,[3] in which the U.S. court directed a Cayman resident to give testimony concerning bank information before a U.S. grand jury, even though the testimony would violate the bank secrecy laws of the Cayman Islands and would subject him to limited criminal penalties.

Some level of secrecy is a characteristic common to both tax havens and non-tax havens. Most countries do impose some level of protection for banking or commercial information. At the same time, however, many countries will not protect information from a legitimate inquiry from a foreign government, particularly where that inquiry is made under a treaty. Tax havens, however, refuse to breach their wall of secrecy, even where a serious violation of the laws of another country may be involved. The distinction is between unreasonably restrictive rules of bank secrecy which

---

[2] Langer and Walker, "The Cayman Islands - An Important Base for Foreign Companies," <u>U.S. Taxation of International Operations</u>, ¶ 8503, Prentice Hall (1978).

[3] United States v. Field, 532 F. 2d 404 (5th Cir. 1976); <u>cert. denied</u>, 429 U.S. 940 (1976).

may encourage the commitment of international tax and other
offenses, and those which pay due regard to the protection
of individual privacy,[4] but which also permit legitimate
inquiry in appropriate cases.

Secrecy is most troublesome when a violation of U.S.
criminal laws is under investigation. It also presents
significant problems to IRS when it attempts to audit legal
transactions. The secrecy may be used as an excuse by a
taxpayer not to produce records, or it may present real
problems preventing IRS access to records.

3. Relative Importance of Banking

Banking tends to be more important to the economy of a
tax haven than it is to the economy of a non-tax haven.
Most tax havens follow a policy of encouraging offshore
banking business. This is done by distinguishing between
resident and nonresident banking activity. Generally,
nonresident activity will not have reserve requirements,
will be taxed differently (if at all), and will not be
subject to foreign exchange or other controls.

One test of the importance of banking to an economy is
the relationship of foreign assets of banks in a country to
that country's foreign trade. When compared to foreign
trade, foreign assets of deposit banks in tax haven jurisdictions
were substantially greater than foreign assets of deposit
banks in non-tax havens. Special statistics developed to
measure the excessive holdings of foreign assets of tax
haven banks indicate that these excess assets[5] are very
large, and have been growing at a rapid rate. For all tax
havens surveyed[6] excess foreign assets grew from $16.7

4/ See Recommendation 833 (1978) on Cooperation Between
Council of Europe Member States Against International
Tax Avoidance and Evasion, ¶¶ 4 and 11(i).

5/ Excess assets are those above the worldwide average
of foreign assets of deposit banks to worldwide
foreign trade. The amount above what this ratio would
yield was the excess assets for that jurisdiction. For
example, 1978 total foreign assets held by deposit banks
in the Bahamas were $95.2 billion. Based on the world-
wide average of deposits to world trade, $1.8 billion
was needed to finance the foreign trade of the Bahamas.
The difference, $93.4 billion, represents excess inter-
national assets and is an indication of assets attracted
because of the tax haven status of the jurisdiction.

6/ For this purpose, Bahamas, Bermuda, Cayman Islands, Hong
Kong, Luxembourg-Belgium (the foreign trade data for the
two countries could not be separated), Netherlands
Antilles, Panama, Singapore, and Switzerland.

billion in 1970 to $272.9 billion in 1978. During the same
period, excess foreign assets in tax havens, as a percentage
of foreign assets held worldwide grew from 12.5 percent to
29.1 percent. When all jurisdictions were compared, only
13 out of 126 have foreign assets which are excessive relative
to the world average in 1979. These 13 are the tax haven
jurisdictions studied and the United Kingdom and France.
The U.K. is an offshore financial center itself, and its
data include the tax havens of the Channel Islands and the
Isle of Man which could not be separated from all other U.K.
data. France has excess deposits, largely because export
financing aid is handled through private banks.

The importance of U.S. banks to the major Caribbean financia
centers is growing. For example, from 1973 to 1979, total assets
of U.S. bank branches increased nine times in the Cayman
Islands, eight times in the Bahamas, and four times in
Panama.[7]

The banking industry has a significant effect on the
economy of the tax haven. Financial business yields revenues
in the form of fees and modest taxes on financial institutions.
The tax haven also benefits from employment of personnel and
rental of facilities. The Bahamas Central Bank estimated
that expenditures of banks and offshore branches in the
Bahamas in 1975 was $32,886,000, including $18,330,000 for
salaries. Licenses and other fees amounted to $1.5 million,
and the banks employed 1,890 (1,650 Bahamians) people.[8]
Informed sources estimate that by early 1978, the banking
sector may have employed 2,100 people (1,897 Bahamians),
paying them salaries in excess of $26 million per annum. An
additional 10,000 jobs may have been indirectly supported.

A comparable survey of the Cayman Islands indicates
that, in 1977, total operating expenditures by Cayman branch
banks were $10.2 million, of which $5.3 million were for
salaries. These branches paid $1.6 million in fees and
employed 433 people, of whom 298 were local citizens.[9]

7/ See Hoffman, Caribbean Basin Economic Survey,
    Federal Reserve Bank of Atlanta, May/June/July 1980,
    at 1.

8/ C.Y. Frances, Central Banking in a Developing Country
    with an Offshore Banking Centre, Central Bank of the
    Bahamas (1978).

9/ Cayman Islands, Department of Finance and Development.

4. Availability of Modern Communications

Many of the countries considered tax havens have excellent communictions facilities, particularly good telephone, cable and telex service linking them to other countries. They may also have excellent air service. For example, the Cayman Islands has excellent telephone and telex facilities. In fact, telephones in the Caymans can be direct dialed from the United Kingdom and Canada. There are two daily non-stop jet flights between Miami and the Caymans, and direct service between Houston and Grand Cayman.

5. Lack of Currency Controls

Many tax havens have a dual currency control system, which distinguishes between residents and non-residents, and between local currency and foreign currency. As a general rule, residents are subject to the currency controls; non-residents are not. However, non-residents will normally be subject to controls with respect to local currency. A company, formed in the tax haven, which is beneficially owned by non-residents and which conducts most of its business outside the tax haven, is generally treated as non-resident for exchange control purposes. Accordingly, a foreign person can form a tax haven company to do business in other jurisdictions. It will not be subject to the tax havens' exchange countrols as long as it is dealing in currency of other jurisdictions and is not doing business in the tax haven.

These rules are adapted to facilitate the use of the tax haven by a person wishing to establish a tax haven corporation to do business in other jurisdictions.

6. Self Promotion - Tax Aggression

Most tax havens seek financial business and promote themselves as tax havens. Considering the potential advantages of attracting financial business, this is an understandable activity from the point of view of the tax havens. Many of these countries view financial business as a relatively stable source of revenue and will actively seek it. Barbados, for example, recently passed banking legislation intended to improve its competitive position as a financial center. Many jurisdictions conduct seminars, and their officials collaborate in articles extolling the virtues of the particular country as a haven. Some tax havens do not hide their disdain for the concerns of other countries in this regard.

7. Special Situations - Tax Treaties

Most well known tax havens do not have an extensive network of tax treaties. There are, however, some exceptions. Knowledgeable persons consider the Netherlands to be a tax haven, notwithstanding its sophisticated and well administered tax system and high tax rates. This is because of its network of income tax treaties, its special holding company legislation, and administration of its tax laws to facilitate the use of Netherlands companies by third country residents. The Netherlands Antilles has an income tax treaty with the U.S., and special Netherlands legislation, similar in effect to a tax treaty, gives the Antilles a tax treaty relationship with the Netherlands.

B. Background

Tax havens, or something like them, have been used for centuries. While some tax havens have evolved through a history of laissez-faire economic policies, others, particularly those specializing in attracting corporations, have been created as a matter of deliberate government policy.[10]

1. Historical Background

People have been looking for ways to avoid taxes for many years. Likewise, governments have been using tax incentives to attract or maintain business for many years.

For example, the ancient city of Athens imposed a tax on merchants of two percent of the value of exports and imports Merchants would detour twenty miles to avoid these duties. The small neighboring islands became safe havens in which to hide merchandise to be smuggled into the country at a later date.[11] In the middle ages, the City of London (as well as other jurisdictions) exempted Hanseatic traders resident in London from all taxes.[12]

In the fifteenth century, Flanders (now Belgium) was a thriving international commercial center. Its government imposed few restrictions on domestic or foreign exchange and

10/ C. Smith, Tax Havens, 1-4 (1959).

11/ D. Wells, Theory and Practice of Taxation, 91 (1900), (Wells).

12/ C. Doggart, Tax Havens and Their Uses, 1-5 (1979), (Doggart).

freed much trade from duties. English merchants supplied the needed raw materials, preferring to sell wool to Belgium rather than to England where they would incur numerous duties.[13/]

Holland (which some consider a tax haven today) was a tax haven during the sixteenth, seventeenth, and eighteenth centuries, applying a minimum of restrictions and duties. The commerce attracted made its ports important.[14/]

International tax avoidance is not new to the U.S. In 1721, the American colonies shifted their trade to Latin America in order to avoid paying duties imposed by England.[15/] The tax morality which developed from this avoidance of English duties has been described as follows: "The fact that the colonists were constantly evading the navigation acts, and made no pretense of paying the duties imposed by England must have had a demoralizing effect, and taught them to evade duties imposed by their own lawmakers . . . ."[16/]

2. Modern Background

The prototype of the modern tax haven is Switzerland, which developed as a "haven" for capital (rather than as a "haven" from tax) for those fleeing political and social upheavals in Russia, Germany, South America, Spain and the Balkans.[17/]

Today, most major havens are also offshore financial centers, that is centers for international borrowing and lending in non-local currency. International banking dates back to the Renaissance, and modern international banking to the early nineteenth century.[18/] Initially, European banks

---

13 A. Barton, World History for Workers, 52 (1922).

14/ Wells, at 74.

15/ Hill, Early Stages of the United States Tariff Policy, 36.

16/ Id. at 36.

17/ Doggart, at 1.

18/ This portion of the report is based to large extent on J. Sterling, Unpublished thesis, John Hopkins University.

grew and branched out to finance the burgeoning international trade. The Bank of Nova Scotia, Canada's second oldest and fourth largest chartered bank, opened its first office in the Caribbean in 1889 in Jamaica.[19]/

Offshore financial centers really began to grow in the 1950's. After World War II, eurocurrency lending (lending by a bank in a currency other than that of its country of residence) grew rapidly. In the 1950's a European market for dollars outside of the U.S. developed. The uncertain world situation, the increased awareness of corporate treasurers of the advantages of depositing dollars abroad (higher interest), and other factors led to an escalating growth in this market. The imposition by the U.S. of the Interest Equalization Tax (IET) in 1963, the increased sophistication of American banks, and the increasing credit controls imposed by the U.S. helped the market to grow. The web of rules in the mid 1960's, including the voluntary Foreign Credit Restraint Program (VFCR) in 1965 and the Offices of Foreign Direct Investment (OFDI) regulations, which required U.S. persons investing abroad to borrow abroad, really launched the offshore market. It was this latter provision which most increased the offshore market. In 1969, the Federal Reserve Board agreed to permit the establishment of shell branches abroad so that smaller banks could compete in the international financial market. Most of these shell branches are in the Bahamas or the Cayman Islands.

3. Present Situation

Today, tax havens thrive in large part because of the presence of foreign banks. As described above, the existence of this financial business clearly brings an economic advantage to the haven in terms of jobs and revenue. It may stimulate tourism and attract wealthy retirees who spend their money in the haven. The financial activities create an infra-structure which can be used by criminals to hide money as well as by legitimate businesses.

C. Reasons for Use of Tax Havens

Before describing the U.S. tax system as it applies to tax haven transactions, it is useful to attempt to understand why business is done there. Obviously, the low rates of tax afforded by tax havens are an inducement. There are, how-ever, uses which do not appear to have a significant tax impact. These include:

19/ See The Bank of Nova Scotia Annual Report, 1978.

(1) confidentiality;

(2) freedom from currency controls;

(3) freedom from banking controls, particularly the reserve requirements.

(4) receipt of higher interest rates on bank deposits and to borrow at lower interest rates.

Often the physical location is not important. Obviously, if one is running a hotel in the Bahamas one must be in the Bahamas, but if one is participating in the Eurodollar market one can do it from New York as well as from Nassau.

Today, most large banks have branch offices in the Bahamas and the Cayman Islands. They are there primarily to participate in the Eurodollar market free of U.S. control. Often they take dollar deposits from foreign persons and lend them to their foreign customers, who are often subsidiaries of U.S. companies. These transactions could be done in the U.S., but the deposits would be subject to reserve requirements imposed by the Federal Reserve. Under these requirements, a portion of any deposit must be held and cannot be lent out, thus that reserved portion cannot produce income. Accordingly, it is more profitable to operate overseas where as much of a deposit as a bank wishes can be lent or invested.

A stable tax haven might also be preferable as a cor- porate situs if one is conducting an active business in a potentially unstable country. For example, a U.S. company wishing to engage in the heavy construction industry in a less developed unstable country, could do so by forming a Bahamian subsidiary, which would then make the investment in that unstable country and conduct the operation. Any profits and assets which need not be maintained physically in that country could be moved out and kept in a branch bank in the Bahamas. In this way, the risk of an expropriation is minimized. By forming a corporation in a tax haven, there is no additional level of tax on the profits, and there is little danger of income being blocked by the imposition of currency controls.

Another reason to use a tax haven is anonymity. Bank secrecy prevents the country in which a tax has been evaded or another crime has been committed from obtaining the documentary evidence needed to prosecute the offender. The huge volume of financial transactions conducted in a tax

haven also gives a certain level of confidentiality to
transactions. Accordingly, a criminal may use a high volume
financial center tax haven such as the Cayman Islands because
the Cayman Islands will not divulge bank information, and
because his transactions are indistinguishable from and can
be lost among other legitimate transactions.

D. Foreign Measures Against Tax Havens

The use of tax havens to avoid or evade taxation is a
problem which affects almost all developed and developing
countries. Problems of international evasion are not new.
In fact, the first tax treaty signed August 12, 1843, was an
agreement concerning administrative assistance between
Belgium and France.[20] Attempts to deal with tax havens
have been undertaken unilaterally, as well as on a bilateral
and multilateral basis. The concern about tax havens is
illustrated by a German-French Memorandum on Tax Evasion
and Avoidance on the International Level.[21]

1. Unilateral Approaches

The developed countries have taken steps to deal with
tax havens. Most have been through tax legislation; some
have involved currency controls.

a. Tax Legislation

Many of the legislative initiatives of other countries
are based on U.S. legislation. Provisions similar to subpart
F (which taxes U.S. shareholders on certain income of controlled foreign corporations) exist in the tax laws of
France, Germany, Canada and Japan.

(i) Provisions similar to subpart F. Under the German
provision, the passive income of a controlled foreign corporation
is deemed to accrue to German shareholders if the income is
subject to a low tax rate, which is defined as a total tax

20/ Manual for the Negotiation of Bilateral Tax Treaties
     Between Developed and Developing Countries, United
     Nations Publications, ST/ESA/94(1979), 29. For a
     historical overview of bilateral and multilateral
     efforts to deal with international evasion and avoidance
     see id, at 29-32.

21/ 14 European Taxation, No. 4, 136 (April 1974).
     The concern with tax havens was made especially clear.

burden of less than 30 percent. The control requirement is satisfied if the German shareholders have more than one-half of the control of the foreign corporation. The existence of a treaty containing the "affiliation privilege," (which treats the income from a foreign subsidiary as tax-exempt in the hands of the German parent company if such company holds a participation of at least 25 percent in the foreign subsidiary) prevents the application of this provision.

The Canadian provision requires that the Canadian shareholder of a controlled foreign affiliate include in income "foreign accrual property income" in proportion to participation. "Foreign accrual property income" includes the affiliate's income from property and businesses other than active businesses, as well as capital gain which is unrelated to active business activity. The percentage ownership required for control, in order to be treated as a shareholder, is similar to that under U.S. law. Like the U.S. and unlike the other provisions modeled after subpart F, there is no requirement that the foreign affiliate be located in a low tax country, or that the income of the foreign affiliate be subject to a low tax.

The Japanese anti-haven law basically provides that Japanese income tax shall be imposed currently upon the pro rata share of the undistributed income of so-called "specified foreign subsidiaries" attributable to Japanese resident or corporate shareholders owning, directly or indirectly, 10 percent of the total shares of the foreign subsidiary. Under the statute, a "specified foreign subsidiary" is defined as a foreign corporation or other legal entity more than 50 percent of the issued shares of which are owned, directly or indirectly, by Japanese residents or by corporations which have a Japanese resident shareholder who owns or belongs to a family shareholding group owning, directly or indirectly, 10 percent or more of the total shares issued by the foreign subsidiary, and which is incorporated in a low tax country. Determination of the latter is to be made by the Minister of Finance on a case-by-case basis.

An exemption from the Japanese statute is provided if the foreign subsidiary: is not a mere holding company; has a physical facility in its country of residence necessary for its business activities; has local management and control; engages in its business activity, principally with unrelated parties or in its country of residence, depending upon the type of activity; has not received greater than five percent of its gross revenues in the form of dividends from other "specified foreign subsidiaries." The Japanese provision, unlike the U.S. subpart F provision, does not define particular types of activities as "tainted," but instead treats certain companies, namely those incorporated in low tax countries, as "tainted." However, the activities of the "specified foreign subsidiary" are crucial to the determination as to whether an exemption is to be applied.

The French provision provides that where an enterprise liable for corporate tax owns, directly or indirectly, at least 25 percent of the shares of a corporation based in a country with a privileged tax regime, the French enterprise will be taxed on the profits (whether or not distributed) of the foreign company in proportion to its rights in the foreign company. The standard used in determining whether a country has a privileged tax regime is whether that country's tax on income and profits is notably less than the French tax. The provision will not apply if the enterprise satisfies the tax authorities that the foreign country is actually engaged in industrial or commercial activities predominantly with unrelated parties.

(ii) <u>Transfer pricing</u>. Most developed countries have adopted transfer pricing rules giving their tax administrators the authority to reallocate income or scrutinize transactions between related parties and disallow costs which are determined not to be arm's length. These provisions apply generally, and are not focused particularly on tax haven transactions.

(iii) <u>Transfers of property abroad</u>. The United Kingdom taxes a United Kingdom resident who has the power to enjoy the income of a foreign person (including a foreign corporation or trust). The income is treated as income of the resident. For it to be taxed, it must have arisen from assets transferred out of the United Kingdom. The provision also treats as income of a U.K. resident any capital sum (including amounts categorized as a loan) that a U.K. resident is entitled to receive with respect to the property transferred, to the extent of income generated by the transferred property. Therefore, if property is transferred abroad by a U.K. resident to a foreign trust and the U.K. resident receives money in the form of a loan from the foreign trust, the amount received by the U.K. resident will be taxed to him to the extent of any income of the trust. This provision should be compared to § 679 of the Internal Revenue Code, which treats a U.S. person who transfers property to a foreign trust as the owner of the portion of the trust attributable to such property, if for such year there is a U.S. beneficiary of any portion of the trust.

The Netherlands has neither a specific provision aimed at tax haven abuse, nor anything comparable to subpart F. However, the transfer of property by Dutch citizens to a foreign corporation which accumulates portfolio income is treated as a sham transaction by the Dutch authorities. The effect is that the foreign corporation would be treated as a Dutch corporation or merely as a collection of Dutch individuals

(iv) <u>Provisions relating to deductions</u>. Specific tax provisions denying deductions with respect to activities carried on in low tax countries exist under French and Belgian law. The French tax code provides that interest, royalties, or consideration for services paid by a person domiciled or established in a foreign country which has a privileged tax regime are deductible for tax purposes, only if taxpayers prove that the expenses incurred correspond to actual operations, and are not abnormal or exaggerated. The definition of privileged tax regime, for purposes of this provision, is a country in which the tax on profits or income is noticeably less than taxes in France. Belgian law contains an almost identical provision. Under both provisions, the burden of proof as to the deductibility of the payments made to the foreign entity shifts to the taxpayer. This is contrary to many other French tax statutes.

The purpose of the French and Belgian provisions, limiting or denying payments with respect to low tax countries is to prevent the taxpayer from deducting payments made to persons in countries with a privileged tax regime for facilities or overvalued services rendered, since the taxpayer must prove that such operation is a normal one. The French tax authorities have found the provision quite effective. However, it deals with merely one part of the tax haven problem. In the normal situation, the aim is to avoid tax on the income generated by the transferred property, rather than to obtain a deduction for facilities provided or services rendered by the foreign entity.

(v) <u>Expatriation</u>. Under German law, a provision similar to §877 of the Internal Revenue Code applies to German citizens or former German citizens who transfer their residence from Germany to a low tax country and who, for five out of the last 10 years, were German citizens or subject to German tax as residents. If such individual

28

retains a significant economic interest in the Federal Republic of Germany or West Berlin after transferring residence abroad, and if the transfer is to a low tax country (a country imposing less than 2/3 of the tax imposed by Germany), then such individual is subject to extended tax liability as a nonresident (which involves taxation of German source income but without certain exemptions available to a nonresident who did not emigrate).

The United Kingdom, under the Capital Transfer Tax Act, imposes a tax on the transfer of property situated in the United Kingdom. The provision applies to a domiciliary, even if he is no longer resident in the United Kingdom. The provision was enacted to prevent a domiciliary from transferring domicile and thereby avoiding all tax on non-U.K. assets. If, however, the individual is not living in the U.K., there is a practical problem of obtaining information to enforce the provision, and of collecting the tax unless assets are still in the U.K.

Under Canadian rules, an individual who expatriates from Canada is subject to a tax on the appreciation of his property on the date he expatriates. The tax is imposed on an amount equal to the value of the property less its basis.

(vi) Special provisions. France has a specific provision aimed at preventing artists incorporating themselves in low tax countries and performing services in France. Under the provision, if proceeds are received by a corporation ("artist corporation") or other legal entity which has its seat of management outside of France in consideration for services rendered by persons domiciled in France, the proceeds are taxed to the persons domiciled in France if: (1) such persons participate, directly or indirectly, in the management, control, or capital of the foreign legal entity; (2) if the persons domiciled in France do not prove that the foreign legal entities are engaged in an industrial or commercial activity other than the rendering of services; or (3) in any case in which the foreign legal entities have their seats of management in a country which is not linked to France by an income tax treaty or has a privileged tax regime. Therefore, if a corporation has its seat of management in a tax haven country and receives payments for services rendered in France by a domiciliary of France, the income received from the rendering of the services is taxed to the individual domiciled in France.

b. Non-Tax Measures

Control of tax haven abuse has not been limited to tax
legislation. Australia dealt with tax haven activities
through foreign exchange controls. Under Australian law, a
transfer of funds overseas requires bank clearance. Under
the Banking Act, the reserve bank is required to refer to
the Australian Commissioner of Taxation any applications
made to the bank for authority to deal in any jurisdiction
listed as a tax haven. The Taxation Department has the
authority to issue a certificate, and may refuse to issue
the certificate if the taxpayer does not satisfy the
Commissioner that the actions proposed in connection with
the application will not involve the avoidance or evasion
of Australian tax. The foreign exchange controls through
the banking system and the requirement of a tax certificate
for transfers to tax haven countries are the principal
methods used by Australia in controlling tax haven abuses.

There is no provision in Australian law comparable to
subpart F; foreign trusts are not regulated, since transfers
are regulated; and there are no provisions restricting
deductions with respect to activities carried on in tax
haven countries. The Australian Government believes that
such provisions are unnecessary, because the foreign exchange
controls and the requirement that a tax certificate be
obtained insure that only bona fide activities in tax haven
countries would be permitted in the first place. However,
notwithstanding the controls, circumvention is possible if
a transfer were made to a non-tax haven country followed
by a transfer to a tax haven country.

France also has exchange controls which regulate the
transfer of property outside of France, but the controls are
general in nature and are not specifically directed at tax
haven abuses.

c. Effectiveness

The effectiveness of legislation against tax haven
abuse varies from country to country. Australian tax authorities
believe that foreign exchange controls and the elimination
of certain Australian territories as tax havens has been
very effective in combating tax haven abuse. However, it
was not clear that this has completely solved the problem.
For example, money could still be invested in a non-tax
haven country and then transferred to a tax haven.

The German experience with tax haven legislation adopted in 1972 has been positive. Prior to its enactment, the German tax authorities had to rely on general principles of tax law. This gave rise to a great deal of litigation and mixed success in courts. The litigation difficulties resulted in a reluctance of German tax authorities to pursue cases of tax haven abuse. With the enactment of the 1972 legislation, the tax administration has actively pursued cases of tax haven abuse. They have noted an increased willingness of taxpayers to settle rather than litigate, and also have noted a decline in use of holding companies in tax havens. Despite the effectiveness of the legislation, there remains a significant problem of illegal transfers and the use of the secrecy laws of tax havens to conceal the transfer of assets.

The French and Japanese provisions modeled after sub-part F are new, and it is too early to ascertain their effectiveness. As discussed previously, France has a provision which shifts the burden of proof to the taxpayer with respect to deductions taken relating to activities in tax haven countries. France has found this provision an effective tool to prevent French taxpayers from deducting payments made to persons in countries with a privileged tax regime for facilities or overvalued services.

Even though the recent tax haven legislation enacted in Western Europe and Japan gives the tax administrations the legal tools necessary to fight tax haven abuse, problems remain due to the circumventing of the provisions by illegal and fictitious transfers and the use of secrecy laws existing in tax havens to frustrate tax authorities.

2. Multilateral Approaches

In the past decade, the growing concern with inter-national tax evasion and avoidance in general, and tax havens in particular, has led to various efforts.

The only multilateral convention dealing specifically with international tax evasion and avoidance is the Con-vention on Administrative Assistance in Tax Matters Concluded by Denmark, Finland, Iceland, Norway and Sweden. This convention was signed on November 9, 1972, and supplemented in 1973 and 1976.

In 1975, the European Economic Community adopted a resolution on measures to be taken to combat international tax evasion and avoidance. The Council of the Community, on December 19, 1977, adopted a directive concerning mutual assistance on direct tax matters.

In April of 1978 the Parliamentary Assembly of the Council of Europe adopted a recommendation on cooperation between Council of Europe member states against international tax avoidance and evasion.[22/] This recommendation recognized an increase in international tax avoidance and evasion, and a lack of efficient cooperation between European tax administrations. The Parliamentary Assembly recommended that the European countries conclude a European multilateral agreement on combating international tax evasion and avoidance, including an exchange of information. It also urged member governments (which include Switzerland) "to abolish unduly strict rules on bank secrecy, wherever necessary, with a view to facilitating investigations in cases of tax evasion or concealing income arising from other criminal activities, while paying due regard to the protection of individual privacy." The Council also recommended that member countries refrain from enacting holding company legislation and take actions to make it more difficult for multinational companies to use tax havens.

The Assembly of the Council of Europe held a colloquy on international tax avoidance and evasion from March 5 to 7, 1980, in an attempt to define international tax evasion and avoidance issues, which might be handled multilaterally, and to define approaches to the problems. The colloquy focused on the relative advantages and difficulties of bilateral as opposed to multilateral cooperation.

The OECD also has addressed the problem of tax avoidance and evasion. The OECD Council adopted, on September 21, 1977, a recommendation calling upon member governments to strengthen their powers to detect and prevent international tax avoidance and evasion, and to develop exchanges of information between tax administrators. A working party of the OECD Committee on Fiscal Affairs is presently considering this problem.

22/ Recommendation 833 (1978).

III. Statistical Data on Patterns of Use of Tax Havens

The data relating to the volume of tax haven use are
summarized in this chapter. The data are not all inclusive.
For each of the categories the available data for the most
important tax havens for that category were included.

A. Levels of Use by U.S. Persons Through Tax Haven Companies

Data on direct investment in tax havens are summarized
below. The data are taken from forms filed by U.S. shareholders of controlled foreign corporations and from surveys
conducted by the Commerce Department. There are large gaps
in data on the direct investment of U.S. persons which are
not corporations. Accordingly, levels of investment through
tax havens is probably understated.

Use of tax havens by U.S. persons is large and apparently growing. The available data, and interviews with
practitioners and IRS personnel, have shown that taxpayers
ranging from large multinational companies to small individuals
are making extensive use of tax havens.

Direct investments in particular are growing much
faster than similar activity in the non-havens. Commerce
Department data reflected in Table 1 show that in 1968 U.S.
direct investment levels in tax haven corporations was $4.7
billion, which represented 7.6 percent of total U.S. direct
investment in U.S. controlled foreign enterprises. In 1978,
U.S. direct investment in tax haven enterprises was $23.0
billion, representing 13.7 percent of total U.S. direct
investment in U.S. controlled foreign enterprises. Between
1968 and 1978, the data show an increase of almost five
times in U.S. direct investment in business formed in tax
havens and about a two and a half times increase in investment
in non-tax haven businesses.

Commerce Department data in Table 1 show that the
earnings of U.S. controlled businesses formed in tax havens
increased from $0.5 billion in 1968 to $4.4 billion in 1978,
an increase of nine times. During the same period, earnings
of U.S. controlled businesses formed in non-tax havens
increased three and a half times from $6.0 billion to $21.3
billion.

These trends are more pronounced in some of the better
known tax havens. For example, direct investment levels in
foreign businesses formed in the Bahamas increased from less
than $0.4 billion in 1968 to $1.8 billion in 1976, approximately
a five fold increase. Over the same period, however, earnings
of those businesses increased seventeen times, from $44 million

to $746 million. In Bermuda, direct investments increased
from $0.2 billion in 1968 to $7.2 billion in 1978, a 37 fold
increase, while earnings increased from $25 million to $959
million, or 38 times. Most of the increases in Bermuda
occurred between 1972 and 1978, which partially reflect the
growth in captive insurance business.

IRS data in Table 2 are limited to figures reported on
the Form 2952 filed by corporate U.S. shareholders of controlled foreign corporations. These data show a similar
trend between 1968 and 1976.[1] There is also evidence that
tax haven jurisdictions are increasingly diverting U.S.
capital away from economically advanced countries that have
highly developed systems of business taxation. In 1968 U.S.
controlled foreign corporations formed in tax havens had
assets of $11.7 billion, which represented 12.1 percent of
the assets of all U.S. controlled foreign corporations. In
1976, such corporations had assets of $55.4 billion, which
represented 17.6 percent of the assets of all U.S. controlled
foreign corporations. IRS data show an almost five fold
increase in the assets of U.S. controlled corporations
formed in tax havens, and a three fold increase in the
assets of non-tax haven corporations.

IRS data in Table 2 show the industrial composition of
controlled foreign corporations formed in the tax havens.
The data indicate that the composition in tax havens differs
from the composition in non-tax havens. For example, assets
of manufacturing companies as a percent of assets of all
companies formed in the tax havens was 13.7 percent in 1976.
In non-tax havens, it was 54.8 percent. In tax havens, the
combined total of assets in finance, insurance and real
estate, wholesale trade, transportation (essentially shipping),
construction and services--typical tax haven industries--was
81.2 percent of total assets. For companies formed in non-
tax havens, for the same year, it was 37.8 percent.

1/ 1976 is the last year for which IRS data are available.

Another indication of relative tax haven use is the
pattern of growth in U.S. ownership of foreign corporations.
Data for the period 1970-1974, and 1974-1979 are taken from
Table 3. These data show that for the period 1970 to 1974
the number of wholly or almost wholly owned tax haven subsidiaries decreased by 2.9 percent, while the comparable
number of non-tax haven subsidiaries increased by 7.6 percent.
For the period 1974 to 1979 this trend reversed. The number
of wholly or almost wholly owned tax haven subsidiaries
increased by 42.7 percent, and the number of wholly owned
non-tax haven subsidiaries increased by 26.4 percent.

The available figures for U.S. investment in other
foreign corporations have always shown a great pro-tax haven
bias. For the period 1970-1974, the number of tax haven
corporations in which U.S. persons owned an interest of 5 to
50 percent increased 164.8 percent, while the increase in
non-tax havens was 57.8 percent. From 1974 to 1979 the
increases were 36.4 percent in the havens and 17.1 percent
elsewhere. Patterns of growth in foreign corporations where
the U.S. interest is from over 50 to 94 percent, reflect a
similar pro-tax haven bias.

There are other indications of significant and increasing
usage of tax haven corporations to conduct business outside
of tax havens. In 1979 U.S. persons owned five percent or
more of the stock of 10,400 tax haven corporations and
52,000 corporations formed in non-tax havens. The relative
importance of those figures is more meaningful when looked
at in terms of ratios of corporations to population. In
1979, there were 55.1 such corporations formed in tax havens
per 100,000 population, and only 1.2 corporations per 100,000
population in non-tax havens. These represent increases
from 32.9 in tax havens in 1970 and from 0.9 in non-tax
havens.

The growth in ownership of Western Hemisphere tax
haven companies is even greater. In 1979 there were 108.1
foreign subsidiaries of U.S. persons per 100,000 population,
about 40 more than in 1970. In non-tax haven areas of the
Western Hemisphere the growth was negligible, from 2.0 per
100,000 of population in 1970 to 2.1 in 1979.

B. Levels of Use by Foreign Persons

Foreign investment in the U.S. through tax havens is
more difficult to measure. The indirect measures from IRS
data on non-resident alien gross income paid by U.S. payors,
and incomplete data from the Commerce Department on direct
investments in the U.S., indicate that the level of inward

investment from the tax havens is very high. In 1978, U.S.
gross dividends, interest and other income payments to
recipients in the havens increased $1.9 billion. These
sums as a percentage of total such payments to all non-
resident aliens were 42 percent. In 1978, payments to
Switzerland alone were about $1.2 billion, which was 26
percent of payments to all non-resident aliens. Payments to
the Netherlands Antilles was another $0.2 billion, which
accounts for an additional four percent of the total.
Thus, there is at least an indication of third country use
of tax havens for investment in the U.S.

A large portion of foreign capital invested in the U.S.
from the tax havens is flowing through business organizations. In 1978, nearly 80 percent of all U.S. gross
income paid to the havens and reported to the IRS on Forms
1042S went to foreign corporations.

The use of income tax treaties with tax havens, and the
relevant data, are discussed in Chapter VIII.

C. Levels of Use by Banks

The presence of international banking facilities is
essential to tax haven use. Initially, in most instances,
assets which are to be invested abroad through a tax haven
would move through the international banking system. The
international deposits by non-banks held in banks resident
in tax havens is a major use of tax havens to hold assets.
Accordingly, this study attempted to measure levels of
banking activity in the tax havens.

The estimates were developed from national source data
in the tax havens, where available, as well as from Federal
Reserve data. In the few cases where complete national
source data were not available estimates were made.

Data for this discussion are taken from Table 4. These
data show that total deposits in banks resident in the tax
havens surveyed were $385 billion dollars at year end 1978.
This figure includes deposits by other banks as well as
deposits from non-banks. Deposits by non-banks were $89
billion at year end 1978. Comparable figures for year end
1968 were $11 billion and $5 billion respectively. The data
show a sustained very rapid growth throughout this period.
This growth occurs both before and after the rapid escalation
in the price of petroleum.

The growth appears to be even more rapid in the case of
deposits in banks resident in the Western Hempishere tax
havens,[2] particularly in the case of deposits by non-banks.

_____

2/ Primarily the Bahamas, the Cayman Islands, and Panama.

At year end 1978 total deposits in these banks (by both banks and non-banks) were $160 billion, and total deposits by non-banks were $32 billion. Most deposits in banks resident in Western Hemisphere tax havens are in branches or subsidiaries of U.S. banks. The Western Hemisphere data are particularly relevant to the U.S. Since to a great extent, the data reflect U.S. use of tax haven banking facilities. This is because of the conveniences of using Western Hemisphere tax havens, including the fact that they are in or near the same time zones as the major money center banks in the U.S.

D.   Levels of Use by Tax Evaders

In the course of this study members of the Unreported Income Research Group of the Internal Revenue Service attempted to estimate the levels of use of tax havens to further non-compliance with U.S. tax laws. Because of the lack of available information, it was not possible to develop reliable estimates. Currency flow projects now underway hopefully will develop data that, when combined with other information, including data developed for this study, will throw some light on illegal use of tax havens.

While the study did not estimate the use of tax havens to hide evasion money, it did develop a methodology which, given a firm commitment of resources over a few years, might be extended to estimate noncompliance as a residual derived from total tax haven funds. If this approach were used, it would first be necessary to estimate total foreign assets in tax havens, including nondeposit assets. (The methodology developed for this study resulted in reliable estimates mainly relating to international deposits held in or through tax havens.) Then, it would be necessary to subtract: (1) funds invested in the tax havens which do not belong to U.S. persons, and (2) funds invested in tax havens which are legally earned and reported to tax authorities.

Another problem with estimating the use of tax havens by tax evaders is that funds may be "laundered" by being deposited in a tax haven bank and immediately withdrawn. The volume of these kinds of transactions is almost impossible to measure because neither data nor adequate methods to estimate such flows are available.

The study team did estimate important aspects of tax haven use, but because of significant data gaps, could not develop a total estimate. Firm evidence was found that total tax haven deposit assets were at least $118 billion at the end of 1978. The findings on Swiss banking data give some insight into the use of tax havens to achieve anonymity. Swiss banks maintain three types of accounts: regular deposit accounts, fiduciary accounts, and security-advisory accounts. Fiduciary accounts consist almost entirely of

deposits by non-residents of Switzerland which are deposited
in banks outside of Switzerland. The deposits are generally
in the name of the Swiss bank, but for the account and the
risk of the depositor. The Swiss banks charge a fee of
between 1/8 and 1/2 percent of the amount of the deposit for
this service. Because this deposit in non-Swiss banks could
be made directly, it can be assumed that a significant portion
of deposits in these accounts belong to persons seeking
secrecy. It is reported that as of the end of 1978 deposits
in fiduciary accounts totaled $29.3 billion.

The security-advisory accounts are essentially trust
accounts which are expensive to maintain. The proceeds of
these accounts are not usually deposited in other banks, but
are used to invest in other financial or fixed assets.
There are no data for these accounts, although based on
estimates[3] and information provided by some knowledgeable
sources, it may be estimated that total assets may range
between $60 and $140 billion. These accounts may hold
bearer shares, and are recognized as an important factor in
the Eurobond market. In any event, such figures could be
used at least to estimate the levels of haven use to buy
anonymity.

3/ M.S. Mendelsohn, Money on the Move, 221 (1980).

38

Table 1

U.S. Direct Investments Overseas in Tax-Haven[1] and Other Areas, 1968-78
(In Million Dollars)

	1968	1970	1972	1974	1976	1978
Tax-Haven Areas						
Earnings of U.S.-controlled foreign business enterprises	469	657	1,012	2,543	3,116	4,354
Reinvested earnings of incorporated affiliates (subsidaries)	202	321	447	892	1,303	1,916
Levels of investment in U.S.-controlled foreign business enterprises	4,697	5,829	7,329	12,053	15,804	23,022
Other Areas						
Earnings of U.S.-controlled foreign business enterprises	6,017	7,366	9,788	16,599	15,912	21,280
Reinvested earnings of incorporated affiliates (subsidaries)	2,238	2,855	4,085	6,885	6,393	10,147
Levels of investment in U.S.-controlled foreign business enterprises	57,210	69,651	82,549	98,025	121,005	145,059

1/ The tax havens covered are: Bahamas, Bahrain, Bermuda, British Islands (covering Anguila, Antigua, British Antilles, British Virgin Islands, Cayman Islands, Monteserrat, Nevis, St. Christopher, St. Lucia and St. Vincent), Costa Rica, Hong Kong, Liberia, Liechtenstein, Luxembourg, Netherlands Antilles, Panama, Singapore and Switzerland.

Source: U.S. Department of Commerce, Bureau of Economic Analysis, unpublished tabulations and Selected Data on U.S. Direct Investment Abroad, 1966-78, Washington, D.C.: U.S. Government Printing Office.

Table 2
Assets of U.S.-Controlled Foreign Corporations in
Tax-Haven and Other Areas, 1968 and 1976

	Total Assets* in			Assets in havens as a percent of assets in all areas
	Tax Havens [1]	Other Areas	All Areas [2]	
	(Amounts in Billion $s)			
1968				
All Industries	11.7	85.1	96.8	12.1
Contract construction	0.2	0.6	0.8	26.5
Manufacturing	1.8	46.7	48.4	3.7
Transportation	1.9	1.9	3.8	50.6
Wholesale trade	2.8	15.9	18.7	15.1
Finance, insurance and real estate	3.7	9.7	13.4	27.8
Insurance	0.1	1.0	1.1	12.8
Holding and other investment companies [3]	1.3	2.4	3.7	34.7
Other	2.3	6.3	8.6	26.7
Services	0.3	2.1	2.3	11.4
Other industries	1.0	8.4	9.4	10.8
1976				
All Industries	55.4	259.0	314.4	17.6
Contract construction	2.2	3.1	5.3	41.8
Manufacturing	7.6	141.9	149.5	5.1
Transportation	9.0	3.1	12.2	74.2
Wholesale trade	10.4	28.9	39.3	24.6
Finance, insurance and real estate	20.9	53.6	74.4	28.0
Insurance	2.4	3.8	6.2	38.5
Holding and other investment companies [3]	8.3	7.8	16.0	51.6
Other	10.2	42.0	52.2	19.5
Services	2.4	7.9	10.4	23.2
Other industries	2.9	20.5	23.2	12.5

[1] Tax-haven areas covered are the Bahamas, Bermuda, Costa Rica, Netherlands Antilles, Other British West Indies (other than Cayman Islands), Panama, Bahrain (for 1976 only), Hong Kong, Liberia, Liechtenstein, Luxembourg, Singapore, and Switzerland.

[2] Sum of two components may not add up to the totals because of rounding.

[3] Excludes bank holding companies which are included in Other.

Source: U.S. Department of the Treasury, Internal Revenue Service, Statistics of Income--1968-1972, International Income and Taxes, U.S. Corporations and Their Controlled Foreign Corporations, Washington, D.C., U.S. Government Printing Office, 1979 and unpublished tabulations on Controlled Foreign Corporations (from Form 2952) of U.S. corporations with assets of $250,000,000 or more (giants) for 1968, 1972 and 1976.

*These were estimated for 1976 since the actual data tabulated from Forms 2952 covered only the assets of CFCs controlled by the giants. To include also the assets of CFCs of smaller U.S. corporations, the data on giants were stepped up based on observed ratios between total CFCs and CFCs of giant U.S. corporations for 1968 and 1972. These ratios were projected forward to 1976 by industry. (The step-up ratio for all industries for 1976 was 1.128 in tax-haven areas and 1.118 in other areas.

Table 3

Patterns of Growth in U.S.-Owned Foreign Corporations
by Area and Percent of U.S. Ownership, 1970-1979

(In Percents)

	1970-74			1974-79		
	CFCs[1] Owned 95-100%	Other CFCs	Other than CFCs[2]	CFCs[1] Owned 95-100%	Other CFCs	Other than CFCs[2]
Bahamas	-32.0	103.2	110.3	18.4	1.0	10.4
Bermuda	82.7	119.2	247.2	19.3	64.9	109.6
British Islands[3]	81.3	281.8	640.0	284.8	290.5	254.1
Costa Rica	37.9	-6.7	86.7	61.3	67.9	36.9
Netherlands Antilles	67.0	108.3	209.5	55.9	152.0	115.4
Panama	-24.1	12.0	218.7	20.0	33.9	23.8
Western Hemisphere Tax-Haven areas	-9.1	56.0	172.2	53.2	45.2	42.1
Bahrain	-	100.0	-	100.0	-	150.0
Hong Kong	4.0	114.0	185.7	85.3	66.4	54.2
Liberia	11.8	39.0	233.0	1.6	65.6	29.7
Liechtenstein	0.8	123.5	118.8	16.9	-0.1	52.9
Luxembourg	2.4	50.0	200.0	8.2	16.7	12.1
Switzerland	1.4	49.8	110.3	20.6	19.9	13.8
Other tax-haven areas	4.2	54.8	155.9	32.5	32.7	29.1
Total tax-haven areas	-2.9	55.4	164.8	42.7	38.8	36.4
Non-tax-haven areas	7.6	32.7	57.8	26.4	14.2	17.1

[1]CFCs stands for Controlled Foreign Corporations, where more than 50 percent of all the voting stock is owned by U.S. shareholders.

[2]To be considered U.S.-owned, there must be at least five percent ownership.

[3]British Islands consist of British Antilles, British Virgin Islands, Cayman Islands, Montesserat, Anguila, Nevis, St. Christopher (also known as St. Kitts), Antigua, Dominica, St. Lucia and St. Vincent.

Source: U.S. Treasury Department, Internal Revenue Service, unpublished tabulations from Form 959.

Table 4

International Banking in Tax-Haven Areas, 1968-1978

(In Billion Dollars)

| | By Non-banks only | | | | By Banks and Non-banks | | | |
| | In Branches and Subsidiaries of U.S. Banks | | In All Banks | | In Branches and Subsidiaries of U.S. Banks | | In All Banks | |
	In the Western Hemi-sphere 2/	In All Areas 3/	In the Western Hemi-sphere 2/	In All Areas 3/	In the Western Hemi-sphere 2/	In All Areas 3/	In the Western Hemi-sphere 2/	In All Areas 3/
1968	n.a.	n.a.	0.3	5.3	n.a.	n.a.	1.5	10.6
1969	n.a.	n.a.	1.3	8.4	n.a.	n.a.	4.8	17.8
1970	n.a.	n.a.	2.0	11.8	n.a.	n.a.	7.5	26.1
1971	n.a.	n.a.	2.7	16.1	n.a.	n.a.	15.4	40.2
1972	n.a.	n.a.	3.9	17.6	n.a.	n.a.	23.5	60.2
1973	3.9	5.2	5.6	23.5	27.3	35.1	35.4	88.3
1974	7.0	9.5	10.6	36.7	37.2	50.3	55.2	130.6
1975	9.7	12.2	13.9	41.8	52.0	65.8	77.9	170.5
1976	13.5	16.5	18.7	50.7	75.2	95.8	112.0	234.1
1977	18.4	21.8	28.2	70.5	88.0	115.8	131.8	296.9
1978	25.9	30.5	31.5	88.7	100.0	130.6	159.5	384.9

(Column group heading: International Deposits 1/ Held in the Tax-Haven Areas)

1/ International bank deposits are foreign and local currency deposits owned by non-residents and foreign currency deposits owned by residents.

2/ The Western Hemishphere tax-haven areas covered are the Bahamas, Bermuda, Caribbean Residual (which include deposits held either in areas such as British West Indies, Barbados and Costa Rica or deposits that should have been, but due to practical difficulties have not been, included in the other Carribbean tax haven estimates), Cayman Islands, Netherlands Antilles and Panama.

3/ In addition to the Western Hemisphere havens, the following areas are covered: Bahrain, Hong Kong, Luxembourg, Singapore and Switzerland.

n.a. - stands for not available.

Source: Unpublished IRS study.

IV. United States Taxation of International Transactions
and the Anti-Avoidance Provisions - An Overview

The Congress has never sought to eliminate tax haven
operations by U.S. taxpayers. Instead, from time to time,
the Congress has identified abuses and legislated to eliminate
them. The result is a patchwork of anti-avoidance provisions,
some intended to deal particularly with tax havens, although
of general application, and some intended to deal with more
general abuse situations, but which might also be used by
the IRS to deal with tax haven transactions.

When dealing with illicit use of tax havens, the substantive
tax rules are rarely the problem (although lack of clarity
often encourages illicit use). Rather, gaps in United States
evidence-gathering ability hinder attempts to prosecute
evaders.

The discussion below seeks to place tax havens within
the context of the U.S. system of taxing international
transactions. When the system is analyzed, it becomes clear
that without appropriate anti-abuse provisions, the U.S. tax
system contains provisions which would encourage the use of
low tax jurisdictions by U.S. persons, and that where anti-
avoidance provisions are not effective, U.S. persons have
positively responded to this encouragement. It is also
clear that tax havens, in and of themselves, do not provide
a U.S. tax advantage; the U.S. tax advantage is provided
only in combination with both the U.S. system of deferral of
taxation of corporate earnings and the U.S. system of consolidated
worldwide foreign tax credits.

It cannot be emphasized too strongly that tax haven
problems cannot be completely divorced from the taxation of
international transactions in general, or from non-tax
policy concerns. Accordingly, some of the materials address
more general problems.

A. Policy Objectives

Stated United States tax policy is decidedly against
tax haven use. However, in practice that policy becomes
ambivalent. It reflects an unresolved conflict between the
following policy objectives:

(1) Maintaining the competitive position of U.S.
businesses investing abroad or exporting;

(2) Maintaining tax equity as between investment in
the U.S. and investment abroad;

(3) The need to provide fair rules for taxing foreign
investment;

(4) Administrative efficiency;

(5) Foreign policy considerations;

(6) Promotion of investment in the U.S.

The result has been policy ambiguities and compromises in legislation which have failed to resolve these conflicts, and which have left U.S. law without a clear focus with respect to tax havens. Concern for administrative feasibility has been practically non-existent.

The development of U. S. taxation of foreign transactions shows a consistent tension between these objectives. For example, Congress introduced the foreign tax credit as part of the Revenue Act of 1918.[1] They did so not only to provide a "just" system, but "a very wise one," without which "we would discourage men from going out after commerce business in different countries or residing for such purposes in different countries if we continue to maintain this double taxation."[2]

Nowhere is this tension more apparent than when it is focused on tax havens. Nowhere is the failure to resolve the policy issues more obvious. Congress over the years, while maintaining deferral of tax on the earnings of foreign corporations controlled by U.S. persons, has at the same time passed numerous anti-avoidance provisions generally intended to solve perceived tax haven-related problems. All have had numerous exceptions, have been complex and difficult to administer, and all have had gaps (many intended, some not).

The tension between the policies and the ultimate attempt to deal with tax avoidance through tax havens, came to a head in connection with the legislative deliberations which resulted in the Revenue Act of 1962 and subpart F of the Code.[3]

---

[1] Revenue Act of 1918, §§222(a) and 238(a).

[2] 56 Cong. Rec. 677-78 (1918).

[3] §§ 951-964.

President Kennedy in his State of the Union Message had recommended that the tax deferral accorded foreign corporate subsidiaries of U.S. corporations be terminated in all cases. His emphasis, however, was on haven practices. He stated that,

"The undesirability of continuing deferral is underscored where deferral has served as the shelter for escape through the unjustifiable use of tax havens such as Switzerland. Recently more and more enterprises organized abroad by American firms have arranged their corporate structures aided by artificial arrangements between parent and subsidiary regarding intercompany pricing, the transfer of patent licensing rights, the shifting of management fees, and similar practices which maximize the accumulation of profits in the tax haven--so as to exploit the multiplicity of foreign tax systems and international agreements in order to reduce sharply or eliminate completely their tax liabilities both at home and abroad."[4/]

The President's recommendation was,

"elimination of the tax haven device anywhere in the world, even in the underdeveloped countries, through the elimination of tax deferral privileges for those forms of activities such as trading, licensing, insurance, and others, that typically seek out tax haven methods of operation. There is no valid reason to permit their remaining untaxed regardless of the country in which they are located."[5/]

The Congress, however, refused to go as far as the President recommended. Rather, it singled out tax haven devices, but did not end deferral for operating companies not considered to be using tax haven devices. The reasons for the transaction approach reflected the policy of maintaining the competitive position of U. S. business overseas. They stated that their bill:

_____

[4/] President's Recommendations on Tax Revision: Hearings Before the House Ways and Means Committee, 87th Cong., 1st Sess. 8 (1961).

[5/] Id. at 9.

". . . does not eliminate tax deferral in the case of operating businesses owned by Americans which are located in economically developed countries of the world. Testimony in hearings before your committee suggested that the location of investments in these countries is an important factor in stimulating American exports to the same areas. Moreover, it appeared that to impose the U. S. tax currently on the U.S. shareholders of American-owned businesses operating abroad would place such firms at a disadvantage with other firms located within the same areas not subject to U.S. tax."[6]

In fact, subpart F as finally enacted was a limited response to President Kennedy's initial proposal. Only the most obvious tax haven issues identified at the time were addressed.

The evidence submitted during the 1961 and 1962 deliberations demonstrated a significant use and rapid growth of tax havens by U.S. multi-nationally based corporations.[7] A memorandum and letter submitted by the Treasury described the various types of operations and the recurrent severe administrative problems in dealing with the operations.[8]

Nevertheless, in reality, subpart F was not drafted in terms of companies formed in tax havens. Rather, it focused on defined activities conducted abroad which were generally considered tax haven devices. While the Congress repeatedly referred to the provision as an anti-tax haven provision, in fact, it can apply in developed countries as well as in tax havens. It is transactional, not jurisdictional. The Congress also provided significant exceptions from the application of subpart F for certain businesses. In 1975 and again in 1976, significant changes in some of the exclusionary rules were made.

---

[6] H. Rep. No. 1447, 87th Cong., 2nd Sess. 57-58 (1962), 1962-3 C.B. 405, 461-462 (H. Rep. No. 1447).

[7] President's Recommendations on Tax Revision: Hearings Before The House Ways and Means Committee, 87th Cong., 1st Sess. 3522 (1961). In 1978, President Carter also recommended elimination of tax deferral in the case of foreign corporations owned by U.S. persons. However, the Congress did not adopt this proposal. See President's 1978 Tax Reduction and Reform Proposals: Hearings Before The House Committee on Ways and Means, 95th Cong., 2d Sess. 19 (1978).

[8] Proposed Amendments to the Revenue Act of 1954: Hearings on H.R. 10650 Before The Senate Committee on Finance, 87th Cong., 2d Sess. 228 (1962).

46

In addition to legislative provisions the U. S. has in force a network of income tax treaties, including some with tax havens. These treaties also reflect a tension between similiar inconsistent policy objectives and, in addition, a policy to encourage foreign investment in the U.S.

While treaties are discussed in a later chapter, it is worth noting at this point that their existence has clearly attracted taxpayers to tax havens. In fact, in at least one case (the Netherlands Antilles), the treaty may have created a tax haven.

B. Basic Pattern

The general rules applicable to international trade and investment apply to income from tax havens as they do to income earned in any foreign jurisdiction. While certain provisions were added to the Code to deal with tax avoidance related to tax havens, there is no provision which on its face deals specifically and exclusively with tax havens per se.

1. General Rules

The U.S. taxes U.S. citizens, residents and corporations on their worldwide income.[9] The U.S. taxes non-resident alien individuals and foreign corporations on their U.S. source income which is not effectively connected with the conduct of a trade or business in the U.S. They are also taxed on their income which is effectively connected with the conduct of a trade or business in the U.S. whether or not that income is U.S. source or foreign source.[10]

Income which is effectively connected with the conduct of a trade or business in the U.S. is subjected to tax at the normal graduated rates on a net basis.[11] Deductions are allowed in computing effectively connected taxable income, but "only if and to the extent that they are connected with income which is effectively connected . . . ."[12] Deductions and credits are allowed only if the taxpayer files a true and accurate return.[13]

---

[9] See § 1 and § 11.

[10] §§871, 881, and 882.

[11] §§ 871(b)(1) and 882(a)(1).

[12] §§ 873(a) and 882(c)(1).

[13] §§ 874(a) and 883(c)(2); Brittingham v. Commissioner, 66 T.C. 373 (1976).

United States source non-effectively connected interest, dividends, rents, salaries, wages, premiums, annuities, and other fixed or determinable income received by a non-resident alien or foreign corporation are subject to tax at a rate of 30 percent of the gross amount received.[14] The net U.S. source capital gains of a nonresident alien present in the U.S. for at least 183 days during a taxable year are taxed at the 30 percent rate.[15] The 30 percent rate on these various income items may be lowered by treaty.

Until 1980, a non-resident alien or foreign corporation could elect to treat all income from U.S. real property (including gains from its disposition, rents or royalties from natural deposits, and certain gains from the disposition of timber) as effectively connected income, and thus have it taxed on a net basis.[16] Once made, an election could not be revoked without the consent of the IRS.[17]

The 30 percent flat rate of tax on non-resident aliens not engaged in trade or business in the U.S. is imposed on payments from U.S. sources. United States source payments are defined in § 861 to include interest paid by a U.S. person and dividends paid by a domestic corporation, with certain exceptions for payments from persons most of whose income is from foreign sources. U.S. source payments also include certain interest and dividends paid by a foreign corporation which earned more than 50 percent of its income from a U.S. business.[18] This gross tax on fixed or determinable income is often reduced or eliminated in the case of payments to residents of countries with which the U.S. has an income tax treaty.[19]

The 30 percent (or lower treaty rate) tax imposed on U.S. source non-effectively connected income paid to foreign persons is collected by means of withholding.[20] The person

---

[14] §§ 871 (a) and 881 (a).

[15] § 871(a)(2).

[16] §§ 871(d)(1) and 882(d)(1).

[17] §§ 871(d)(2) and 882(d)(2).

[18] §§ 861(a)(1)(C) and 861(a)(2)(B).

[19] Treaties are discussed in Chapter IX.

[20] §§ 1441 (individuals) and 1442 (corporations).

48

required to withhold is specifically liable for the tax but is indemnified under the Code against any claims for the withholding tax other than claims by the U.S.[21/] Statutory exceptions from withholding are provided, including one for income effectively connected with the conduct of a trade or business within the U.S.[22/]

Under the regulations, the obligation to withhold in the case of dividends depends upon the recipient's address. In the case of interest and royalties, it depends on a certification by the taxpayer. Thus, withholding on a dividend payment is required if the shareholder's address is outside of the U.S., but not if the address is inside the U.S.[23/] An exemption from withholding can be claimed on the basis of U.S. citizenship or residence.[24/]

Certain exemptions from the gross tax are provided. Bank account interest is defined as foreign source interest and, therefore, is exempt.[25/] Likewise, interest and dividends paid by a U.S. corporation which earns less than 20% of its gross income from U.S. sources is defined as foreign source income and is exempt.[26/] Exemptions are also provided for certain original issue discount and for income of a foreign government from investments in U.S. securities. Our treaties also provide for exemption from tax in certain cases.

Worldwide taxation can result in double taxation of foreign source income. The U.S. seeks to mitigate this double taxation by permitting a dollar-for-dollar credit against U.S. tax imposed on foreign source income. The limitation to foreign source income is computed on a world-wide consolidated basis. Here all income taxes paid to all foreign countries are combined to offset U.S. taxes on all foreign income. A credit is also provided non-resident aliens and foreign corporations, but only for certain foreign taxes imposed on foreign effectively connected income.[27/]

21/ § 1461.

22/ § 1441(c)(1).

23/ Treas. Reg. § 1.1441-3(b)(3).

24/ Treas. Reg. § 1.1441-5(a) and (b).

25/ § 861(a)(1)(A) and (c).

26/ § 861(a)(1)(B) and (a)(2)(A).

27/ § 906.

2.   United States Taxation of Property Held by a Foreign Trustee

For tax purposes, foreign trusts in general are treated as non-resident alien individuals. To qualify as a foreign trust, the entity must be both a "foreign trust," as defined in § 7701(a)(31) and Treas. Reg. § 301.7701-4, and considered to be a non-resident or foreign situs entity.[28]

Because it is taxed as a nonresident alien, a foreign trust which has U.S. source income not effectively connected with its conduct as a U.S. trade or business, would be taxed at the flat 30 percent rate on certain passive income and gains. Also, interest on amounts deposited with U.S. banks that is received by the foreign trust is not considered U.S. source income and, therefore, not taxed to the trust. If such interest, however, is "effectively connected" with the conduct of a U.S. trade or business, it may still be taxable.[29]

A foreign trust which is engaged in a U.S. trade or business is taxable at the normal graduated rates on all income effectively connected with the conduct of that trade of business, whether such amounts are sourced within or without the U.S.[30] Prior to 1980 legislation, a foreign trust, as a non-resident alien, could make the special election under § 871(d) in the case of "real property income" as defined in § 871(d)(1).

A foreign trust which is not a grantor trust can be used to defer U.S. tax on income from property, even when held for the benefit of a U.S. person. In 1962, the Congress first dealt with tax avoidance by the use of foreign trusts. The beneficiaries of foreign trusts created by U.S. persons were subjected to an unlimited throw-back rule at the time of the ultimate distribution of accumulated income.

In 1976, the Congress passed legislation intended to eliminate the deferral privilege accorded foreign trusts created by U.S. persons for the benefit of U.S. beneficiaries. Under that legislation, a U.S. person who directly or indirectly transfers property to a foreign trust is treated as the

---

[28] See Rev. Rul. 60-181, 1960-1 C.B. 257; B.W. Jones Trust v. Commissioner, 46 B.T.A. 531 (1942), aff'd, 132 F.2d. 914 (4th Cir. 1943).

[29] §§ 861(a)(1)(A) and 861(c).

[30] § 871(b).

owner for the taxable year of that portion of the trust attributable to the property transferred, if for the year there is a U.S. beneficiary for any portion of the trust.[31] Therefore, the U.S. grantor is taxed on the income.

3. Taxation of Corporations and Their Shareholders

The U.S. taxes corporations and their shareholders under the so-called "classical" system of corporation taxation, a system under which a corporation and its shareholders are separately taxed. In general, corporate earnings are taxed to the corporation and not to its shareholders, and a shareholder is taxed only on dividends received.

The same system governs the taxation of foreign corporations and U.S. persons who are shareholders of foreign corporations. In general, the earnings of the foreign corporation are not taxed until the shareholder receives a dividend from the corporation. Also, the general jurisdictional rules described above apply to a foreign corporation with U.S. shareholders, even if those shareholders control the corporation. Accordingly, a foreign corporation controlled by U.S. persons is taxed only on its income from U.S. sources and on its foreign effectively connected income.

A shareholder of a corporation may also be taxed when he sells or exchanges his stock of the corporation, or when he transfers property to it or receives property from it. The Code, however, contains numerous provisions providing for nonrecognition of gain in such cases.

A corporation can be easily utilized to the tax advantage of its shareholders. In the domestic context, the advantage can generally occur because of the differential in rates of tax between corporations and individuals. In the foreign context that differential may be much larger, and if a tax haven is used, the rate of tax imposed on the corporate earnings may be zero.

Absent the anti-avoidance provisions in the law, corporations can easily be manipulated by U.S. shareholders engaged in foreign transactions. In the simplest case, a U.S. person could, in a transaction which qualifies for non-recognition treatment, transfer income producing assets (such as stock or bonds) to a foreign corporation organized

---

[31] § 679(a)(1).

in a zero tax jurisdiction. The income earned by the foreign
corporation would not be taxed by the U.S. or by the zero
tax jurisdiction. The assets remain under the control of
the U.S. person, but the income would not be taxed until
repatriated. The shareholder would be taxed on the sale of
the stock, but at favorable capital gains rates. If the
shareholder holds the stock until he dies, it is subject to
U.S. estate tax but passes to his heirs free of income tax
at its value as of the date of his death. His heirs could
then liquidate the foreign corporation free of income tax
(because of the step-up in basis by reason of the shareholder's
death) and return the property to the U.S. to start again.
Or, they could maintain their ownership in the foreign
corporation and shelter the income.

Another manipulation could occur if a parent corporation selling goods overseas forms a foreign corporation
in a tax haven to make those sales. The parent would then
sell the goods to the subsidiary at a small or zero profit,
and the subsidiary would sell them to the ultimate customer
at a substantial mark-up. The profit on the sale would not
be taxed by the U.S. and could accumulate free of tax in a
tax haven.

In order to curtail what it, from time to time, categorized as abuses, the Congress has periodically adjusted
the system of taxation and the non-recognition provisions of
the Code. Because of the resulting anti-abuse provisions,
the simple manipulations just described are not possible.

C. Anti-Abuse Measures

Since the adoption of the income tax in 1913, Congress
has incorporated into the tax laws numerous provisions intended to correct perceived deficiencies. Some were intended
to mitigate double taxation, while others were intended to
deal with abuse. There follows a summary of the anti-abuse
measures. While most are technically applicable to foreign
corporations, those that have not been specifically tailored
to foreign corporations tend not to be useful to curb tax
haven abuse.

1. Accumulated earnings tax. The accumulated earnings
tax was the earliest anti-abuse measure.[32] As originally
adopted, if a corporation were formed or fraudulently availed
of to accumulate income, then each shareholder's ratable

---

[32] Revenue Act of 1913.

share of the corporation's income would be taxed to him. The provision was amended in 1921 to impose a penalty tax on a corporation when it unreasonably accumulated earnings for purposes of avoiding income tax of the shareholders by permitting the earnings and profits of the corporation to accumulate instead of being distributed. The operative test is accumulation beyond the reasonably anticipated needs of the business. The 1921 structure continues in use today.[33] The tax clearly applies to the U.S. source income of a foreign as well as a domestic corporation.[34]

2. Transfer pricing. In 1921, the Congress gave the Commissioner the authority to "consolidate accounts for related trades or businesses" for the purpose of "making an accurate distribution or apportionment of gains, profits, income, deductions, or capital between or among such related trades or businesses."[35] The provision was replaced in 1928 by the predecessor of § 482, which provided for the allocation of gross income or deductions between or among related trades or businesses.

In 1968, in response to Congressional proding during the Revenue Act of 1962, the IRS published revised detailed regulations setting forth the standards it will apply in shifting income among related entities to prevent tax avoidance.

Today, §482 is one of the most important anti-avoidance provisions in the law, and is, along with subpart F, the central focus of IRS international enforcement efforts. In 1979 the tax value of § 482 adjustments proposed by international examiners was $500 million, which represented 36 percent of the tax value of all adjustments proposed by the international examiners.

3. Sections 367 and 1491. In 1932, the Congress, recognizing that the various Code provisions permitting nonrecognition treatment for gains realized in certain exchanges and reorganizations involving foreign corporations constituted "serious loophole[s] for the avoidance of taxes,"[36] enacted the predecessor to § 367. That section and its successors have uniformly provided that a taxpayer seeking nonrecognition treatment for gains realized on certain foreign transfers must show to the "satisfaction" of the

---

[33] §§ 531-537.

[34] § 532(a).

[35] Revenue Act of 1921, § 240(d).

[36] H.R. Rep. No. 708, 72d Cong., 1st Sess., 20 (1932), 1939-1 C.B. (Part 2) 457, 471.

Commissioner, that the transaction does not have as one of its principal purposes the avoidance of Federal income taxes. Nonrecognition treatment requires a ruling issued under that provision.

Today's version of § 367 distinguishes between transfers from the United States and all other transfers. For transfers from the United States, non-recognition treatment is not available unless, pursuant to a request filed not later than 183 days after the beginning of a transfer, it is established to the satisfaction of the Commissioner that the exchange does not have as one of its principal purposes the avoidance of Federal income taxes. For all other transfers (foreign to foreign and foreign to U.S.) a ruling is not required, but the rules governing the tax consequences are provided in regulations which can deny non-recognition to the extent necessary to prevent tax avoidance.[37]

Also, in 1932 the Congress dealt with a second aspect of the transfer problem and enacted the predecessor to § 1491. That section imposed an excise tax upon the transfer of stock or securities by a U.S. person to a foreign corporation as paid-in surplus or as a contribution to capital, or to a foreign estate, trust, or partnership. The tax was measured by the difference between the fair market value of the property at the time of transfer and its basis.[38] The difference is reduced by the amount of any gain recognized by the transferor on the transfer. Section 1491 was amended in 1976 to apply to transfers of any property and to increase the excise tax to 35 percent from 27 1/2 percent. The excise tax does not apply to a transfer described in § 367 or a transfer for which an election has been made under § 1057.[39] In lieu of the payment under § 1491, the taxpayer may elect under §1057 to treat a transfer described in § 1491 as a taxable sale or exchange, and to recognize gain equal to the excess of the fair market value of the property over its adjusted basis.[40]

---

[37] See Revenue Act of 1932, § 112(k); Revenue Act of 1934, § 112(i); Revenue Act of 1936, § 112(i); Revenue Act of 1938, § 112(i); 1939 I.R.C. § 112(i).

[38] H.R. Rep. No. 708, 72d Cong., 1st Sess., (1932), 1939-1 C.B. (Part 2) 457, 494.

[39] § 1492.

[40] § 1057.

4. _Personal holding companies_. The undistributed personal holding company income of a personal holding company is subject to a penalty tax of 70 percent. This provision, added to the law in 1934 and extensively revised in 1937 and 1964, was intended to thwart the creation of so-called incorporated pocketbooks and the transfer of services to corporations organized by the provider of those services. The Congress, in adopting this provision, acknowledged that the accumulated earnings tax was not working to prevent some significant abuses in the area.

A corporation is a personal holding company if at least 60 percent of its adjusted ordinary gross income is personal holding company income (passive investment income and certain personal services income), and more than 50 percent in value of its stock is owned by five or fewer individuals. The tax is imposed on the corporation (not the shareholders), and provision is made for relief from the tax to the extent a "deficiency dividend" is paid.

A foreign corporation can be a personal holding company. However, if all of its outstanding stock during the last half of the year is owned by nonresident aliens, then it is not a personal holding company.

5. _Foreign personal holding companies_. In 1937, the Congress, in response to a request of President Roosevelt and the Report of the Joint Committee on Tax Evasion and Avoidance of the Congress of the United States[41]/, again acted against incorporated pocketbooks. This time, it focused on those incorporated abroad by U.S. persons. The result was the foreign personal holding company provisions. It is of interest that Congress focused on corporations domiciled in countries such as the Bahamas and Panama, which had little or no corporate income tax (at least on foreign source income) and which are today considered to be tax havens.

The U.S. shareholders of a foreign personal holding company are taxed on their proportionate share of the corporation's undistributed foreign personal holding company income. A foreign corporation is a foreign personal holding company if at least 60 percent of the corporation's gross income for the year is foreign personal holding company

---

[41]/ H.R. Doc. No. 337, 75th Cong., 1st Sess. (1937).

income, and if more than 50 percent in value of the corporation's outstanding stock is owned (directly or indirectly) by not more than five individuals who are citizens or residents of the U.S.

Foreign personal holding company income includes passive income such as dividends, interest, royalties, and annuities, gains from sale of stocks, securities, and future transactions in certain commodities, income from an estate or trust or the sale of an interest therein, income from certain personal service contracts, compensation for the use of corporate property by 25 percent shareholders, and rents, unless they constitute 50 percent or more of the gross income of the corporation.

The foreign personal holding company provisions take precedence over the personal holding company provisions, thus, a foreign corporation which meets both tests is treated as a foreign personal holding company.[42/] Generally, they take precedence over the subpart F provisions.[43/]

6. Section 269. In 1943, the Congress enacted the predecessor of §269[44/], which grants to the Secretary the power to disallow a tax benefit if the principal purpose of the acquisition of control of a corporation, or of the acquisition by a corporation from another corporation of property with a carryover basis, is evasion or avoidance of Federal income tax by securing the tax benefit. This provision applies to foreign corporations as well as domestic corporations.

7. Foreign investment companies. Despite the provisions described above, activities perceived as abusive continued. One of those activities was the establishment of foreign investment companies which sold shares widely among U.S. individuals.

In connection with the 1962 Act, Congress attacked the problem of the foreign investment company which avoided being a personal holding or foreign personal holding company because it avoided the shareholder test by selling shares widely to U.S. persons. These companies, often organized in jurisdictions which did not tax their income, could invest in securities or other passive assets and accumulate income offshore.

42/ § 542(c)(5).

43/ § 951(d).

44/ 1939 I.R.C. § 129.

The Revenue Act of 1962 adopted §§ 1246 and 1247 as an alternative means of attacking these companies. Under § 1246 a U.S. shareholder realizes ordinary income on the sale or redemption of his stock in a foreign investment company, to the extent of his ratable share of its earnings accumulated by the company after 1962 and during the time the shareholder held the stock.

Under § 1247, a foreign investment company could, prior to 1963, elect to have its U.S. shareholders taxed substantially like the shareholders in a domestic regulated investment company. This meant that the shareholders had to receive a distribution of 90 percent of the company's ordinary income, and any capital gains realized by the company were taxed to the shareholders.

8. Controlled foreign corporations. In 1962 Congress enacted subpart F which taxes U.S. shareholders of controlled foreign corporations on their proportionate share of certain categories of undistributed profits from tax haven activities and certain other activities of the foreign corporation. A controlled foreign corporation is defined as a foreign corporation in which more than 50 percent of the voting power in the corporation is owned by U.S. shareholders. A U.S. shareholder is a United States person who owns directly or indirectly 10 percent or more of the voting stock of a foreign corporation. In contrast, the ownership test for foreign personal holding company status is ownership by five or fewer individuals of more than 50 percent in value of the stock of the foreign corporation. There is no minimum ownership threshhold for a shareholder's interest to be taken into account for foreign personal holding company purposes.

The categories of income subject to current taxation under subpart F are foreign personal holding company income, sales income from property purchased from, or sold to, a related person if the property is manufactured and sold for use, consumption or disposition outside the country of the corporation's incorporation, service income from services also performed outside the country of the corporation's incorporation, for or on behalf of any related person, and certain shipping income. The Code refers to these types of income as "foreign base company income." Basically, this provision is designed to prevent tax avoidance by the diversion of sales or other types of income to a related foreign corporation which is incorporated in a country which imposes little or no tax on this income when it is received by that corporation since it arose in connection with an activity taking place outside of that country. In addition, the Code provides for the current taxation of the income derived by a controlled foreign corporation from the insurance of U.S. risks. Foreign base company income, income from the insurance of U.S. risks, and certain other income are collectively referred to as subpart F income. The Code also provides under subpart F that earnings of controlled foreign corporations are to be taxed currently to U.S. shareholders if they are invested in U.S. property.

In 1976, subpart F income was expanded to include boycott generated income, and illegal bribes or other payments paid by or on behalf of the controlled foreign corporation directly or indirectly to a government official. Neither of these later items necessarily involves tax havens.

Subpart F contains certain exclusions from foreign base company income. Income from the use of ships in foreign commerce is excluded to the extent that the income is reinvested in shipping assets.[45/] Foreign base company income also does not include any income received by a controlled foreign corporation, if it is established to the satisfaction of the Commissioner that neither the creation or organization of the controlled foreign corporation receiving the income nor the effecting of the transaction giving rise to the income through the controlled foreign corporation has as one of its significant purposes the substantial reduction of income taxes.

There is also the 10-70 rule: if foreign base company income is less than 10 percent of a controlled foreign corporation's gross income, then none of its income is foreign base company income, and if more than 70 percent of its gross income is foreign base company income, then its entire gross income is treated as foreign base company income. If the percentage is between 10 percent and 70 percent, then the actual amount of foreign base company income is treated as such.

[45/] As originally enacted, shipping income was excluded without regard to reinvestment.

Income derived from the insurance of U.S. risks is subpart F income, if the controlled foreign corporation receives premiums in respect of insurance or reinsurance in excess of five percent of the total premiums and other considerations it received during its taxable year. For purposes of applying the insurance of U.S. risks rules, a controlled foreign corporation in certain cases includes one of which more than 25 percent of the total combined voting power of all classes of voting stock is owned by U.S. shareholders

9. <u>Dispositions of stock of controlled foreign corporations.</u> The Revenue Act of 1962 also introduced § 1248 to the Code. That section requires a U.S. shareholder who disposes of his shares in a controlled foreign corporation to report any gains on the disposition as a dividend, to the extent of the earnings and profits of the foreign corporation accumulated after 1962. Accordingly, this rule can be beneficial because foreign taxes paid or accrued by the corporation may be credited against U.S. taxes of a domestic corporation.

10. <u>Dispositions of patents to foreign corporations.</u> The Revenue Act of 1962 also adopted § 1249, which requires that gain from the sale or exchange of patents, copyrights, secret formulae or processes, or similar property rights to a foreign corporation by a person controlling that corporation, is to be treated as ordinary income rather than capital gain. The House-passed bill had included, as a category of subpart F income, income from patents, copyrights, and similar property developed in the U.S. or acquired from related U.S. persons. The income to be included was royalty income, and a constructive royalty if the foreign corporation used the property itself.[46] The Senate rejected the House approach because of difficulties it foresaw in determining constructive income.[47]

---

[46] H. Rep. No. 1447, 61, 1962-3 C.B. 402, 465.

[47] S. Rep. No. 1881 87th Cong., 2d Sess. 109-111 (1962) (S. Rep. No. 1881), 1962-3 C.B. 703, 815.

V.   Patterns of Use of Tax Havens

The figures in Chapter III, and our interviews indicate
that tax havens are being used by U.S. persons investing
overseas, and by foreign persons investing in the U.S. Not
all of this use is tax motivated. Much, however, is. Some
of the transactions are clearly legitimate, being within the
letter and the spirit of the law. Other transactions are
fraudulent, although proving the necessary willfulness to
establish a criminal case may not be possible. An overriding
problem is that the complexity of the law, the difficulties
in information gathering, and administrative problems within
the IRS often make it difficult to distinguish between the
two.

This chapter begins with a brief discussion of the
distinction between tax avoidance and tax evasion. It then
describes how assets can be transferred to tax havens in the
context of the Code provisions which seek to insure that the
transfers themselves are not abusive. This chapter then
describes the activities which are being carried on in tax
havens within the context of United States tax laws which
apply to those transactions.

The transactions described begin with corporations and
multinationals. They illustrate how existing rules are
utilized in a legal way. The descriptions also point out
how, in some instances, unscrupulous taxpayers arrange their
affairs so that they appear legal, but are in fact fraudulent.
More abusive transactions are also described. In Chapter VI,
transactions which have been investigated as frauds are
discussed. In Chapter VII, options for administrative and
legislative changes are presented. These might help rationalize
the taxation of tax haven transactions, and make the rules easier
to administer.

A.   Tax Avoidance v. Tax Evasion

Many consider tax haven transactions evil per se
simply because there is a tax haven involved. Others look
at the tax system as something to be manipulated, viewing
tax havens as a piece in that game. They see little wrong
in using a tax haven transaction to avoid taxes that they
know are due, provided that transaction is reported. Others
will use the complexities of the law to hide income or
create deductions. In truth, often the question of whether
a tax haven transaction is legitimate or illegitimate,
whether it is tax avoidance or tax evasion, is in the eyes
of the beholder.

Whether or not a tax haven transaction is tax avoidance or tax evasion or something else depends in part on how you define those terms. In fact, the terms have probably never been adequately defined. The term "avoidance" is particularly imprecise. Furthermore, "avoidance" has certain connotations which in themselves seem to import evil doing although not quite to the extent that evasion does. The problems with distinguishing in this area and in using these terms have been described as follows:

> The term tax avoidance itself has unfortunate connotations; it is considered as referring to an attitude of unethical and, indeed, unlawful behavior, although it is actually a neutral term. In the pejorative sense the term tax evasion should be used, which indicates an action by which a taxpayer tries to escape his legal obligations by fraudulent means. The confusion arises from the fact that sometimes taxes are avoided -- by the use of perfectly legal measures -- against the purpose and spirit of the law. Where this is the case, the taxpayer involved is abusing the law and he is blamed for it, although, no penal measures can be taken against him.[1]

Rather than attempt to define the terms with any pre-decision, we have identified four categories of use, ranging from completely legal (from a tax point of view) to fraud:

(1) Non-tax motivated use, transactions involving tax havens where no U.S. tax impact results. An example is a U.S. branch bank in a tax haven which is fully taxable by the United States and where the source of income is not changed.

---

[1] J. van Hoorn Jr., "The Uses and Abuses of Tax Havens", Tax Havens and Measures Against Tax Evasion and Avoidance in the EEC, Associated Business Programs (London, 1974).

(2) A transaction which has a tax effect, but which is completely within the letter and the spirit of the law. An example is the formation of a subsidiary in a tax haven to conduct a shipping business or the formation of a subsidiary in a tax haven to conduct a banking business, where all of the necessary functions are performed by the tax haven entity in the tax haven.

(3) Aggressive tax planning that takes advantage of an unintended legal or administrative loophole. An example of this might be establishing a service business in a tax haven to provide services for a branch of that business located in a third country. A further example might be the use by a multinational corporation of artificially high transfer pricing to shift income into a tax haven. Often, the parties know full well that, if the transaction is thoroughly audited, a significant adjustment will probably be made. They rely on difficulties in information gathering and on complications to possibly avoid payment of, or at least to postpone payment of, some tax.

(4) Tax evasion; an action by which the taxpayer tries to escape his legal obligations by fraudulent means. This might involve simply failing to report income, or trying to create excess deductions. This category can also be broken down into two subcategories: (a) evasion of tax on income which is legally earned, such as slush funds; (b) evasion of tax on income which arises from an illegal activity, such as trafficking in narcotics.

In this chapter, patterns of use of tax havens are described. At times, the transactions are so complicated and the information gathering problems so difficult that it may not be possible to distinguish between the various categories. The lines become murky because the law is murky and the information is incomplete.

B. Transfers to a Tax Haven Entity

United States persons doing business abroad continue to use tax havens in traditional ways. They will form a corporate entity in a tax haven and use it to carry out their foreign operations. The use of a tax haven company has significant advantages. From a U.S. tax point of view, it may give the benefit of deferral or enable a U.S. parent corporation to absorb excess foreign tax credits. It may also decrease the overall foreign tax burden of a taxpayer or affiliated group of corporations, and may allow a company to do business overseas free of currency or other controls. Generally, in order to use a tax haven entity, property must be transferred to it.

1. Transfer Pricing

United States taxpayers may attempt to shift assets and income to low or no tax countries from high tax countries through transfer pricing. Where this shifting is at arm's length and within the guidelines set by the IRS and the courts, it is perfectly legitimate. There often are honest disagreements as to what is an appropriate charge or price. This happens very often because taxpayers find the §482 regulations difficult to deal with. If the price is too high, the IRS can allocate the income. Transactions generally not permissible under IRS regulations and for which an allocation may therefore be appropriate can take numerous forms, as follows:

a. Payment of interest from the U.S. or another high tax country to a tax haven affiliate at above market rates.

b. Payment of royalties from the U.S. or other high tax country to a tax haven affiliate at higher than fair market value rates.

c. Sale of property by an entity located in a high tax country to an affiliate in a tax haven at a low price, followed by a sale by the tax haven entity at a high price.

d. Transfer of income producing assets, such as stocks, bonds or other securities, or patent rights, from a U.S. person or from any affiliate of a U.S. person in a high tax country to an affiliate in a tax haven at a low cost.

e. Payment of management, service or other fees to a related entity which has not in fact performed services; or payment for services performed but at a price above fair market value.

f. Leasing of tangible property to a tax haven entity for less than fair market value.

g. Transfer of components for less than market value, to a tax haven affiliate for assembly, followed by a sale of the finished product at a high price.

In many cases, in addition to shifting assets to the tax haven entity, the transactions will result in deductions for the high tax country entity which is income shifting. For example, the payment of interest by a U.S. corporation

to a foreign affiliate results not only in the shifting of
the interest to the tax haven, but in a deduction for interest
expense to the U.S. company. Likewise, if a U.S. company
develops technology, deducts the development expenses, and
then transfers the technology to the tax haven affiliate
for sublicensing or for use in its trade or business without
adequate compensation, not only is income-producing property
transferred to the tax haven entity, but the U.S. affiliate
has been able to take deductions for expenses without having
to realize the income that accrues from the expenses.

A somewhat related problem is the failure of a U.S.
company to properly allocate to a tax haven affiliate expenses
it incurs for that affiliate. For example, a U.S. company
may provide managerial services for a tax haven affiliate,
and fail to charge for them. In addition, it may fail to
allocate expenses which it incurs and which are, in reality,
for the tax haven affiliate. A greater foreign tax credit
may be available because of this failure to properly allocate
expenses.

2. Transfers of Assets Other than by Transfer Pricing

Another method for transferring property to a tax haven
entity is by a tax free reorganization or other exchange.
In the case of transfers from the U.S., the general non-
recognition provisions of the Code operate only if the
transferor receives a ruling from the IRS that the exchange
did not have as one of its principal purposes the avoidance
of Federal income taxes.[2]

a. Transfers to Tax Haven Corporations--Scope of §367.

Section 367 was originally intended to prevent taxpayers
from permanently circumventing the tax ordinarily payable on
the disposition of appreciated assets.[3] When created, the
tax avoidance concept was thus of limited scope.

---

[2] § 367.

[3] See H.R. Rep. No. 708, 72d Cong., 1st Sess. 20 (1932);
and S. Rep. No. 665, 72d Cong., 1st Sess. 26-27 (1932).

To illustrate the loophole they sought to close, the
House and Senate gave this example in their report:

A, an American citizen, owns 100,000 shares of
stock in corporation X, a domestic corporation, which
originally cost him $1,000,000 but now has a market
value of $10,000,000. Instead of selling the stock

The IRS, however, expanded this scope by looking to other consequences of asset transferral. In addition to the complete avoidance of tax on realized appreciation from investment assets, the IRS considered the potential for temporary deferral of tax and also the deferral of tax on other income produced by the transferred asset, e.g., interest and dividends, in determining whether a tax avoidance purpose was present. Application of the tax avoidance concept was thus enlarged to include both the nature of the transferred assets and the nature of their subsequent use.

The breadth of this inquiry was reduced by the IRS in 1968, in response to the 1962 enactment of subpart F. [4] The IRS announced, in Revenue Procedure 68-23, [5] that its

---

> outright, A organizes a corporation under the laws of Canada to which he transfers the 100,000 shares of stock in exchange for the entire capital stock of the Canadian company. This transaction is a nontaxable exchange. The Canadian corporation sells the stock of corporation X for $10,000,000 in cash. The latter transaction is exempt from tax under the Canadian law and is not taxable as United States income under the present law. The Canadian corporation organizes corporation Y under the laws of the United States and transfers the $10,000,000 cash received upon the sale of corporation X's stock in exchange for the entire capital stock of Y. The Canadian corporation then distributes the stock of Y to A in connection with a reorganization. By this series of transactions, A has had the stock of X converted into cash and has it in complete control.

When this provision was adopted, Canada was considered to be a tax haven.

[4] See J. Sitrick, "Section 367 and Tax Avoidance: An Analysis of the Section 367 Guidelines" 25 Tax L. Rev. 429 (1970).

Mr. Sitrick, formerly of the Office of Tax Legislative Counsel (International), states that

> . . . while the importance of section 367 was reduced considerably by reason of the 1962 legislation, the section retains importance in transactions with which the provisions of subpart F were not intended to deal directly. [25 Tax L. Rev. at 442.]

[5] 1968-1 C.B. 821.

concern would be limited to the nature of the assets transferred, i.e., to their inherent potential for income and gain.[6]

The IRS also announced in Revenue Procedure 68-23, at §3.02(1), that when the transferred assets are "...to be devoted by the transferee foreign corporation to the active conduct, in any foreign country, of a trade or business... [the transaction will ordinarily receive favorable consideration] Although apparently in conflict with the new policy to leave consideration of post-transfer use to subpart F, adoption of this "active business" criterion was not intended to provide a means for determining whether tax avoidance would flow from the post-transfer activity itself. Rather, it was included to test the avoidance potential of the individual asset, the thought being that property used in an active trade or business would not be transferred with a principal view to the realization of its appreciation or enjoyment of its income outside the taxing jurisdiction.[7] Therefore, the active business requirement does not impinge on the deferral permitted by subpart F.[8]

In 1976, the Congress amended § 367 to remove the pre-transaction filing requirement in all cases, and the ruling requirement in certain cases.[9] None of the statutory changes significantly clarified the meaning of tax avoidance.[10]

---

[6] See Rev. Proc. 68-23, §§ 3.02(1)(a)-(d) (describing certain "tainted" assets), § 3.01(2), and § 3.03(1)(a).

[7] See also § 3.02(1)(a)(iv) of Rev. Proc. 68-23.

[8] Section 367 clearance will not be granted if property transferred to a foreign corporation will be used to conduct a trade or business in the United States. To this extent, the subsequent use test retains vitality under § 367.

[9] Tax Reform Act of 1976, § 1042.

[10] H.R. Rep. No. 94-658, 94th Cong., 1st Sess. 239-40 (1976), 1976-3 C.B. (Vol. 2) 931-2; and S. Rep. No. 94-938, 94th Cong., 2d Sess. 261-2 (1976), 1976-3 C.B. (Vol. 3) 299-300.

As presently construed, § 367 is of limited utility in tax haven related tax administration. While it does prevent the transfer of certain assets with income-producing potential, it will not prevent the transfer of an active business which may then be conducted free of subpart F. For example, a tax free transfer can be used to enable a U.S. manufacturer to take advantage of a tax exemption granted by one country to attract manufacturing and the low rates of tax afforded by a tax haven on passive investment income.

Section 367 can be used only to deny non-recognition for a transfer to a corporate entity, and therefore its impact is limited to permitting a tax (often a capital gain tax) on appreciation. In many cases it is unclear that anything of value has been transferred. For example, an engineering company which is to perform services in the Middle East may be able to form a subsidiary corporation in a tax haven without a §367 ruling. Arguably, under Revenue Ruling 79-288,[11] no ruling would be required if, before the transfer, the parent had no rights under the tax haven's law to use, and protect from unauthorized use, the parent's name. However, a ruling may be required for the transfer of the active business or for the transfer of goodwill.

b. Transfers Not Reorganizations

Section 367 does not affect a transfer to a trust, a partnership, or a corporation where the reorganization provisions are not applicable in any case. Instead, the § 1491 excise tax might apply.

Like § 367, § 1491 was intended to prevent taxpayers from transferring appreciated property to foreign entities to avoid United States tax on the gain. Today, § 1491 is broad, covering almost all transfers to almost all foreign entities. There are, however, exceptions which can be abused. Further, like § 367, the IRS does not interpret § 1491 as taking into account post-transfer use of the assets transferred in determining whether it operates. Therefore, if the transfer fits one of the exceptions, the § 1491 excise tax does not apply.

Legislative exceptions to the § 1491 tax are provided (1) for transfers to a tax exempt organization, (2) if the transfer is not in pursuance of a plan having as one of its principal purposes the avoidance of Federal income taxes, (3) if § 367 applies to the transfer, or (4) if an election to recognize gain on the transfer is made.[12]

---

[11] 1979-2 C.B. 139.

[12] § 1492.

Attempts have been made to avoid or evade §1491 by the following transactions:

1.   A transfer of unappreciated or slightly appreciated property, or a transfer of slightly appreciated property with respect to which a § 1057 election has been made.

2.   A transfer to a friendly foreign foundation which is a tax exempt organization.

3.   A transfer of ordinary income property (subject to the excise tax, but at a lower rate of tax than the ordinary rates).

4.   A transfer at death by operation of law rather than by devise.

5.   A transfer through a conduit, such as a shell U.S. corporation which has no assets with which to pay the § 1491 tax, or through a friendly non-resident alien to a trust for the benefit of the U.S. transferor or his family.

Some of these transactions are fraudulent. The use of a foreign intermediary to pass property to a foreign trust, for example, is a willful attempt to evade or defeat tax. The willful failure to file the required return (Form 926) is punishable under § 7203. The same is true of the transfer to a friendly foreign foundation where the real intent is that the property will be used for the benefit of the transferor or his family.

To the extent that the transactions described above are permitted by the Code, they reflect Congressional policy determinations. For example, the fact that § 1491 is avoided by a § 1057 election or the realization of a small amount of income reflects a Congressional policy of protecting the U.S. tax on the gain inherent in the property. Not subjecting to U.S. tax the income earned from the property after transfer is a deferral issue, and occurs because of Congressional policy decisions as to the scope of the trust rules or other anti-avoidance rules.

Similarly, § 1491 will not apply to a transfer to a
foreign trust by a non-resident alien who then becomes a
United States resident. Section 1491 can also be avoided by
a United States expatriate transferring property after
renouncing citizenship. Both gaps could be closed by legislation
subjecting at least some transfers to §1491. Once again,
however, any problems are caused by Congressional decisions
as to the scope of the United States taxing jurisdiction.

C. Transactions Through a Controlled Entity

Today, major corporations conduct varied activities in
tax havens. During consideration of the 1962 Revenue Act,
the IRS described certain categories of tax avoidance devices
used by U.S. taxpayers doing business overseas. Some appear
to be used today and in some cases their use has grown;
others have been substantially eliminated. Corporations
continue to divert income to foreign subsidiaries which
engage in no real activity abroad. They continue to organize
foreign subsidiaries to carry on the same type of business
activity previously conducted by the domestic parent and to
divert income through improper pricing arrangements and
through the transfer of valuable income producing assets,
both tangible and intangible, to tax haven entities. Diversion
of income through improper expensing also continues. Foreign
transportation and reinsurance still continue to a significant
degree.

Patterns of use by industry groups is apparent. For
example, the petroleum industry makes significant use of
tax havens. It uses them by forming companies in tax havens
to carry out the traditional functions of shipping and
refining and selling petroleum, and for newer activities
including transshipping.

The insurance industry also continues to make extensive
use of tax havens. Foreign insurance companies doing business
in the United States often have a Bermuda or Cayman subsidiary
through which they reinsure risks written in the United
States. Many United States multinational companies have
captive insurance subsidiaries located in Bermuda.

The construction industry and other service industries
are making increasing use of tax havens. The growth in
these industries appears to have been the fastest of any
industry group.

Tax havens are an overwhelming factor in the shipping industry. Many United States companies own shipping companies formed in tax havens (most often Liberia or Panama).

Commercial banks have extensive operations in tax havens, operating there mostly through branches, although some U.S. banks have subsidiaries in tax havens. As the data in our tax haven levels estimate show, this use has grown enormously in the past few years, with a great deal of the growth in the Bahamas.[13]

The heavy equipment industry also tends to utilize sales companies in tax havens. In a few cases manufacturing or assembly operations have been conducted in tax havens. Most manufacturing and assembly operations, however, are conducted in low cost areas offering tax incentives to attract industry, such as Taiwan, Korea, the Phillippines, Ireland, and Puerto Rico, which were generally not addressed in this study. At times, a tax haven corporation is formed to make the investment in the manufacturing tax haven.

1. Tax Planning -- Minimizing Tax and Maximizing the Foreign Tax Credit

United States taxpayers use tax havens in legal tax planning for one of three purposes or a combination of them: (1) to minimize United States tax on a transaction or on investment income; (2) to increase foreign source income free of foreign tax to enable the taxpayer to credit more foreign income taxes; and (3) to minimize foreign taxes which might otherwise be imposed on a transaction.

Tax haven entities can be used to minimize taxes. If the goal is to avoid U.S. tax on the income from a transaction, the transaction would have to be structured to avoid the application of subpart F and the foreign personal holding company rules. It would also have to comply with the §482 pricing regulations. Prior to 1976, foreign trusts could be used for this purpose, but this use has been substantially curtailed, although not totally eliminated. Avoiding or deferring U.S. tax on the income might be accomplished by, for example, keeping within the de minimis exception from subpart F, or by conducting transactions which subpart F does not tax.

---

[13] See Chapter III, supra. See New York Times, Friday, March 24, 1977, at A1.

In some tax haven transactions may result in U.S. tax liability under subpart F or the foreign personal holding company provisions. In other cases, the IRS may shift income to or from the tax haven entity under the intercompany pricing rules and accordingly minimize the tax avoidance potential of the haven entity. In some cases, however, unless the income is treated as U.S. source income, taxing the tax haven entity's income to the U.S. parent under subpart F has no real U.S. tax effect, because the U.S. parent is in an excess foreign tax credit position and foreign taxes imposed on non-tax haven income will in any event offset any U.S. tax which may be imposed on the subpart F income. In fact, at times, a planning goal is achieved if income can be shifted from the United States to a tax haven so as to absorb excess credits from taxes paid to high tax countries. Some practitioners believe that most large multinational companies are at or near an excess credit position, and that any changes to tax more tax haven income will affect small companies, not the larger ones. Nevertheless, the larger companies are using tax havens to significant advantage.

A U.S. taxpayer can credit foreign taxes on a dollar-for-dollar basis against its U.S. tax imposed on foreign source income. The limitation is computed on a worldwide basis so that taxes paid to high tax countries can offset U.S. taxes on income earned in low tax countries such as tax havens. The foreign tax credit is available up to the U.S. tax rate. If the foreign taxes paid or accrued in a taxable year exceed the U.S. rate, the excess can be carried back or carried forward for a limited number of years. If they cannot be used within that period, they are lost.

Assume, for example, that U.S. corporation X has taxable income of $10 million, $5 million from U.S. sources and $5 million from Country A. Country A imposes a tax of 50 percent, or $2.5 million in this case. X's U.S. tax before

credit is $4.6 million (46% of $10 million). X's foreign
tax credit limitation is $2.3 million ($5,000,000 ÷ $10,000,000
x $4,600,000) which leaves X with a $200,000 excess credit.
Its worldwide tax burden is $4.8 million. If this same
pattern recurs annually so that X will not be able to use
the excess credits in other years, then X has an additional
cost of $200,000 per year.

Assume, however, that X can structure its transactions
to convert $1.0 million of its U.S. source income to foreign
source income in a tax haven which does not tax that income.
For example, X could form a Bahamian company and sell through
it to generate foreign base company sales income, or it
could transfer working capital to be invested by the Bahamian
company. In either case, X would be taxed under subpart F
on the income of the Bahamian company. Thus, X is still
taxed by the U.S. on $10 million and its U.S. tax before
credit is still $4.6 million. However, X's foreign tax
credit limitation is now $2.76 million ($6,000,000 ÷ $10,000,000
x $4,600,000). X can therefore credit its entire Country A
tax of $2.5 million bringing its worldwide tax burden down
to $4.6 million.

If the above transactions are not conducted at arms
length the income might be reallocated to the U.S. under
§482. Also, the IRS may have an argument for disregarding
the tax haven company under §269. If, however, the transactions
cannot be restructured a tax advantage has been gained.

The same worldwide tax reduction can be accomplished by
reducing foreign taxes, which is at times easier than minimizing
United States taxes. Often foreign laws are not as well
developed as United States laws and foreign tax administrators
may not be as sophisticated as United States tax administrators,
or have the resources which are available to the United
States. If foreign taxes can be minimized so that they do
not exceed the United States foreign tax credit limitation,
a cost of doing business has been reduced. Thus, an alternative
approach in the above example would be to try to shift
income from Country A to the tax haven.

2. Holding Companies

One of the most significant uses of a tax haven corporation is as a holding company. Holding companies are used to control other companies through stock ownership, as investment vehicles, or to collect income such as dividends, loan interest, and royalties or licencing fees. The company will either distribute the funds to the parent or it will reinvest the funds, in some cases lending them to affiliates.

Generally, the company will be established in a tax haven which imposes little or no income tax on the earnings of the company, and which imposes no withholding tax on the distributions and payments it will make. If possible, a tax haven with a widespread treaty network will be used so that payments to the holding company will incur relatively low rates of tax in the source country. A country with a special tax regime for holding companies might be chosen. Thus, many holding companies are established in Switzerland, Luxemborg, Liechtenstein, or the Netherlands (which becomes a tax haven by reason of its treaty network).

The holding company is formed in the tax haven, and assets are transferred for nominal consideration or in a tax free reorganization transaction. The company then either collects dividends, in the case of stock, or in the case of patents, relinquishes these rights to other foreign corporations and receives royalties.

Initially, the Congress addressed holding company abuse by individuals and sought to eliminate that abuse by the foreign personal holding company provisions.[14] Widely held companies, however, were free to obtain the benefits of deferral by the formation of a holding company in a tax haven. In 1962, the Congress sought to prohibit corporate holding companies by including, as a category of subpart F income, foreign personal holding company income.[15] In doing so, they recognized "the need to maintain active American business operations abroad on an equal competitive footing with other operating businesses in the same countries", but saw "no need to maintain the deferral of U. S. tax where the investments are portfolio types of investments or where the company is merely partially receiving investment income."[16]

---

[14] §§ 551-558.

[15] § 954(a)(1).

[16] H. Rep. No. 1447, 87th Cong., 2d Sess. 62 (1962); S. Rep. No. 1881, 87th Cong., 2d Sess. 82 (1962).

For subpart F purposes, foreign personal holding company income is defined as that term is defined for purposes of the foreign personal holding company provisions,[17] but with numerous modifications, generally intended to exclude actual business income and income received from a related company in the same country as the receiving company.

There is still significant use of tax haven holding and investment companies. In 1976, controlled foreign corporations formed in tax havens and classified as holding companies and other investment companies reported assets of $8.3 billion. This figure represents more than half of the worldwide assets of such companies.

The foreign personal holding company provisions may be circumvented by transferring the income producing assets to an active business rather than to a holding company. Under subpart F, if the foreign base company income of a controlled foreign corporation is less than 10 percent of gross income, no part of the gross income for the taxable year is treated as foreign base company income. Accordingly, if a substantial non-base company income producing business is being conducted, passive income can be sheltered, provided the passive income is less than 10 percent of the gross income of the controlled foreign corporation. The amount sheltered can be large. For example, if a foreign subsidiary has gross income of $10 million, none of which is base company income, over $1 million in passive income could be shifted to it and sheltered. In fact, there are base companies with over $1 billion in gross non-base company income. Such a company could shelter more than $100 million in passive income.

A holding company can also be used to advantage to change U.S. source income into foreign source income to absorb excess foreign tax credits. For example, X, a U.S. multinational corporation, has cash invested in CD's in a U.S. bank. The income is U.S. source income taxable in the U.S. The interest income could be turned into foreign source income simply by placing the cash in a foreign bank. However, there is a separate foreign tax credit limitation for bank interest income to prevent just such planning. Instead, X contributes the cash to Y, its tax haven holding company. Y deposits the cash in a foreign bank. The interest Y receives on the deposit is foreign personal

---

[17] § 553.

holding company income taxable to X under subpart F, but as
a dividend not subject to the separate limitation for interest
United States source interest income has been converted into
foreign source income against which foreign taxes may be
credited. This transaction is perfectly legal, and is done
often.

Some persons have attempted to avoid paying U.S. tax on
the personal holding company type income of their foreign
corporation, circumventing the personal holding company
income provisions by claiming that the income of the foreign
corporation is derived from the active conduct of a banking
or financing business, one of the exclusions from foreign
personal holding company income.[18] In many cases the
schemes are fraudulent. In others, however, the issue is
not so clear because the form of establishing a bank and
engaging in the banking business is followed.

For example, in an attempt to create a colorable claim
of entitlement to this exclusion, an individual or a company
organizes a bank or finance company in a friendly tax haven
jurisdiction, such as St. Vincent, that has little or no
control over its local banks. The bank may engage in various
activities. For example, it may lend funds to related
parties and receive the income free of tax. It may also
engage in some limited banking activity, such as selling
CD's to foreigners, and then relending the proceeds for use
in its controlling shareholders business or for use by
others. If the taxpayer is successful in avoiding audit,
or, in the unlikely event that he is sustained in the
argument that his foreign corporation is engaged in the
banking business, the personal holding company type income
can be accumulated in the tax haven free of tax. St. Vincent
shell banks have allegedly been used to defraud banks and
other businesses in the United States.[19]

3. Sales Activities

A tax haven corporation may be used as a sales company.
The sales company may buy from or sell to affiliates or may
engage in sales only with unrelated persons. Transactions
with affiliates will frequently be priced to minimize the
tax liability of the affiliated group. Generally, this
means that the sales will be structured to maximize the
profit of the tax haven affiliate.

---

[18] §954(c)(3)(B).

[19] See New York Times, Tuesday, Oct. 21, 1980, D-5.

Prior to the Revenue Act of 1962, U.S. companies had established a significant number of sales companies in tax havens. The Congress sought to limit this use by including in the U.S. shareholder's income "foreign base company sales income".[20] Foreign base company sales income is the income of a controlled foreign corporation derived from (1) the selling of property purchased from a related person, or (2) the buying of personal property for sale to a related person, if the property is produced outside the country under the laws of which the controlled foreign corporation is created or organized and the property is sold for use outside of that country.[21] Commission income from those sales is also included.

The crucial element in foreign base company sales income is a purchase from or a sale to a party related to the controlled foreign corporation. If the transactions are with unrelated parties, there is no foreign base company income.

Under this provision, income earned by a Bahamian corporation from the sale to unrelated Italian customers of goods purchased from a German affiliate would be foreign base company sales income. Income earned by the Bahamian corporation from the sale to unrelated Italian customers of goods purchased from an unrelated German supplier would not be foreign base company sales income.

Despite subpart F, some sales activity continues in tax havens. Attempts may be made to circumvent subpart F. A U.S. company can arguably avoid the foreign base company sales income provisions by licensing an unrelated foreign company to manufacture goods, and having a tax haven subsidiary purchase those goods for sale to customers in a third country.

The 10 percent de minimis exception can be used to shelter enormous amounts of income. Foreign tax haven corporations wholly owned by a U.S. corporation have had gross income of more than $1.0 billion from purchasing and selling from and to unrelated persons. The companies also earned shipping income and had passive investment income. There was no subpart F income because the sales activity was with unrelated parties, the transportation income was exempt, and the passive income was sheltered by the 10 percent de minimis exception.

---

[20] § 954(a)(2).

[21] § 954(d)(1).

In the petroleum industry, trading companies have been
formed by the major integrated companies, and also by small
oil companies commonly known as oil resellers, which do not
have production of their own. The majors will often use the
trading companies for dealing with unrelated parties. If
the trading company is actually engaged in this business,
the activity is specifically outside the scope of subpart F.
In many cases, however, all of the decisions regarding the
purchases and sales by the trading company are made in the
United States. In some cases, the business functions of the
parent are duplicated by the foreign subsidiary. There may
be two buying and selling organizations, one engaging in
domestic business and the other in foreign with respect to
the same oil. It is difficult to determine who is really
doing what for whom. Similar patterns may exist in the
grain industry.

While trading companies are legitimate tax planning
tools, fraudulent arrangements may be structured to look
like trading companies. Often, information gathering problems,
including lack of access to tax haven records, make it
difficult to prove criminal fraud. Transactions are, at
times, arranged with friendly third parties to avoid purchases
and sales with a related party. For example, oil company X
forms subsidiary corporation Y in a tax haven. Y is to
engage only in the buying and selling of foreign oil.
Usually, Y buys foreign oil from an unrelated party and
sells that oil to an unrelated third party. It is believed,
however, that at times swapping arrangements are entered
into under which Y buys from an unrelated party and sells to
an unrelated friend at a high price. The friend then sells
to X, the U.S. parent, at its cost or at cost plus a small
profit. In reality, Y has sold oil to X at a price which is
too high. If the facts were known, the IRS could reallocate
the income to X under § 482, and Y would have subpart F
income. Because of the frequency of transactions, the
fungibility of oil, and the lack of adequate records, it is
difficult for the IRS to establish the substance of the
transaction.

Trading companies were involved in the so called "daisy
chain" scheme that was used to attempt to avoid the Department of Energy price control regulations. In one case, a
U.S. company bought domestic oil and sold it to a tax haven
corporation, which the U.S. company claimed was not an
affiliate. The oil was sold through a number of different
companies, and then the same oil was purchased by the U.S.
corporation's foreign subsidiary, which sold it to other
parties and then back into the United States. The initial

sale by the U.S. company to the tax haven company was at a
low controlled price. The oil was eventually sold back into
the United States at the higher world price. The substantial
markup was left in the offshore companies. The persons who
control the U.S. company also control the tax haven company,
but evidence which can be introduced in a court is not
available.

The foreign base company sales income provisions may
be avoided by structuring an entity as an assembly operation
rather than as a sales company. Foreign base company sales
income does not include income from the sale of property
manufactured, produced, grown or constructed by the controlled
foreign corporation in whole or in part from property which
it purchased.[22] Property is considered manufactured,
produced, grown or constructed by the subsidiary if it is
substantially transformed prior to sale or if the property
purchased is used as a component of the property sold.[23]
The substantial transformation test is subjective. The
component test in the regulations can be met through a cost
test or a subjective test. Purchased property is used as a
component if the operations conducted by the selling corporation
in connection with the property purchased and sold are
substantial in nature and are manufacturing, production or
construction of property.[24] In addition, the operations
of the selling corporation, in connection with the use of
the purchased property as a component part of the personal
property which is sold, is considered the manufacture of a
product if, in connection with the property, conversion
costs of the corporation are 20 percent or more of the total
cost of the goods sold.[25]

---

[22] Treas. Reg. § 1.954-3(a)(4).

[23] Treas. Reg. § 1.954-3(a)(4)(ii) and (iii).

[24] Treas. Reg. § 1.954-3(a)(4)(iii).

[25] For an example of the application of the manufacturing
exception see, Dave Fischbein Mfg. Co. v. Commissioner,
59 T.C. 338 (1972), acq. 1973-2 C.B. 2, in which a bag
assembly operation was conducted by a Belgian corporation
wholly owned by a U.S. corporation. The Belgian company
bought components from its U.S. affiliates, and some
minor parts locally, assembled them in Belgium, and then
sold them worldwide. The court simply disagreed with
the contention of the IRS that the activities were not
manufacturing.

A U.S. company can, therefore, form a subsidiary in a
tax haven, sell components to the subsidiary which assembles
them, and take the position that no foreign base company
sales income is earned on the sale of the property which
includes the components. The 20 percent safe harbor is
relatively easy to meet. In addition, the subjective tests
in the regulations are difficult for the IRS to deal with
because of problems of access to books and records, personnel,
and the manufacturing plant itself.

The assembly operations may be subject to scrutiny
under the intercompany pricing rules. The IRS may reallocate
income from sales between the haven subsidiary and its
affiliates.[26] In addition, allocations might be made on
the grounds that an affiliate is performing services for the
tax haven subsidiary[27] or that an affiliate has licensed
intangibles (such as a trademark) to the subsidiary without
adequate compensation.[28] There are, however, information
gathering problems in applying these rules.

Also included in foreign base company sales income is
income of a branch of a controlled foreign corporation
operating outside of the country in which the controlled
foreign corporation is incorporated, if the use of the
branch has substantially the same tax effect as if the
branch were a wholly owned subsidiary corporation of the
controlled foreign corporation.[29] The regulations assume a
substantially similar tax effect if the branch is taxed at a
somewhat lower rate than it would have been in the country
where the subsidiary is incorporated.[30] Under this rule,
if a tax haven company is organized in Panama, and has a
selling branch in a low tax country, the branch rule will
operate, because Panama imposes a corporation tax on business

---

[26] § 482; Treas. Reg. § 1.482-2(e)(1)(ii).

[27] Treas. Reg. § 1.482-2(b).

[28] Treas. Reg. § 1.482-2(d).

[29] § 954(d)(2).

[30] Treas. Reg. § 1.954-3(b)(1).

income from Panamanian sources. If, however, the base
company is formed in the Cayman Islands (which has a zero
rate of tax) it can establish a branch in a second country
and not be subject to the branch rule.[31]

A pattern of doing business has developed to take
advantage of the branch rule and the 10 percent foreign base
company de minimis rule. A U.S. company wishing to take
advantage of a tax holiday offered by a country which is
trying to attract manufacturing plants, forms a subsidiary
in a tax haven with which the United States has a tax treaty
and transfers to it the requisite capital and technology.
The tax haven company constructs the manufacturing plant in
the tax holiday country and its production is exported and sold
to unrelated persons. Assuming the initial transfer qualifies
under § 351, a favorable § 367 ruling would ordinarily be
issued because the property will be used in the active
conduct of a trade or business.[32] The manufacturing profits
are not taxed to the U.S. parent because they are not foreign
base company income. The sales profits are not foreign base
company sales income because of the local manufacturing
test. In addition, the earnings can be reinvested in the
tax haven substantially free of tax if the income from those
earnings is less than 10 percent of the foreign corporation's
gross income. The tax haven entity is used because while
the tax holiday country does not tax the export manufacturing
profits it would tax the passive income earned on retained
earnings at a high rate. The tax haven may tax these earnings
but at a very low rate of tax. The retained earnings of the
tax haven company might also be reinvested in active business
assets free of tax. The tax effect is the avoidance of the
tax holiday country tax, not necessarily U.S. tax.

4. Services and Construction

The service and construction industries have increased
their use of tax haven entities enormously. The data demonstrate rapid growth in assets invested through tax haven
entities in both of these industries. The growth greatly
exceeds the growth in other industries, despite subpart F's
application to services and the existence of detailed § 482
allocation regulations applying to services.

---

[31] Of course, if the second country is a high tax country,
then to the extent that the branch is subject to tax in
that second country there is no overall tax avoidance.
However, by careful planning, some second country
tax can often be avoided.

[32] See Rev. Proc. 68-23, 1968-1 C.B. 821, 823.

For 1976, earnings of controlled foreign corporations
formed in the tax havens are estimated at $330 million in
the service industries and over $500 million in construc-
tion. These companies are estimated to have assets of $2.4
billion and $2.2 billion respectively. In 1976, controlled
foreign corporations formed in the tax havens held 23 percent
of the worldwide assets of service companies and 42 percent
in construction. These figures represent an increase from 11
percent and 26 percent respectively, from 1968.

Subpart F income includes foreign base company services
income. Foreign base company services income is defined as
income from the performance of technical, managerial, engineering, architectural or like services outside of the country
of incorporation of the controlled foreign corporation, if
such services are performed for, or on behalf of, a related
person.[33/] Services which are performed for, or on behalf
of, a related person include (i) direct or indirect compensation
paid to a controlled foreign corporation by a related person
for performing services, (ii) performance of services by a
controlled foreign corporation which a related person is
obligated to perform, (iii) performance of services with
respect to property sold by a related person where the
performance of services constitutes a condition of sale, and
(iv) substantial assistance contributing to the performance
of the services by the controlled foreign corporation furnished
by a related person or persons.[34/] A related party provides
substantial assistance to a controlled foreign corporation
if the assistance furnished provides the controlled foreign
corporation with the "skills" which are a principal element
in producing the income from the performance of the services
or the cost to the controlled foreign corporation of the
assistance is 50 percent or more of the total cost to the
foreign corporation of performing the services; assistance
is not taken into account unless it assists the subsidiary
"directly" in the performance of the services.[35/]

Despite these provisions, little income tax has been
collected from the service or construction industries in
havens. According to IRS statistics, includable income of
controlled foreign corporations in the services industry was

[33/] § 954(b)(3).

[34/] Treas. Reg. § 1.954-4(b)(1).

[35/] Treas. Reg. § 1.954-4(b)(2)(ii)(b) and (e).

approximately $5.7 million in 1975 and in the construction industry was approximately $2.6 million.

The foreign base company services income concept was drafted with manufacturing-related services in mind. Congress stated that "as in the case of sales income, the purpose here is to deny tax deferral where a service subsidiary is separated from manufacturing or similar activities of a related corporation and organized in another country primarily to obtain a lower rate of tax for the service income."[36] Today, the services which appear to be making the greatest use of tax havens are independent construction, natural resource exploration, and high technology services, which are not related to manufacturing. A portion of a business which is conducted in the U.S. can simply be excised from the U.S. business and transplanted to a tax haven. The services are not being performed for a related party, but rather are being performed for unrelated parties. The income is being accumulated free of tax.

The problems with the service rules are generally due to the approach taken by the Congress, which, in effect, mandates regulations requiring difficult line drawing. It is unclear what facts and circumstances are necessary for the IRS to assert that substantial assistance has been rendered to the foreign subsidiary. The regulations do not establish guidelines, other than two examples which are not particularly helpful. One example indicates that if a contract for the provision of services is supervised by employees of the U.S. parent corporation who are temporarily on loan to the subsidiary, then substantial assistance is rendered to the subsidiary by the related person, and the income from the performance of the contract is foreign base company income.[37] If, however, the contract is supervised by permanent employees of the subsidiary, and the U.S. parent only provides clerical assistance, then such assistance is not substantial and income from the contract is not

---

[36] S. Rep. No. 1881, at 84, 1962-3 C.B. 703, 790.

[37] Treas. Reg. § 1.954-4(b)(3) example (2).

foreign base company services income.[38/] The example also
indicates that if permanent employees of a controlled foreign
corporation oversee a contract with no substantial assistance
rendered by a related person, then no foreign base company
services income arises from the performance of the contract.[39/]

The determination of whether an employee is permanent
or temporary presents a very difficult factual issue. By char-
acterizing employees as permanent employees of a controlled
foreign corporation, a U.S. shareholder can take the position
that the transactions in question do not produce foreign
base company services income.

The factual issue of what constitutes substantial
assistance has arisen in connection with a number of services,
including offshore drilling. In a prototype case, a U.S.
parent establishes a foreign subsidiary in a tax haven to
conduct offshore drilling operations outside of the subsidiary's
country of incorporation. The officers of the parent may
negotiate the drilling contracts and then enter into an
agreement with third parties as officers of the subsidiary.
The parent corporation is not liable on the contracts and
does not guarantee performance of the contracts. The parent
may lease the equipment necessary to conduct the drilling
operations at the safe harbor arms-length charge under the
§ 482 regulations. The day-to-day drilling operations are
managed and performed by on-site employees of the foreign
subsidiary, who are characterized as permanent employees.
The joint officers of the parent and the subsidiary perform
various managerial services for the subsidiary. In many
cases, there will be little or no tax imposed on the service
income by the country in which the services are performed.

Arguably, the parent renders minimal rather than substantial
assistance to the foreign subsidiary, and therefore income
from the drilling operations is not foreign base company
services income. On the other hand, it may be argued that
the income received by the subsidiary is foreign base
company services income because the assistance rendered by
the parent in the form of overall direction of the subsidiary
drilling contracts is substantial. The issue is difficult
to resolve, particularly since important facts may be known
to employees of the foreign subsidiary who cannot be compelled
to testify.

[38/] Treas. Reg. § 1.954-4(b)(3) example (3).

[39/] Treas. Reg. § 1.954-4(b)(3) example (3).

A construction company will also often use a subsidiary formed in a tax haven to conduct its construction projects abroad. A construction project generally will consist of three phases: (1) a prospectus phase during which the plans for the project are outlined; (2) a planning phase during which actual detailed plans will be drafted; and (3) a construction phase during which a construction manager is placed on the construction site to supervise the project.

The initial prospectus will often be prepared and promoted by a U.S. company. If the company is successful in obtaining the contract, the contract will be signed by officers of the offshore subsidiary of the U.S. company, who may also be officers of the U.S. parent. Supervision of the construction will be conducted by the offshore company through an on-site manager who is an employee of that company, but who at one time may have been an employee of the U.S. parent. He may have obtained all of his knowledge and skills from the U.S. parent.

As with the drilling rig situation, it may be difficult to establish that the services were performed for or on behalf of a related person. Once the company develops substance overseas, so that fewer of its managerial services are being performed by the U.S. parent, it becomes more difficult for the IRS to make the substantial assistance case.

The Commissioner may be able to allocate some of the services income from the services to the U.S. parent under § 482. The regulations under § 482 provide that where a member of a controlled group of entities performs managerial or technical services "for the benefit of, or on behalf of, another member of the group" without charge, an allocation may be made to reflect an arms-length charge for those services.[40/] The test of whether the services were performed for the benefit of or on behalf of the parent is, as with the subpart F tests, a very difficult subjective test for the IRS to apply.

Agents believe that a few of these cases are in fact abusive. An example of such a situation might be the nego- tiation and agreement of a construction contract by the U.S. parent but, at the last minute, having the contract signed

---

[40/] Treas. Reg. § 1.482-2(b).

by an officer of the tax haven subsidiary. This contract is
valuable and in some cases there has therefore been a transfer
of assets and gain should have been reported or the profits
from the activity should have been reported. Failure by a
sophisticated, well-advised taxpayer to report may be fraud,
but it would be difficult to establish.

Some companies have been able to accumulate significant
income overseas by leasing equipment to a tax haven subsidiary
to be used in the service business. By manipulating the §
482 rental safe harbor rule and the fair market value of the
equipment, significant income can be accumulated in the tax
haven company. This income can be used to create substance
in the tax haven company, which makes the arrangement between
the two companies even more difficult to challenge.[41]

5. Transportation

U.S. companies are engaged in the transportation industry
in tax havens (primarily shipping) to a significant degree.
As of December 31, 1977, 687 foreign flag vessels were owned
by U.S. companies or foreign affiliates of U.S. companies.[42]
Four hundred eighty-eight of these were tankers. Three
hundred eighty-five vessels were registered in Liberia, and
88 were registered in Panama. In 1976, approximately 74
percent of the assets of controlled foreign corporations
engaged in the transportation business were held by companies
formed in tax havens.[43] This represents a substantial
increase over 1968 when 50.6 percent of assets were in
companies formed in tax havens. Most of this use is completely
legal. While there can be significant tax savings, the
structures are within the spirit and letter of the law.

Two aspects of U.S. law encourage the use of tax haven
subsidiaries for carrying on the transportation business:
(1) the reciprocal exemption from U.S. income tax of foreign
flag ships which engage in traffic to and from the U.S.; and
(2) the deferral of tax on the income of foreign corporations
controlled by U.S. shareholders, whether or not they are
engaged in activities involving the U.S. In addition, U.S.
source rules operate to minimize U.S. tax even when the
vessels are shipping to the U.S.[44]

---

[41] See safe harbor rental rule in Treas. Reg. § 1.482-2(c).

[42] U.S. Department of Commerce, Maritime Administration,
Foreign Flag Merchant Ships owned by U.S. Parent Companies,
April 1979.

[43] See table 2 in Chapter III.

[44] See § 863, and Treas. Reg. § 1.863-4.

Earnings derived from the operation of a ship documented under the laws of a foreign country which grants an equivalent exemption to citizens or corporations of the United States are exempt from U.S. tax.[45] To qualify for the exemption, the foreign country granting the exemption must be the country of registration of the vessel.[46]

Under a provision adopted by the Tax Reduction Act of 1975, subpart F income includes foreign base company shipping income;[47] this is income derived from or in connection with the use of any vessel in foreign commerce and income derived from or in connection with the performance of services directly related to the use of any such vessel or from the sale, exchange or other disposition of the vessel. Prior to 1975, shipping income was excluded from subpart F. Amounts reinvested in the shipping business are still excluded. Amounts of previously excluded shipping income which are withdrawn from investment in the shipping business are included as subpart F income in the year of withdrawal. Accordingly, a company can continue to reinvest its earnings in the prescribed categories of assets, and not realize subpart F income.

We have been advised that while it was anticipated that most companies would be able to qualify for the exclusion through reinvestment, in fact, because of the glut of oil tankers, some companies may be forced to report subpart F shipping income for lack of reinvestment opportunities within the next few years. Moreover, this provision may be irrelevant to major petroleum companies because they are in an excess credit position.

A relatively new development in the petroleum industry is the transshipment of oil, which originated in 1972 when the use of super tankers became necessary. The super tankers load their cargo in the producing countries and transport it to the Caribbean where the oil is unloaded and stored by a related corporation, or by an independent transshipping company. When needed, the oil is loaded on smaller vessels which bring it to the United States. A terminalling charge of $.13 to $.17 per barrel has been paid by the refiner to the transshipper for the removal and storage of the oil.

---

[45] §§ 872(b)(1) and 883(a)(1).

[46] Rev. Rul. 75-459, 1975-2 C.B. 289.

[47] § 954(f).

However, some transshippers have charged as much as $.30 a barrel, and the Department of Energy has apparently permitted $.27 a barrel. In the usual case, the oil will remain in the terminal for no more than 30 days. The terminalling company is an offshore tax haven company. Because this is a relatively new phenomenon, the full extent of use is not known, but it is generally assumed to be significant. It is known that most oil imported from the Persian Gulf is transshipped One tax benefit can be deferral of the tax on the profit from the transshipping. If the transshipper is an affiliate, overcharging can mean a shifting of income from the U.S. to the tax haven affiliate.

6. Insurance

No deduction is allowed for self insurance. To circumvent this rule, many companies find it advantageous to form a wholly owned insurance subsidiary known as a "captive insurance company" to insure risks of the parent or its affiliates. If the company is considered an insurance company for tax purposes, and if it assumes the full risk (does not reinsure), it can invest the entire premium and realize income most of which would be free of tax.[48/]

In the prototype case, the U.S. company forms a Bermuda company to engage in the insurance business. The captive must have a minimum paid-in capital of $120,000. The captive enters into an insurance contract with its parent, pursuant to which it will insure risks of its U.S. parent or of foreign subsidiaries of the U.S. parent. In most cases the captive enters into a reinsurance contract with an unrelated insurance company. Under this contract, the unrelated insurance company assumes the risk which had been assumed by the captive. The captive invests the premium, and then, at the end of the insurance period, pays over the reinsurance premium, retaining a small percentage of it. In addition, it retains the profit realized on the invested premiums. This investment income is earned because, while the insurance premiums are paid in advance by the insured, the reinsurance premiums are not paid by the captive until the end of the coverage period.

48/ Most captives are formed in a tax haven. Some have been formed in the United States in Colorado, which has a captive insurance company law relieving captives of many of the reserve and other requirements normally imposed on insurance companies. A Colorado captive is subject to Federal income tax, but at the favorable insurance company effective rates.

In addition to significant tax advantages, a captive
also provides business advantages. It can underwrite
insurance which is not available in the commercial insurance
market, or is available only at a high premium or with large
deductibles.[49/] It can be established in jurisdictions
which free it from many State controls. Bermuda has been
the foremost situs for captives, although the Cayman Islands
is attempting to attract captive business, as are other
havens.[50/]

The earnings of a captive insurance company are potentially
subject to tax under subpart F, but only to the extent those
earnings are from the insurance of U.S. risks. Subpart F
income includes income derived from the insurance of U.S.
risks,[51/] which includes U.S. property and U.S. residents.[52/]
If the premiums for insuring U.S. risk do not exceed five
percent of total premium of the foreign company, then the
subpart F provisions do not apply.[53/] For purposes of the
subpart F insurance provisions, a foreign corporation is a
controlled foreign corporation if more than 25 percent of
the total combined voting power of all classes of stock of
the corporation is owned directly or indirectly by U.S.
shareholders on any day of the taxable year.[54/] However,
the 25 percent rule, rather than the normal 50 percent rule
for controlled foreign corporations, applies only if the
gross amount of premiums or other consideration in respect
of the reinsurance or the issuing of insurance on U.S. risks
exceeds 75 percent of the gross amount of all premiums or
other consideration received.[55/]

Subpart F has not been useful in dealing with captives.
First, there is a U.S. tax advantage to being taxed as an
insurance company, and the subpart F income of the company
would be computed by applying the insurance company rules.
Accordingly, a U.S. company may choose to form a captive
even if its income will be taxed.

[49/] See O'Brien and Tung, "Captive Off-Shore Insurance
Companies," 31 N.Y.U. Inst. on Fed. Tax., 665, 719 (1973).

[50/] See "A Survey of Offshore Captives," Tax Haven and Shelter
Report, 4 (August 1978).

[51/] § 952(a)(1).

[52/] § 953(a)(1).

[53/] § 953(a).

[54/] § 957(b).

[55/] Id.

Second, the insurance company rules are considerably narrower than the foreign base company income provisions, and therefore apply in fewer cases. The provision is limited to income from insuring U.S. risks.[56] The foreign risks of affiliates, therefore, may be insured without generating subpart F income. The foreign personal holding company rules generally do not apply to the passive income of the foreign insurer,[57] and certain amounts relating to reserves for foreign risks can be invested in U.S. property without being taxed to the U.S. shareholders as an increase in investment in U.S. property.[58] Arguably, however, insuring the foreign risks of affiliates will generate foreign base company services income.

The IRS has sought to deal with captives outside of subpart F. It has ruled that a premium paid by a domestic corporation and its affiliates to a captive insurance company, either directly or through an intermediary independent insurance company which reinsures with the parent's captive, is not deductible because there is no economic shifting or distribution of risk of loss with respect to any of the risk carried or retained by the wholly owned foreign subsidiary. To the extent that an unrelated insurer retains the risk, or to the extent that the risk is shifted to an unrelated insurance company, the premiums are deductible.[59] IRS has also ruled that the so-called "insurance premiums" paid by domestic subsidiaries of a U.S. parent were to be considered distributions of dividends to the parent, and then as a contribution to capital of the foreign subsidiary by the parent. Also, the ruling held that the companies were not insurance companies for tax purposes. This view was upheld by the Tax Court in Carnation Company v. Commissioner.[60]

----

[56] § 953(a).

[57] § 954(c)(3)(B); see § 954(c)(3)(C), which excludes from subpart F investment yields on an amount equal to one-third of the premiums earned on certain insurance contracts, provided they are not attributable to risks of related persons.

[58] § 956(b)(2)(E).

[59] Rev. Rul. 77-316, 1977-2 C.B. 53.

[60] 71 T.C. 400 (1978), appeals pending (9th Cir. 1978).

Under the IRS view, therefore, the deduction of premiums
paid to a captive would be denied, and, in the case of
premium payments for insurance by foreign subsidiaries to
the captive, there would be a constructive dividend to the
parent which would be taxable income, followed by a contribution
to the capital of the foreign captive. The foreign captive
would not have subpart F income because it would not be
engaged in the insurance business. Because the amounts are
contributions to capital rather than premium income, the
foreign corporation does not have any gross income from the
purported insurance transactions, hence it does not have any
foreign source income for purposes of the foreign tax credit
limitation.[61]

The IRS has ruled, however, that where the company is
not a wholly owned captive, but rather is owned by a group
of taxpayers, premiums will be deductible.[62]

Despite IRS attention to this area, the data show that
significant captive insurance business continues. In some
cases the captive insurance companies are beginning to
write small amounts of insurance for unrelated third parties.
In one case a captive has reached the point where 70 percent
of the risk insured by it is risk of unrelated parties. By
insuring some unrelated risk, it is intended that the company
will be deemed an insurer and the premium paid by the domestic
parent will be deductible. Because income from insurance of
foreign (even if related) risk is not subpart F income, it
can be expected that captives will continue to grow if
taxpayers can avoid the holding of Carnation. Captives have
also begun to underwrite open market business by participating
in "pools" in order to improve their chances of being considered
an insurance company.[63] Because the premiums from the related
and unrelated income are not fragmented for tax purposes, substantial amounts of income arguably can be shifted to a captive
if it writes some unrelated risk.

_____

[61] See Carnation Company, Id.

[62] Rev. Rul. 78-338, 1978-2 C.B. 107, holding that a foreign
insurance company owned and organized by 31 domestic
companies was a viable insurance company.

[63] "A Survey of Offshore Location for Captives", Tax Haven
and Shelter Report, 4 (August, 1978).

Another method of attempting to circumvent the Carnation case, and the IRS position, is the use of a so-called "rent-a-captive". Under this scheme, the taxpayer enters into an insurance contract with an unrelated U.S. commercial insurer that in turn enters into a reinsurance agreement with a tax haven company and cedes most of the premium to it. Payments of the reinsurance premiums are made at the time the taxpayer pays the premium so that the cash balances are held by the tax haven company. The taxpayer then purchases nonvoting preferred stock in the tax haven company. The shares have a value equal to a fixed percentage of the premium of the primary policy. After a period of years, the taxpayer gets a return of the capital paid for the preferred shares plus investment income on the capital and loss reserves The taxpayer can borrow an amount equal to its capital and pay interest to its preferred account.

The promoters take the position that the premiums are deductible, and that the income of the tax haven company will accumulate free of tax, because the company's share dispersal will be such that it will not be a controlled foreign corporation. In addition, they claim that there will be adequate risk shifting if properly structured so that the premiums will be deductible. Finally, they point out that large multinational corporations can benefit because the income realized when the preferred shares are redeemed will be considered foreign source income which will increase allowable foreign tax credits.

7. Banking

United States banks continue to conduct significant business through offshore financial centers. Generally, the business is conducted in branch form and the income generated is taxed currently by the U.S., subject to the availability of the foreign tax credit as limited by the overall foreign tax credit limitation. In some cases, however, U.S. banks establish holding companies and other subsidiary corporations in the havens to conduct trust or other businesses. A few of the large U.S. banks have a presence in most, if not all, of the tax havens.

The use of tax havens by banks is large and growing. Many major banks now have trust companies in the havens. These companies are not subject to U.S. tax under subpart F. Wholly owned subsidiaries of U.S. banks in the Bahamas, Cayman Islands, Netherlands Antilles, Panama, Hong Kong, Luxembourg, Singapore, and Switzerland had combined surplus and undivided profits of over $500 million at the end of 1979. The total earnings of subsidiaries of large banks in these tax havens were $96 million in 1976.

91

D. Transactions Through An Entity Which Is Not Controlled

The anti-avoidance provisions which apply to foreign transactions generally require that the foreign entity being scrutinized be controlled by a U.S. person. Without control, many of the reports by which transactions with potential U.S. tax consequences are identified arguably do not have to be filed, and the powers to compel production of records are unclear.

The subpart F or foreign personal holding company provisions apply to a foreign entity only if that entity is controlled by U.S. persons. Income is attributed to U.S. persons under subpart F only if the foreign corporation is a controlled foreign corporation.[64] A foreign corporation is a controlled foreign corporation if more than 50 percent of the total combined voting power of all classes of its voting stock is owned, or is considered as owned, by U.S. shareholders.[65] A U.S. shareholder is a U.S. person who owns 10 percent or more of the voting stock of the foreign corporation.[66] There is no equity or value test for purposes of determining whether or not a corporation is a controlled foreign corporation.

The regulations make clear that arrangements to shift nominal voting power to non-U.S. shareholders, when actual control is retained, will be disregarded.[67] The IRS has successfully defended this regulation in court. All of the litigated cases involved domestic corporations attempting to "decontrol" their foreign subsidiaries through the issuance of voting preferred stock to non-U.S. shareholders.[68]

Nevertheless, if real decontrol can be achieved, subpart F does not apply. A foreign corporation can be structured so that U.S. persons own one-half or less of its voting stock, but more than one half of the equity in the corporation

---

[64] § 951(a).

[65] § 957(a).

[66] § 951(b).

[67] Treas. Reg. § 1.957-1.

[68] Garlock, Inc. v. Commissioner, 489 F. 2d 197 (2d Cir. 1973), cert. denied, 417 U.S. 911 (1974); Kraus v. Commissioner, 490 F. 2d 598 (2d Cir. 1974), aff'g. 59 T.C. 681 (1973); Koehring Co. v. United States, 583 F. 2d 313 (7th Cir. 1978). But see, CCA Inc. v. Commissioner, 64 T.C. 137 (1974), acq. 1976-2 C.B. 1.

through, for example, the use of voting preferred stock.
Because there is no value test, the corporation (assuming
that actual control cannot be proved) is not a controlled
foreign corporation.

Moreover, a U.S. shareholder must own or be considered
as owning 10 percent or more of the total combined voting
power of the foreign corporation. Accordingly, a foreign
corporation may be formed with its stock owned by 11 U.S.
shareholders, each owning nine percent of the corporation's
stock, and it will not be a controlled foreign corporation
subject to tax under subpart F. In addition, it will not be
a foreign personal holding company because the ownership
test under those provisions is ownership by five or fewer
individual shareholders of more than 50 percent in value of
a foreign corporation's outstanding stock.

Methods have developed for maintaining actual voting
control, while achieving technical decontrol for subpart F
purposes. One such method is the issuance of "stapled",
"paired", or "back-to-back" stock. A domestic parent corporation
forms a tax haven subsidiary and then distributes ratably to
its shareholders its stock of the foreign subsidiary. The
shares of the two companies are tied together so that they
can be transferred only as a unit. The IRS has ruled, in
the domestic context, that the result is a brother/ sister
relationship between the two corporations, rather than a
parent/subsidiary relationship, and that the distribution of
the subsidiary's stock is a distribution of property includable
in income as a dividend distribution to the parent shareholders.[69]
The result of the published IRS positions is that controlled
foreign corporation status is avoided.

The distribution may be treated as a dividend to the
shareholders of the U.S. company. If, however, the subsidiary is not valuable at the time its stock is distributed,
decontrol may be achieved at little cost. In addition, the
distribution may qualify as a tax free reorganization.

In one case a U.S. company spun off to its shareholders
the stock of its wholly owned tax haven subsidiary. Within
a few years, the gross income of the tax haven company grew
to well over $100 million.

_____

[69] Rev. Rul. 54-140, 1954-1 C.B. 116. See also Rev. Rul.
80-213, 1980-28 I.R.B. 7. Stapled stock may also be
used to avoid the boycott provisions of § 999 of the
Code, and with a DISC to avoid taxation of DISC income
at the corporate parent level.

Another method for attempting to avoid the subpart F provisions is to do business through a controlled foreign corporation which is a partner in a foreign partnership. The foreign base company sales income and the foreign base company services income rules apply to transactions with related persons. The term related person does not include a partnership controlled by a controlled foreign corporation.[70/] Accordingly, a U.S. person could arguably form a controlled foreign corporation which in turn would enter into a partnership with an unrelated person and enter into base company type transactions through the partnership. Even if the other person had a relatively small interest in the partnership (for example, 10 percent), the related party status, and thus subpart F, would be avoided.[71/]

Promoters have sold decontrol through fraudulent schemes which attempt to avoid all reporting requirements and thus IRS scrutiny. For example, the May 1980 issue of the Journal of Taxation describes a scheme in which a Panamanian corporation establishes a British Virgin Islands (BVI) trust for the benefit of the Mexican Red Cross, contributing to the trust a nominal sum of money. The trust then organizes a Hong Kong company. Ninety-six percent of the stock is issued to the trust and four percent is issued to the U.S. person who is the investor. The BVI trust then has the U.S. person assume management and control over the Hong Kong company.

The promoters apparently take the position that the Hong Kong company is neither a controlled foreign corporation nor a foreign personal holding company, because control is in the BVI trust which is a foreign trust created by a foreign grantor and having a foreign beneficiary (the Mexican Red Cross). Further, the promoters take the position that the U.S. investor does not have to file a Form 959 because the U.S. person acquired less than five percent of the stock of the foreign corporation. Under this theory, no other return would have to be filed. The Mexican Red Cross never gets anything because the company never pays dividends. Instead, its profits are "lent" to the U.S. investor.

[70/] See § 954(d)(3).

[71/] See MCA Inc. v. United States, 46 AFTR 2d 80-5337 (D.C. C.D. Cal. 1980), holding that a partnership consisting of a controlled foreign corporation and an employee trust was a corporation related to the controlled foreign corporation. Lack of separate interests among the partners caused the alleged partnerships to be treated as corporations. See Toan, "Foreign Base Company Services Income," Subpart F – Foreign Subsidiaries and Their Tax Consequences, Feinschreiber, ed., 132 (1979).

In another scheme, the 50 percent threshhold has been combined with improper transfer pricing in a fraudulent scheme to syphon patent royalties into a tax haven holding company. For example, U.S. company X wants to license a patent from unrelated foreign licensor Y. It is anticipated that the royalties will be $100 per year. X's after tax cost would be $54 ($100 less $46 tax). Instead, X and Y form tax haven corporation Z in a treaty country. Y licenses the patent to Z which sublicenses to X for $200 per year. X deducts the $200. While X's cost is $200, its after tax cost is $8 ($200 less $92 less $100 in the tax haven corporation) Further, the $100 X owns in the tax haven corporation can earn investment income free of U.S. and local tax. X will not have subpart F income because it does not own more than 50 percent of the stock of Z. The scheme is fraudulent, but cloaked in legitimacy. The participation of the unrelated licensor may make it difficult for the IRS to establish improper transfer pricing.

The application of the §482 rules may also be avoided through decontrol. In order for §482 to be applied, the organizations dealing with one another must be owned or controlled, directly or indirectly, by the same interests. The regulations define the relationship broadly, stating that "the term control includes any kind of de facto control, direct or indirect, whether legally enforceable, and however exercisable or exercised...."[72] Nevertheless, control still must be found in order for a § 482 allocation to be possible. Therefore, in cases where decontrol is achieved, arguably not only do subpart F and the foreign personal holding company provisions no longer apply, but allocations can no longer be made under § 482.

E. **Principal Patterns of Abusive Tax Haven Use Predominently by Promoters and by Individual Taxpayers**

Individuals use tax havens in many of the same ways and for many of the same reasons as do multi-national companies. Thus, many of the structures described above are used by individuals. Promoters, including tax practitioners, have also been advising individuals to use tax havens to abuse the tax structure. Some of these uses are highlighted below.

1. **Background**

The earliest anti-avoidance legislation, the predecessors of §§ 367, 1491 and the foreign personal holding company and personal holding company provisions, were intended to deal with abusive tax avoidance by individuals. In a letter to

---

[72] Treas. Reg. § 1.482-1(a)(3).

President Roosevelt, Secretary of the Treasury Morgenthau
cited numerous instances of the abusive use by individuals
of holding companies in the Bahamas, Panama, and Canada
(then a haven). The uses included creation of artificial
deductions by means of loans made to individuals by their
personal holding company, removing assets (three million
dollars in one case) to a Bahamian company, with the individual
shareholder then filing returns in successive years from
such diverse places as New Brunswick, Maine, British Columbia,
Jamaica, and expatriation by a retired army officer who
immediately established Bahamian corporations to hold and
sell his securities.[73]

Many of the most flagrant abuses of holding companies
seem to have been curtailed. Significant use of tax havens
by individuals, however, is still possible and much of it
does not comport with Congressional intent. There appears
to be a growing use of tax havens for small transactions.

2. Patterns of Use

Described below are some of the abusive schemes we have
seen by which individuals have attempted to use tax havens
to avoid U.S. tax.

a. Investment Companies

A promoter forms P, a Bermuda company, which in turn
forms a Bermuda subsidiary (S) to engage in speculative
trading in commodity futures and forward contracts. All of
the stock of P is held by U.S. persons. All trading is to
be done by S. S receives a ruling from Bermuda authorities
that it is exempt from current and future Bermuda taxes.
The promoter takes the position that neither P nor S will
incur U.S. tax because: they are foreign corporations; will
not conduct business in the U.S.; will not have any U.S.
source income; P's share dispersal among U.S. persons will
be such as to avoid controlled foreign corporation or foreign
personal holding company status; and capital gain on the
disposition of P's shares will be afforded by avoiding
§ 1246, because the company did not register under the
Investment Company Act of 1940 and was not engaged in trading
or dealing in securities.

---

[73] See report of the Joint Committee on Tax Evasion and
Avoidance of the Congress of the United States, 75th
Cong., 1st Sess., No. 337 (1937) at 1.

The Congress adopted §1246 in 1962 in an effort to limit what it considered an abuse which had arisen by persons forming investment companies in tax havens with shares being sold to U.S. persons. Prior to 1962, the company was not taxed, and the U.S. shareholders were taxed at the favorable capital gain rates when the shares were sold or redeemed. Section 1246, however, applies only to a company which trades in securities. Arguably, commodities futures contracts are not securities, and thus §1246 does not apply. In addition, the company would not be a personal holding company because of its share dispersal.[74] In any event, personal holding company income does not include income from trading in commodities.[75] Furthermore, if the commodity transactions are executed in the U.S. through a U.S. broker, S will not be engaged in trade or business in the U.S. and the short-term capital gain realized on the sales will not be taxed in the U.S. because it is not fixed or determinable income.

S might be subject to the accumulated earnings tax on its U.S. source income if its earnings are accumulated beyond the reasonable needs of the business. In an attempt to avoid this result, S will distribute dividends to P. P will not be subject to the accumulated earnings tax because it does not have U.S. source income. However, § 269 might apply to enable the IRS to disregard S, in which case P would have to distribute the income to its U.S. shareholders or pay the accumulated earnings tax.

b. Trading Company

A promoter forms a company in the Grand Cayman Islands, citing the company's tax-free status there. The promoter purchases 50 percent of the shares in the company, and the other 50 percent are sold to 20 unrelated U.S. individuals. Each person who purchases shares signs a contract obligating himself to pay up to $10,000 over a period of 18 months. The agreement provides that the profits will be split fifty-fifty between the shareholders and the corporation during the 18-month period. Afterwards, all of the profits will belong to the corporation, with the shareholders receiving distributions. The promoters take the position that there is no U.S. tax because the company is not a controlled

---

[74] § 542(a)(2).

[75] See § 543.

foreign corporation or a foreign personal holding company, because it does not meet the "more than" fifty percent ownership test. The promoters also take the position that the $10,000 payment is a deductible reimbursement for expenses, and not an investment in assets.

c. Holding Companies

Foreign companies have been used in an attempt to shelter royalty or similar income. In one case a U.S. person purchased the movie rights to a series of books. A Swiss corporation was formed, with a U.S. individual receiving 50 percent of the stock and a U.S. distributor receiving 50 percent of the stock. The individual transferred the movie rights to the Swiss corporation. The Swiss corporation then gave the distribution rights to the film to the U.S. distributor. Royalties are paid to the Swiss company, which claims that activities of the corporation are conducted by the Swiss company in Switzerland. Under the U.S.-Swiss treaty, the royalties are exempt from tax by the U.S. The company has accumulated millions of dollars and has paid only limited dividends. The U.S. individual shareholder has borrowed millions from the company, and has paid only interest. Most of the company's retained earnings are invested in the U.S. in CD's, or are invested in the Eurobond market. The company claims that it is engaged in an active business and that it does not have subpart F income. In fact the shareholders should be taxed on the loans to them under § 956.

d. Shelters

Abusive tax shelters present the IRS with one of its most serious compliance problems. The IRS has identified approximately 25,000 different shelter promotions in recent years. These involve roughly 190,000 returns and perhaps as much as five billion dollars in potential adjustments.

A recent, and apparently growing, phenomenon is the interjection of an offshore jurisdiction into the shelter scheme. A tax haven may be used in an attempt to hide the fact that a transaction upon which a deduction is based never took place, to hide the promoter's profit, or to hide the list of investors. Also, losses may be transferred to an investor's account in a tax haven and the ownership relationship with the account hidden. Tax haven shelter activity appears to have increased markedly over the past few years; and, in a few cases, previously domestic shelter schemes have moved off-shore in later years.

(i) Commodities. We have identified a number of cases where offshore entities or locations were used to faciliate alleged commodity transactions. Generally, these are so called "tax spreads" which seek to give the investor a tax advantage by generating large ordinary losses in year one, and then long-term capital gain in year two. The benefit to the taxpayer is the difference between the tax saved on the ordinary loss and the tax paid on the capital gain. A Treasury Bill-GNMA straddle is entered into to produce ordinary loss on the T-Bill leg and long term capital gain on the GNMA leg. The purpose is to convert ordinary income in one year into long term capital gain in the immediately succeeding year. The taxpayer liquidates his loss by covering the short sale on the T-Bill leg. The taxpayer then borrows money to cover the loss from a broker located in the Bahamas, and locks in the gain by entering into a contract to deliver the GNMA's at the current price in twelve months. At the end of the twelve month period, the taxpayer delivers the GNMA's and realizes long term capital gain. There is evidence that the transactions may never have taken place. In one case, a revenue agent estimates that there may be as many as 1,500 investors and deductions of as much as $150 million.

Another scheme has been marketed over a four year period to at least 500 taxpayers. The IRS has identified 40 income tax returns for two taxable years which were involved with this tax shelter on which losses were deducted in excess of $4,000,000.

Salesmen for the taxpayer will approach wealthy individuals and advise them that they have a perfectly legitimate tax shelter device which will allow the investor to double his money in one year. It is explained that the marketing organization will set up for the taxpayer a foreign trust which will be located in a tax haven jurisdiction. The foreign trust will be a grantor trust which will have the taxpayer as its sole beneficiary. The trust will be formed ostensibly for the purpose of investing in gold and silver with the idea of making a profit.

The investor puts up $20,000 in cash which constitutes the corpus of the trust. The trust subsequently becomes a limited partner in a limited partnership formed in Liechtenstein or another tax haven. The limited partnership is a foreign partnership not doing business in the United States which would not be subject to United States income tax. The stated business of the partnership is investing in gold or silver with the intent of making a profit.

Next, three simultaneous contracts are entered into.
In the first contract, the partnership borrows from a foreign
bank $1,200,000 payable one year from the date of the loan
with interest at the rate of 10% per annum, so that the
interest during the first year would be $120,000. The
general partner is supposed to pay the interest. The trust
as a limited partner would enter into an agreement stating
that the trust would be responsible for the payment of the
interest in the event of default. Next, the partnership
purchases gold or silver valued at $1,200,000 which is
pledged as collateral for the $1,200,000 bank loan. Finally,
the partnership enters into a contract to sell the gold or
silver one year from the date of the contract at a profit
of 10% or $1,320,000.

The taxpayer is advised that as a result of these
transactions during the first year the partnership pays
interest in the amount of $120,000, has no income, and thus
has a loss in the amount of $120,000 which would flow through
the trust to the individual investor. Assuming the taxpayer
is in the 50 percent tax bracket, the $120,000 deduction
would be worth $60,000 in tax savings to the taxpayer.
Thus, for an investment of $20,000, the taxpayer has recouped
his initial $20,000 plus he has received a profit of $40,000
payable by the United States Government. He has thus managed
to double his money with no risk.

During the second taxable year, the trust should have
capital gain of $120,000 with no offsetting deductions.
Thus, the ordinary loss has been converted into capital
gain. However, the taxpayer may enter into a similar arrangement
during the second taxable year. The trust will have neither
gain nor loss because the $120,000 gain resulting from the
first series of transactions will be offset by an interest
deduction of $120,000 resulting from the second set of
transactions. Thus, by entering into similar arrangements
each year on the anniversary date of the contracts, the
taxpayer may postpone indefinitely the recognition of gain.

In point of fact, none of these transactions takes
place, although the taxpayer-investor is lead to believe
this is a legitimate tax shelter which can be used to offset
income taxes.

In reality, the promoter of this tax shelter utilizes
the services of foreign attorneys, accountants, nominee
corporations and foreign banks for the purposes of creating
documentation of transactions which are not consummated.
Thus, the investor will be furnished with letters and a
contract from foreign attorneys which purportedly establish

the validity of the gold or silver transaction as well as the bank loans and interest payments. These documents will then be provided to the IRS upon audit to substantiate the taxpayer's claimed deductions.

The promoter uses the services of a nominee tax haven corporation which receives the investor's original $20,000 investment. This money is deposited in a bank located in a tax haven jurisdiction in an account under the name of the nominee corporation. Subsequently, the taxpayer arranges through the use of a United States corporation to "borrow" money from the bank in which has been deposited the investor's original $20,000. The promoter, in turn, borrows this money which he uses for personal living expenses.

A similar straddle was arranged through a domestic trust. In order to avoid partnership reporting, a domestic trust was formed for the benefit of the investor. The domestic trust then becomes a beneficiary of a Bahamian trust. The Bahamian trust realizes the brokerage losses, which are distributed back to the domestic trust and in turn to the U.S. taxpayers.

Offshore commodity schemes to defraud the consumer rather than the IRS have also been marketed. Commodity brokers may establish accounts in a tax haven and structure commodity trading losses through those accounts. The broker will deny ownership of the accounts. In some cases, such an account has been used to defraud the investor. For example, a Cayman company sells silver options to investors. If the investor decides to exercise the option, he is told that the silver has been lost or that the company is insolvent. The investor has lost his investment.

Both the Securities and Exchange Commission and the Commodities Futures Trading Corporation are investigating offshore commodity schemes.

(ii) Movies. A U.S. promoter forms a corporation in Liechtenstein which purchases a low grade movie. The movie is then sold to a U.S. partnership for up to fifty times the purchase price. The consideration paid by the partnership might be 10 or 15 percent of the inflated sales price in cash and a nonrecourse note for the remainder. The cash remains in the Liechtenstein corporation and the note is never paid. The investors receive a statement from the promoter showing the payment of interest and other fees for a particular year, and take deductions accordingly.

(iii) <u>Foreign situs property</u>. A number of cases have
been identified in which the property which is the shelter
investment is located in a foreign country which may or may
not be a tax haven. Even where the property is not in a
tax haven, the investment vehicle (partnership or trust) or
the promoter may have a tax haven address. One case involved
the sale of an interest in a South African mine. Each
investor paid a 20 percent "advanced" royalty in cash and
signed a non-recourse note guaranteed by a Cayman insurance
company for the balance. The investors deduct the start-up
costs, and the promoting entity (which it is alleged is
owned by U.S. persons) retains the advanced payment. Revenue
agents involved estimated that they had identified $30
million in deductions through this shelter, and that investors
may have taken as much as $150 million in deductions.

Other cases involving South and Central American gold
mines were identified. The shelter vehicles had in fact
purchased mining claims but their valuations were too high.
In the case of one promotion, we have identified a number of
returns with deductions for "mining development costs" of as
much as $175,000. It would be difficult for the IRS to
refute the valuation, if that were necessary, because of the
lack of availability of expert witnesses.

e. <u>Foreign Trusts</u>

Foreign trusts have been an important vehicle for tax-
free investment by U.S. persons, in or through tax havens.
Prior to 1962 a trust afforded the deferral advantages of a
foreign corporation, and in addition could accumulate passive
income without foreign personal holding company consequences.
In 1962, Congress subjected beneficiaries of foreign trusts
created by U.S. persons to an unlimited throw-back rule at
the time of the ultimate distribution of accumulated income.
The distributed income itself was taxed whether it represented
gross income from sources within or without the United
States. Unless distributed, however, the income could be
accumulated tax free in a tax haven.

In 1976, Congress dealt more directly with foreign
trusts by removing the deferral privilege for foreign trusts
created by a U.S. person if the foreign trust had or acquired
United States beneficiaries. Today, a U.S. person who
directly or indirectly transfers property to a foreign trust
is treated as the owner for the taxable year of the portion
of the trust attributable to the property transferred, if
for the year there is a U.S. beneficiary of any portion of
the trust.[76] The provisions apply to both direct and

[76] § 679(a)(1).

indirect transfers, and include transfers by gift, sale, exchange or otherwise. An exception is provided for transfers by reason of the death of the transferor. In addition, an exception is provided for any sale or exchange of property at its fair market value in a transaction in which all of the gain to the transferor is realized at the time of the transfer and is recognized either at that time or is returned as is provided in § 453.

Generally, a trust has a U.S. beneficiary unless the trust instrument provides that no part of the income or corpus may be paid or accumulated for the benefit of the U.S. person. Attribution rules are provided under which a foreign corporation is treated as a U.S. beneficiary if more than 50 percent of the total combined voting power of all classes of stock is owned, or is considered owned, by U.S. shareholders under § 958. A foreign partnership is treated as a U.S. beneficiary if any U.S. person is a partner of the partnership directly or indirectly. A foreign trust or estate is considered a U.S. beneficiary if the foreign trust or estate has a U.S. beneficiary.

The Tax Reform Act of 1976, while significantly curtailing the ability of U.S. persons to use foreign trusts, did not eliminate them. Some practitioners believe that foreign trusts may still be used to a U.S. tax advantage, either by structuring transactions to avoid § 679 or by the using rules of § 679 to achieve certain tax advantages. Most are abusive, and in any event distributions of property from a foreign trust would incur the onerous interest charge on accumulation distributions imposed by §668.

A foreign trust may be used to avoid the corporate anti-abuse provisions in some cases. For example, if a foreign trust is not a § 679 trust, then a sale by the trust of stock of a controlled foreign corporation will not be subject to the ordinary income rules of § 1248, because § 1248 applies to a U.S. person who sells or exchanges stock in a foreign corporation. Likewise, gain on the sale of collapsible corporation stock (which should be taxable as ordinary income) would be deferred until the proceeds are distributed to the beneficiaries. Some claim that the stock can be transferred to the trust by a long-term installment sale thus qualifying for the sale or exchange exception.

Section 679 does not apply to any transfer by reason of the death of the transferor, nor does it apply to an inter vivos trust after the death of the transferor. Therefore, a foreign trust can still be used as an estate planning tool. Distributions would, however, be taxed to the beneficiaries, and the interest charge imposed by § 668 would apply to those distributions. In the alternative, an inter vivos trust can be created, and property transferred to it. A U.S. grantor can transfer non-income producing property with appreciation potential to the trust. The transferor is subject to tax on the income from the property but, because the property is non-income producing he will pay no tax. Further, if the property generates losses, the grantor will receive the benefit of those losses during his lifetime. After his death, the property can be sold and the assets invested in income producing property, with the income accumulating for the benefit of the beneficiary. While distribution will incur tax and an interest charge, some beneficiaries attempt to take the income out in the form of "loans" which are not taxed unless they are detected.

Section 679 does not apply to a sale or exchange of property at its fair market value in a transaction in which all of the gain to the transferor is realized at the time of the transfer and is recognized either at such time or is returned as provided in § 453. Accordingly, a U.S. person can purchase property, wait for it to appreciate slightly (to qualify for the "gain realized exception"), and then sell it to a tax haven trust which he created. He will realize gain but take back a long-term installment note at stated interest, thereby according current reporting of that gain.

Some practitioners seem to be taking the position that § 679 is avoided if a § 1057 election is made for a transfer to a foreign trust.[77] A combination of these exception provisions might then be used in conjunction with a foreign trust to accelerate the recognition of gain without disposing of property, by transferring appreciated inventory to a foreign trust, making a § 1057 election (thereby recognizing gain), and then, when the inventory is needed back, liquidating the trust. The gain could be used to offset expiring net operating loss carryovers. The inventory would come back at a stepped-up basis, so that sales of the inventory would not generate income (unless the inventory had further appreciated).

---

[77] § 679(a)(2)(B).

A foreign trust can be used to generate losses for the benefit of the grantor (this can also be done with a domestic trust). One scheme which has been described is for a U.S. grantor to transfer property to a foreign trust for the benefit of foreign beneficiaries. In the years when there are significant losses, a beneficiary can establish residence in the U.S., thereby flowing the losses through to a U.S. resident. If it appears that the trust will earn income for a year, the beneficiary can return to his own country. It is unlikely that such a scheme really happens often.

Section 679 applies only to transfers by U.S. persons. A nonresident alien emigrating to the U.S. may, prior to assuming resident status, make a transfer to a foreign trust with a U.S. beneficiary, and not be subject to § 679 when he becomes a U.S. resident. Similarly, a nonresident alien individual spouse who intends to make a § 6013 (g) or (h) election to be treated as a U.S. resident could make the transfer in a year before the first year to which the election is to apply.[78/] If a foreign trust does not have U.S. beneficiaries in the year of a transfer by a foreign person, and if the foreign beneficiaries become U.S. beneficiaries at the same time the transferor becomes a U.S. person, neither § 679 (a) (1) nor § 679 (b) (concerning trusts acquiring U.S. beneficiaries) applies. Consequently, the § 679 rules are avoided and income can be accumulated abroad free of tax for the benefit of a person who is not a U.S. resident. However, any distribution will incur the §668 interest charge.

f. Double Trusts

A number of persons have been promoting a fraudulent scheme known as so-called "double trusts" or "triple trusts" as a method for avoiding U.S. income taxation. Over 200 returns which appear to involve these trusts have been identified.

Under one such scheme the taxpayer agrees with a promoter to enter into a "double trust" arrangement. After payment of a large fee to the promoter, the promoter arranges for a foreign person to create a trust in a tax haven. The foreign creator appoints the taxpayer as trustee and the taxpayer transfers assets to the trust. The assets may range from real estate to an active business. The foreign person then creates a second trust in the same tax haven and names the

---

[78/] Sections 6013(g) and (h) permit certain nonresident alien individuals married to U.S. citizens or residents to make an election to be treated as U.S. residents.

first trust as trustee of the second trust. The beneficiary of the second trust may be a friendly foreign "Credit Union". The trustee is given broad powers to deal with trust property.

The first trust will earn the income and the trustee will distribute it to the second trust. The second trust will, from time to time, make distributions in the form of gifts or loans to the taxpayer or his family. If the assets of the first trust include an active business in the U.S., the trusts should, and many of them do, file an income tax return. Many of these returns eliminate taxable income by reporting the payment of a "contingent royalty", presumably to the second trust. Some of the returns identified indicate that the offshore entity is purchasing supplies and selling them to the United States party at an inflated price. The profit is being accumulated in the tax haven, or is being returned to the taxpayer as a gift or a loan.

Section 679 will apply to these trusts if the U.S. person (or any U.S. person) is a beneficiary. The indirect transfer rule may apply to the second trust if the "expenditures" are fraudulent, as may be the case. In the case of the transfer of business assets, §679 clearly applies. The ultimate beneficial interest, which may be shown by the receipt of a "gift" or "loan", is owned by a U.S. person. If U.S. persons are not the ultimate beneficiaries, then § 679 does not apply, but § 1491 should apply to the transfer.[79]/

The double trust problem is a compliance problem--proof of the existence of the foreign trusts, the U.S. beneficiaries, the fraudulent nature of deductions, etc., must be obtained. Once obtained, § 679, 1491, or the grantor trust rules should apply. Identification of returns (if any) involving double trusts is an important step.

g. Generating Deductions

Tax haven entities have been used to generate deductions other than shelter deductions. An example of a scheme is contained in an article about recent IRS successes in the Tax Court. The cases involved transactions planned by Harry Margolis, a west coast attorney. According to the Wall Street Journal, an investor would arrange to "borrow" $50,000 from an entity called Anglo Dutch Capital Co., which the government alleged existed only on paper. Then the investor would invest the loan proceeds in Del Ceiro Associates, another entity the article alleges was controlled by Mr. Margolis With $5,000 in real cash, the taxpayer would prepay a year's

---

[79]/ See Rev. Rul 80-74, 1980-1 C.B. 137.

interest on the loan he supposedly got from Anglo Dutch.
But, according to the Journal, the "investment" in Del Ceiro
would turn sour, and the client would take a total deduction
of $55,000 for his loss plus the interest he paid on his
loan. The Tax Court has found this case and others like it
to be shams.

There are over 800 additional cases docketed against
clients of Mr. Margolis. If each case had to be tried
separately, it would take years to resolve them.

h. Expatriation

U.S. persons can leave the U.S. and renounce their
citizenship in order to avoid paying U.S. taxes. For example,
if a U.S. person owns appreciated property, he may move to a
low tax haven such as the British Virgin Islands or Bermuda,
establish residence and renounce his U.S. citizenship, and
then obtain a British passport which enables him to move
around the world. In some cases, the U.S. person may even
expatriate to a country such as Canada, which gives an
immigrant a basis in his assets equal to their fair market
value as of the date residence is established.

United States tax law limits the advantage of expatriation
for tax purposes, by retaining jurisdiction to tax the
expatriate in limited cases.⁸⁰/ Under the Code, the expatriate
would be taxed on his U.S. source income and his foreign
source effectively connected income. For purposes of this
provision, income from U.S. real estate, stock or securities
of a U.S. corporation, and debt of a U.S. person, would be
considered U.S. source income taxable to the expatriate.
This provision applies only to income earned within ten
years of the date of expatriation. No tax is imposed on
foreign source income, including income from the disposition
of appreciated foreign assets.

In addition to permitting expatriation to avoid U.S.
tax on foreign assets, the U.S. law is difficult to administer.
Once the U.S. person has removed himself from U.S. jurisdiction,
various schemes can be used to dispose of U.S. assets in a
manner which makes it difficult to detect.

In one case a U.S. person, allegedly to avoid U.S.
capital gains tax on over $20 million in appreciation,
expatriated and almost immediately sold his appreciated
stock in a foreign corporation.

80/ § 877.

F. Use by Foreign Persons Doing Business in or Residing in the U.S.

Foreign persons investing in the U.S. or doing business in the U.S. make extensive use of tax havens. The most widely publicized use is that of the Netherlands Antilles for investment in U.S. real estate. Much has been written on this subject, and it has been extensively studied by various branches of the Federal Government. It is discussed in Chapter VIII dealing with treaties. Legislation enacted in December 1980 will subject foreign persons to tax on their gain from the sale of United States real property. Often, foreign investors' use of tax havens is connected with treaty shopping, which is also discussed in Chapter VIII.

1. Banks

Foreign banks may use tax havens as investment vehicles or otherwise in connection with U.S. business.

Foreign banks conduct business in the United States through branches, agencies, and subsidiaries (a branch takes deposits, but only in the form of large denomination CD's; an agency does not accept these deposits). In many cases foreign banks first came to the U.S. to finance imports to this country and to finance sales of raw materials to their home countries. Today, many function as full service commercial banks, and some U.S. subsidiaries of foreign banks are among the largest commercial banks.

It appears that most large foreign banks have subsidiaries or branches in tax havens. While their investments are not necessarily funneled through tax havens in all cases, havens nevertheless play an important role in their tax planning. In a few recent instances, foreign persons have formed a tax haven corporation to acquire significant interests in major U.S. banks.

For example, dollars may be loaned to U.S. customers or to foreign customers. In either case, the loans may be "booked" at Nassau or the Cayman Islands, and the interest paid to the home office. The bank often takes the position that there is no U.S. business income from this type of transaction, and that any interest paid is free of tax because of a tax treaty. The reason is that a foreign corporation engaged in a trade or business within the U.S. is taxable at normal rates on its income which is effectively connected with the conduct of a trade or business within the U.S.[81] Income from a security (which would include a note)

---

[81] § 882(a).

which is from U.S. sources, and derived by a foreign corporation
in the banking business, is treated as effectively connected
income only if the securities are "attributable" to the U.S.
office.[82]   Loans which are "booked" abroad are not attributable
to a U.S. office, and therefore the interest from the loans
is not effectively connected.[83]

Under the IRS regulations, it would appear that U.S.
source interest on loans booked overseas is not effectively
connected with the conduct of a trade or business in the
U.S., and therefore the interest is not taxable on a net
basis by the U.S. If the U.S. has a tax treaty with the
home country of the bank, and the interest is paid to the
home country, then the treaty rate of tax (often zero) will
apply. Accordingly, there is no U.S. tax on the transaction.

However, in the case of foreign source interest, the
IRS position is that active participation by the U.S. office
is sufficient to make the income effectively connected.[84]

The problems with the foreign source interest rules are
largely administrative. Lack of cooperation in supplying
books and records, and in permitting tax haven employees to
be interviewed, makes it difficult for the IRS to determine
whether the haven company or the U.S. office negotiated the
loan. In addition, the "booking" rule in the effectively
connected regulations makes it easy for a bank to choose the
tax treatment of its U.S. source loan transactions.

2. Insurance

Foreign insurance companies do business in the U.S.
through branches or through U.S. subsidiary corporations.
The trend seems to be toward incorporating the branches.
The IRS Office of International Operations appears to have
no tax haven problems with foreign insurance companies,
although the companies do reinsure a part of their domestic
risk through tax havens (most often Bermuda, but in some
cases the Caymans).

---

[82] Treas. Reg. § 1.864-4(c)(5)(ii).

[83] Treas. Reg. § 1.864-4(c)(5)(iii)(2).

[84] Rev. Rul. 75-253, 1975-1 C.B. 203.

3. Entertainment Industry

Foreign entertainers appear to make extensive use of tax havens in structuring their U.S. and foreign business. An entertainer or a group of entertainers may establish a corporation in a tax haven with which the U.S. has a treaty (most often the Netherlands Antilles or Switzerland), and enter into a long term employment contract with that corporation The corporation then contracts with a U.S. promoter to arrange tours for the entertainers. The proceeds from the tour are paid to the tax haven company, and that company then pays the entertainer an annual salary.

The corporation also contracts with a U.S. distributor for the distribution of records. Profits from the sale of the records are paid by the U.S. distributor to the tax haven company, and the company takes the position that the amounts are royalties and that the treaty benefits apply. In the case of the Swiss and Netherland Antilles treaties, this means that the amounts are not taxed by the U.S. This issue is discussed in Chapter VIII, relating to treaties.

4. Trading and Sales Companies

A foreign corporation may invest in the U.S. through a tax haven. The treaty shopping issues of this form of investment are discussed in Chapter VIII.

In some cases, a foreign corporation selling into the U.S. through a U.S. subsidiary will establish a second subsidiary in a tax haven. The U.S. subsidiary will sell to or purchase from the tax haven subsidiary, often at prices which are not arms length. These transactions should be subject to a § 482 adjustment. In some cases, however, the IRS is not aware of the ownership of the tax haven entity, and therefore an appropriate § 482 adjustment is not made.

This is a problem of administrative detection, which can probably best be dealt with by good solid auditing. In addition, a schedule might be prepared to be attached to the Form 1120 filed by a U.S. subsidiary of a foreign corporation. The schedule would request information necessary to enable the revenue agent to consider a § 482 adjustment.

5. Aliens Resident in the U.S.

It is generally believed that there are a large number of aliens living in the U.S. who claim to be nonresidents, but who in fact spend substantial amounts of time here and for all practical purposes might be considered residents.

Many of these persons own expensive apartments and have no
other permanent abode. An alien may enter this country as
a tourist, advise Immigration that he will be here for from
60 to 90 days, and then, within the 60 to 90 day period,
leave to travel or to visit his offshore bank. He then
returns and gives Immigration the same story.

The alien will often transfer his assets to a holding
company or a trust located in a tax haven. His money will
be invested in U.S. bank accounts, the Eurobond market, or
in other financial assets. The assets may also be invested
in U.S. real estate. Because the alien claims to be a
nonresident alien and does not consider any of his income as
being from U.S. sources, he does not report any of this
income on U.S. returns.

Aliens are able to avoid tax, and the IRS is unable to
deal with them because of: a lack of reporting; a lack of
information concerning payments to the aliens; a lack of
coherent information disseminated to the IRS; and the absence
of a clear definition of the term "residence."

There is little that can be done about the lack of
reporting of income or obtaining information on receipts of
income, unless a readily administerable definition of residence
is developed and information concerning the comings and
goings of aliens is made available to the IRS.

Under U.S. law, a non-resident alien not engaged in
trade or business within the U.S. is taxed only on his U.S.
source income, but a resident alien is taxed on his worldwide
income. Accordingly, while the determination of resident
status can have an enormous impact, there is no precise
definition of the term. The regulations[85] define a resident
as one "actually present in the United States who is not a
mere transient or sojourner." The length of his stay and
its nature are factors to be considered. No definite rule
is provided. The IRS has, however, ruled that presence in
the U.S. for one year creates a presumption of residence.[86]

---

[85] Treas. Reg. §1.871-2(b).

[86] Rev. Rul. 69-611, 1969-2 C.B. 150.

VI. Use of Tax Havens To Facilitate
Evasion of U.S. Taxes

The use of tax havens by earners of illegal income
(particularly narcotics trafficers) has generated significant publicity over the years. The extent of this type of
use, and the extent of use for tax evasion purposes in general,
is not definitively known. The statistical study undertaken
in connection with the Tax Haven Study has not given us an
estimate of the level of this use although the study does
show enormous and growing levels of financial activity and
accumulation of funds in tax havens.[1]/

Our study has been able to conclude that there are a
large number of transactions involving illegally earned
income and legally earned income which is diverted to or
passed through havens for purposes of tax evasion. We
identified approximately 250 criminal cases (either currently
active or closed within approximately the past three years)
involving offshore transactions. This number of cases
is an indication of a significant level of use.

Many of the cases identified were closed without prosecution, often because the evidence was not available to establish a key element in a case. Almost every case involved
either an offshore entity such as a trust or corporation or
a foreign bank account.

A fair statement of the problems in dealing with this
type of activity is that of Assistant Attorney General (Tax
Division) Ferguson in his statement to the Oversight Committee of the Ways and Means Committee:[2]/

> "As you might expect, evasion
> of United States taxes through sham
> business transactions involving foreign
> entities is difficult to detect, hard
> to recognize when found, and, where
> foreign witnesses and documents are
> crucial, sometimes impossible to prove
> in court. Even the most transparent

1/ See Chapter III, infra.

2/ The Use of Offshore Tax Havens for the Purposes of
Evading Income Taxes: Hearings Before the House Sub-
committee on Oversight of the Committee on Ways and
Means, 96th Cong., 1st Sess. 18 (1979).

transactions are likely to have
sufficient documentation to satisfy
a surface inquiry by an auditor and
enough complexity to discourage a
deeper look. Furthermore, being
dependent on form and multiplicity
of steps, such transactions will
utilize entities in tax haven jurisdictions offering business and banking
secrecy to conceal their lack of
substance."

A. Prior Efforts To Investigate Offshore Cases

Over the past two decades, Revenue Agents and Special
Agents have conducted a number of investigations involving
tax havens.

During 1957 and 1958, special agents in the Manhattan
District attempted to establish the identity of persons
making large deposits of currency in New York banks for
subsequent transfer to secret (numbered or coded) Swiss bank
accounts. During one three month period, a New York bank
filed 81 currency forms reflecting deposits of $1.1 million
under 77 different names and addresses. These deposits were
transferred to coded accounts in specified Swiss banks.
Investigation by eight Special Agents revealed that all 77
names and addresses given to the bank by the depositors were
fictitious; the depositors could not be located.

Follow-up investigations of other currency deposit
forms did locate depositors who had transferred funds to
numbered Swiss bank accounts. The reasons for maintenance
of the accounts ranged from engaging in complicated international commercial transactions to political refugee situations. Although it was suspected that some of these transactions involved tax evasion or other violations of U.S.
law--including narcotics, securities law, and smuggling--the
inability to secure information on the accounts from Switzerland contributed to the lack of success in developing any
cases for prosecution.

The investigations served to increase concerns of law
enforcement authorities about the potential for using secret
foreign bank accounts for illegal purposes, and suggested a
need for tighter regulation or better reporting of international currency transfers. Accordingly, during the summer

---

3/ Forms TCR-1 (predecessor of Form 4789).

of 1960, a conference was held in the National Office of IRS
to develop means for controlling illicit international money
flows. None of the ideas put forth at the conference was
implemented, in part because they required legislation. It
was felt that the lack of proof that secret foreign bank
accounts were in fact being used for tax evasion purposes
made prospects poor for legislation to require improved
reporting on international currency transfers.

From 1966 through early 1967, IRS agents worked with
the U.S. District Attorney for New York City, who was then
conducting a grand jury investigation of the use of foreign
banks by suspected "underworld" figures. IRS agents assisted
in examining bank records and correspondence of taxpayers
who opened and funded Swiss accounts by making deposits in
U.S. branches of Swiss banks. In early 1967, a task force
was formed to coordinate Examination, Criminal Investigation
and Office of International Operations activities regarding
secret foreign bank accounts. Although these efforts improved
IRS knowledge of the use of secret foreign bank accounts,
audits of 130 taxpayers identified via grand jury investigation were disappointing in terms of taxes collected, due
to lack of adequate documentation and perhaps also due to
the inexperience of audit personnel in dealing with cases
where pertinent records were beyond the reach of U.S. law.

As an outgrowth of these efforts, a project known as
"Swiss Mail Watch" and later as the "Foreign Bank Account
Project", was initiated to identify U.S. taxpayers receiving
mail from Swiss banks. From January 8 to May 2, 1968, with
the assistance of the postal authorities, IRS monitored mail
received in a New York post office. Swiss bank mail was
identified by the postage meter numbers used by the Swiss
banks, and the outside of envelopes mailed by the Swiss
banks to individuals and firms in the U.S. was photocopied.
From this monitoring, a list of 8,500 taxpayers was prepared,
from which 168 taxpayers were selected for audit by 16
agents in two districts. The audits resulted in the assessment of about $2 million in taxes and penalties, less than a
third of which was attributable to the foreign bank accounts.
The audits indicated that only about a fifth of the taxpayers used their Swiss accounts as a depository for unreported
income or to avoid the interest equalization tax, and that
the unreported income in such cases was not substantial.
Because of the inability to obtain corroborating testimony
and documentation from the Swiss banks, no prosecutions
resulted.

Subsequently, two more mail watches were initiated, one during the period January 2 through February 2, 1969, and the last from December 27, 1970 through February 4, 1971. The 1969 mail watch identified about 21,500 taxpayers who appeared to have Swiss bank accounts, and the 1971 mail watch identified another 20,000 to 25,000 taxpayers who appeared to have such accounts. However, no IRS audit was initiated as a result of these later mail watches.

The Foreign Bank Accounts Project was discontinued for a combination of reasons. A mutual assistance treaty was being negotiated with Switzerland which, it was hoped, would permit Swiss banks to provide bank account information about Americans suspected of crimes. It was believed that use of the mail watch data would jeopardize the treaty negotiations. In addition, a Senate Subcommittee on Constitutional Rights was raising questions about the propriety of developing computerized files of suspected tax violators. Finally, some officials believed that the audit results, and failure to develop prosecution cases, were disappointing in terms of resources expended; staff costs were estimated at 2,318 staff days, at a salary of $260,000. They also believed that this technique did not offer a long-term solution to the foreign bank account problem. The issue was also being addressed by the House and Senate Banking and Currency Committees; the result was the enactment of the Bank Secrecy Act 4/ on October 26, 1970, which became effective upon publication of implementing regulations in July 1972.

Other investigative efforts were initiated during the 1960s and early 1970s. One was an investigation (sometimes referred to as the "Bahamas Project") of a West Coast attorney who appeared to be promoting the use of tax havens to evade the taxes of well-to-do clients. A lengthy examination resulted in criminal prosecution, and a trial that lasted six months. The attorney was acquitted, but hundreds of civil tax cases, involving over $100 million in taxes, resulted against his clients. Most of these civil cases are still pending in the Tax Court.

In another effort, a special agent from the IRS Reno District established liaison with a police department official of Grand Cayman Island, who subsequently furnished limited information concerning bank accounts of U.S. citizens. This effort, called "Project Pirate," was terminated in 1975.

4/ P.L. 91-508.

Records do not indicate that any successful audits or criminal prosecutions resulted from this information. In 1976, the Caymans strengthened their bank secrecy laws, making it a crime for any person to reveal information about bank accounts in the Cayman Islands.

The above investigative efforts were examined in considerable detail in several Congressional hearings. These hearings gave principal attention, however, to an effort termed "Operation Tradewinds," and to an offshoot termed "Project Haven."

Operation Tradewinds was an information gathering effort by IRS agents in the Jacksonville, Florida District to obtain information from Bahamian bank employees about the identity of U.S. taxpayers using Bahamian trusts and bank accounts. Information was obtained from informants passing on the information through Americans acting as intermediaries to IRS agents.

Operation Tradewinds produced considerable useful information, resulting in audit deficiencies recommended in 45 cases, and several criminal prosecutions, before the operation was suspended in January 1975. It also developed the information which gave rise to Project Haven.

Project Haven was initiated in 1972 in connection with an investigation of a narcotics trafficker, who it was learned had dealings with a Bahamian bank. A confidential informant was used to obtain Bahamian bank documents regarding this individual; in the process the informant learned that the Bahamian bank was receiving and disbursing funds on behalf of U.S. citizens whose identities were not revealed to the correspondent U.S. banks in Miami, New York, and Chicago.

The confidential informant, having developed a social relationship with a Bahamian bank official, learned that the bank official was planning to travel to the U.S. in January 1973, with a stop-off in Miami. At the banker's request, the informant arranged a date for the banker. While dining out, the banker left his briefcase in his date's apartment. She had previously given the informant a key to the apartment. The informant entered the apartment, removed the briefcase, had it opened by a locksmith, and made the documents therein available to IRS agents for photocopying. After photocopying, the documents were replaced and the briefcase returned to the apartment, all without the banker's knowledge.

The documents identified over 300 U.S. citizens and firms having accounts with that Bahamian bank. A large number of civil and criminal investigations were initiated on the basis of this information. The criminal cases (about 6 dozen in all) were initially investigated by several grand juries, and were finally consolidated in 1975 under one grand jury in the Southern Judicial District of Florida. One of the criminal cases reached the Supreme Court,[5]/ which ruled that the defendent lacked standing to object to admissibility of evidence obtained by the "briefcase caper," since the defendant's (as distinguished from the banker's) constitutional rights were not violated.

B. Narcotics Related Cases

Much of the concern with tax havens centers on their use by narcotics traffickers. Over the past few years there have been numerous Congressional hearings directed at problems involving the use of havens by narcotics traffickers. The press has, from time to time, reported on alleged use.

Tax havens are ideally suited to the purposes of the narcotics trafficker. The trafficker's goal, once he has sold his product, is to cleanse his money or to hide it so that he can put it to use without it being attributed to him as unreported income. A tax haven facilitates achievement of this goal by providing a veil of secrecy over parts of the transaction, so that the taxpayer cannot be definitely tied to the flow of funds. Furthermore, the tax haven's infrastructure, which often includes modern banking and communications facilities, serves to facilitate rapid movement of funds.

The problem can be illustrated by a simple case. A narcotics trafficker arranges for a carrier to carry $50,000 cash in a suitcase to the Cayman Islands, where it is deposited in a small private bank. The small bank then transfers the money to an account at the branch of a large money center bank. The U.S. narcotics trafficker then borrows $50,000 from a Canadian bank. Both the U.S. trafficker and the Canadian bank claim the loan is simply a signature loan to the individual. In fact, the loan is effectively secured by the Cayman deposit. The IRS, however, is unable to establish the connection and therefore cannot prosecute. The IRS may be able to identify the money leaving the U.S. by use of

_____

5/ United States v. Payner, 46 AFTR 2d 80-5174 (1980), rev'g 590 F. 2d 206 (6th Cir. 1979).

currency transaction reports and records of wire transfers.
It may see the money entering the U.S. The veil of secrecy
prevents tying the two together. While Canada might give
the U.S. information pursuant to a treaty request, the
information may not be sufficient to tie the taxpayer to the
Cayman account. To a great extent, it is the highly developed
and sophisticated banking and communications infrastructure
in the tax haven which makes it possible to move the money
swiftly and efficiently.

In general, there does not appear to be much that is
new or exceptionally sophisticated in the methods used by
narcotics traffickers to move their money. For example, in
a standard pattern a courier deposits cash in a U.S. bank
and the money is then wired to a haven bank account. From
there it can be moved with relative ease.

Many narcotics cases do not involve offshore transactions at all. In addition, in some cases foreign jurisdictions which are not tax havens are utilized. For example,
Mexico and Canada have been used because of their proximity
to the U.S. and perhaps because of their lack of taint. A
transaction with the Cayman Islands is suspect; a transaction with Canada is not. Our current investigations
indicate, however, that many narcotics transactions do
involve offshore activity. The Florida Cash Flow Project
has uncovered some.

It would appear that the most effective methods for
dealing with narcotics traffickers have been intensive well
coordinated inter-agency grand jury investigations. These
investigations have the advantage of enabling one person
(the Assistant U.S. Attorney) to provide direction and
coordination. They also enable agents from various agencies
to work more closely together with a common goal. Furthermore, a joint investigation brings together a number of
different disciplines and expertise. Finally, it enables
the IRS to avoid some of the coordination problems caused by
the disclosure rules of § 6103.[6]

Other successful methods of uncovering large scale
narcotics operations have involved the use of informants or
undercover operators to launder money through financial
institutions.

---

[6] See, for example, "Narcotics Agents Track Big Cash
Transactions to Trap Dope Dealers", The Wall Street
Journal, November 26, 1980, A-1.

Caution must be exercised in applying resources in the narcotics area. The CID agent is a highly trained financial investigator who is capable of dealing with sophisticated cases. Too much pressure to apply resources without identifying adequate and proper cases could lead to a waste of these valuable people by having them recommending termination assessments against low level drug dealers. This kind of problem was encountered in the early 1970's, and in the opinion of some resulted in some overreaching. The use of termination and jeopardy assessments at one time or another became disproportionate.

C. Patterns of Use of Tax Havens for Evasion

A brief description of the general categories of transactions which we identified follows. In many of these cases, the only reason prosecution was possible was because an informant was available.

1. Double Trusts

The IRS has under investigation a number of promoters of so-called double trusts or family estate trust schemes. There are at least two grand juries and numerous civil investigations. The schemes seem to be concentrated in the western part of the country.

The schemes, while differing somewhat from promoter to promoter, generally involve having an unrelated party set up a trust in a haven. The first trust then sets up a second trust which it designates as the beneficiary of the first trust. Some promoters also use a third trust. The U.S. taxpayer may appoint himself as the trustee of the first trust, and then appoint the first trust the trustee of the second trust, and so on. The U.S. person transfers his assets or his right to earn income, or both, to the first trust in exchange for certificates of ownership. The income then flows to the second trust, which may make "gifts" or "loans" to the U.S. taxpayer.

Some of the returns indicate that the offshore entity is purchasing supplies and selling them to the U.S. party at an inflated price. The profit is being accumulated in the haven, or is being returned to the taxpayer as gifts or loans.

There is no way of knowing how many persons having an interest in these trusts have dropped out of the tax return filing population.

2. Secret Bank Accounts

Generally, these cases involve unreported income being diverted to a bank account located in a tax haven. Many of the taxpayers under investigation are alleged narcotics traffickers. The money is most often diverted from the U.S. by physically removing it from the country or by wire transfers. If money is diverted by wire transfer it must first be deposited in a U.S. bank. A currency transaction report may have to be filed by the bank. However, the depositor may give a fictitious name, or may simply leave the country before a report can be investigated.

In one case, the taxpayer was the sole shareholder of a corporation which acted as a sales agent for a major foreign corporation. The taxpayer's corporation received commissions for the sales activities performed, which were properly recorded on the books of the corporation. However, the corporation received additional commission payments from the foreign corporation which were not accounted for on its books and records. Pursuant to a direction by the shareholder, these additional commissions were wired by the foreign corporation to a numbered bank account in Switzerland maintained by the taxpayer. The special agent examined the records of the foreign corporation, which indicated that the wire transfer had been made, and also interviewed foreign corporate officials who stated that the taxpayer had directed them to transfer the funds into the numbered Swiss bank account. However, the foreign corporate officials subsequently refused to cooperate, and prosecution of this case had to be declined by District Counsel due to the lack of available witnesses and documentary evidence subject to the compulsory jurisdiction of the United States courts.

In another case recently prosecuted by the United States Attorney's office, the United States was able to successfully prove that corporate receipts had been diverted to a foreign bank account. In this case, a United States corporation purchased machinery and equipment from a Puerto Rican corporation. The purchase agreement and the payments made were properly reflected both on the books of the corporation and on the corporation's tax return. However, additional agreements had been entered into, in connection with the purchase of the machinery and equipment, which were not reflected on the corporate books and records or on the tax returns. These agreements provided that if the machinery and equipment sold to the U.S. corporation were not delivered by a certain date, then the Puerto Rican corporation would be liable for lease payments at a stated rental per month. When the Puerto Rican corporation failed to deliver the equipment and machinery on the specified date, it became liable for the rental payments which were subsequently paid.

In receiving payment, the U.S. corporate officials arranged it so that the proceeds from the payment were used to purchase certificates of deposit in a nominee name in Puerto Rico. Subsequently, the proceeds from these certificates of deposit were deposited in a bank account in the Cayman Islands, in the name of a Cayman corporation whose stock was held by nominees. The amount in the Cayman bank account was eventually divided up among the corporate officials, in proportion to their stock ownership.

The corporate offical who masterminded the scheme, an attorney familiar with the methods used by the IRS to prosecute tax crimes, advised the other participants that the money from the bank account should only be spent in such a way so that it left no trace, in order to avoid the IRS' making a net worth and expenditures case against the shareholders

Successful prosecution in this case was made possible by an informant, an uninvolved corporate employee, who furnished the IRS with information of the details of this scheme, as well as with copies of bank statements for the Cayman Islands bank account and with an agreement drawn up by a Cayman Islands attorney reflecting the fact that the nominal shareholders of the Cayman corporation were merely acting as nominees for the corporate officals. Other corporate officials also testified at the trial under grants of prosecutorial immunity.

Also involved in this case was the use of a corporate jet to ferry cash secretly out of the country. In this scheme, the corporation sold component parts of heavy construction equipment for cash, without reporting the sales of the components on the books and records of the corporation. The pilot of the corporate jet would then meet someone at a U.S. airport who would hand him a brief case. The pilot was instructed to fly to the Cayman Islands and to give the brief case to an attorney. The brief case contained cash representing the unreported sales proceeds, and was deposited by the Cayman Islands attorney in the secret bank account mentioned above.

3. U.S. Taxpayers Using a Foreign Corporation - Substance Over Form

In some cases, taxpayers form corporations in tax havens, ownership is not denied, and the required returns are filed. Cases may, for example, involve sales subsidiaries. In at least one case, a large company had formed and used a captive insurance company. Most of the recommendations for prosecution were declined either by Chief Counsel or the Tax Division.

Other cases appear fraudulent but necessary evidence
cannot be obtained. In a recent routine civil examination
of a return, it was discovered that substantial amounts had
been deducted as business expenses relating to rental property
which was not owned by the taxpayer. Upon further examination,
it was discovered that the rental property was owned by a
trust with the trustee being a bank located in a Caribbean
tax haven. The taxpayer was listed as the United States
agent for the trust. It was also determined that the taxpayer
was listed as the agent for the bank, which was the sole
shareholder of several corporations doing business in the
United States with which the taxpayer had formerly been
associated. Because information was received that the
taxpayer had unreported consulting fees, as well as unreported
capital gain income, the case was referred to Criminal
Investigation for investigation.

During the investigation, it was determined that returns
had been filed by all of the corporations and trusts, and
reflected the items of income and expense involved. No
evidence was produced to substantiate the allegations of
unreported consulting fees or unreported capital gain income.
However, since the taxpayer refused to cooperate, and because
of commercial secrecy laws in the Bahamas, no information
could be obtained concerning the trusts or the corporations
and their relationship to the taxpayer. In addition, no
financial records of any of these organizations could be
examined to determine if unreported income of the taxpayer
was being diverted to these entities. Accordingly, because
of the lack of evidence to substantiate allegations of
unreported income, and because, at most, the case involved a
question of substance over form, District Counsel and Criminal Investigation agreed that the investigation should be
discontinued.

4. Shelters - Commodity Transactions

We have identified a number of cases where offshore
entities or locations were used to faciliate alleged commodity transactions. Generally, these are so called "tax
spreads" which seek to give the investor a tax advantage by
generating large ordinary losses in year one, and then long-
term capital gain in year two. The benefit to the taxpayer
is the difference between the tax saved on the ordinary loss
and the tax paid on the capital gain. A tax haven entity may
be used in these schemes to conceal the fact that transactions
never take place, or to conceal the promoter's profit. Some of
these transactions were discussed in Chapter V, supra., and
an option for dealing with these schemes on a technical
basis is presented in Chapter VII, infra.

5. Income Generated Overseas Deposited in a Foreign Bank Account

A taxpayer who was an employee of a large United States multinational tire and rubber manufacturer, through the use of a nominee bank account in Switzerland, was able to receive large amounts of kickbacks, from sellers of raw materials to his employer corporation, which were deposited in the Swiss bank account and which were not reported for federal income tax purposes.

The taxpayer approached a seller of natural rubber and suggested that the seller have one of its subsidiary companies increase the sales price paid by the employer company for rubber purchased from the subsidiary. The increased sales price would then be partially kicked back to a subsidiary of the employer corporation, with the difference between the amount of first kickback and the increased purchase price being transferred to a Swiss bank account.

In order to avoid having the Swiss bank account traced to him, the taxpayer persuaded an officer of the foreign selling corporation to set up the bank account in the officer's name. The foreign corporate official made arrangements with the Swiss bank so that the taxpayer had full authority over the account. The initial deposit to this account was $25,000.

In addition to this arrangement, the taxpayer also arranged to have kickbacks paid by another corporation which sold raw materials to his corporation. This second kickback scheme was falsely recorded on the books and records of the selling corporation. Records of this corporation indicated that the amounts which were kicked back represented consulting fees paid to the first foreign corporate official mentioned above. Checks were made in the name of the foreign corporate offical and were deposited to the Swiss bank account which bore his name. Subsequently, the taxpayer or an agent of his withdrew these amounts from the Swiss bank account. The amount of kickbacks which were deposited and withdrawn based upon this scheme amounted to $220,000.

The foreign corporate offical was unaware of this scheme with the second selling corporation. In point of fact, he was not a consultant to the selling corporation nor had he received any of the monies in question, all of which had been withdrawn for the use of the taxpayer. This case resulted in a successful criminal prosecution. The taxpayer was sentenced to three years imprisonment.

6. Slush Funds

Most of these cases were identified in the mid 1970's. They generally involved large companies which were facilitating the payment of bribes or kickbacks to persons in foreign countries, who assisted in the sales of products by the U.S. company. Usually, the slush fund money was generated by increasing the contract price and having the excess paid into a foreign account. In most cases the funds used for the bribes were generated overseas. Other cases involved payments to sales agents in a foreign country, with the commissions being funneled to foreign government officials.

Most of these cases appear to have been developed from data provided by the company to the Securities and Exchange Commission as part of a voluntary disclosure program. The IRS initiated approximately 200 criminal investigations. Only about four of these cases resulted in a conviction or a plea of guilty.

7. Use of a Foreign Entity To Step-up the Basis of U.S. Property

A number of cases have been identified where a foreign entity was apparently used by a U.S. taxpayer to step-up his basis in property and thus obtain higher depreciation deductions on his U.S. tax return. In one case, a shelter promoter allegedly established a Cayman Islands company. The promoter then purchased slum property and sold it to the Cayman entity at a low price. The Cayman entity sold the property to a U.S. limited partnership at a greatly inflated price in exchange for cash and notes. The limited partnership then marketed interests in the slum property.

8. Repatriation of Funds

One problem that the tax evader faces is obtaining the use of funds which he has failed to report as income. Various schemes are resorted to so that the taxpayer can justify his use of the funds.

In one case, agents of an alleged narcotics dealer placed $2.5 million in the Panamanian account of a Panamanian corporation. The Panamanian company had a U.S. subsidiary which it capitalized by cash contributions. The U.S. company had made major investments in the U.S. The taxpayer was a salaried employee of the U.S. company.

Perhaps the most common form of repatriation of evasion
money is a loan from a foreign entity to the taxpayer. In
one case IRS was able to track deposits into a Canadian
bank which had a branch in the Cayman Islands. The loans
were fully documented, but the authenticity of the documentation
was questionable. There was no proof which would be admissible
in court of the connection between the Cayman deposits and
the Canadian loans. Without evidence from the Cayman Islands,
we cannot refute the authenticity of the loans. In another
case, the taxpayer's lawyer told the IRS agent that any net
worth figures that they developed could be explained through
fully documented loans. The agent was told that the loan
papers would be produced when the allegations were made.

Another pattern is for a tax haven entity to make payments
to third parties on behalf of the taxpayer. Still another
method of using the funds is to make indirect payments for
the benefit of children or relatives of the taxpayer. This
is often done through a trust disbursing the funds. In one
case a closely held U.S. company owned a valuable asset.
The asset was sold to a Cayman Island trust which had as its
beneficiary the children of the shareholders of the U.S.
company. The corporation then licensed the asset back from
the trust and paid substantial license fees to the trust.
It was alleged by the taxpayer that an unrelted party controlled
the trust. This could not be refuted because of the unavailability
of witnesses and records from the Cayman Islands.

D. Informants and Undercover Operations

Informants are a useful means of developing leads in
havens. Often, they are the only vehicle with which to
breach the wall of secrecy. Even if an informant cannot
supply documentary evidence, leads developed from information
supplied by an informant may often provide the missing
pieces in an investigation. In the case of a narcotics
related investigation or an organized crime case, an informant
may be the only lead with which to develop a case worthy of
prosecution.

IRS special agents are advised that informants are
often necessary in order to complete an investigation and
acquire essential evidence. This can include "undercover
work".7/ Since 1977 CID has held regional and district

7/ See IRM 9372.1.

seminars on developing, handling, and paying informants. In
order to place new emphasis on the need to develop informants,
CID has prepared a new film which, after some testing, will
be disseminated nationally. This film presents the latest
techniques for identifying informants, extracting information
from them, controlling informants, and making payments to
informants. It also highlights the pitfalls which must be
watched for in dealing with informants.

The IRS is authorized to pay rewards for information
leading to the detection and punishment of any person guilty
of violating the tax law.[8/] The payments are generally
limited to 10 percent of the additional tax, penalties, and
fines collected because of the information.[9/]

In addition, the IRS can pay informants for specific
information or to lay the groundwork for the later pro-
curement of information.[10/] The instructions to the special
agents also provide for "confidential expenditures" for the
purchasing of information.[11/] They also make clear that it
is the policy of the IRS to maintain the confidentiality of
the identity of informants and that superiors, while they
have a right to know who an informant is, will generally not
inquire as to his identity unless the knowledge is necessary.[12/]

Since 1977 the IRS has developed an increased number of
cases by the use of informants. The number of cases initiated
because of information furnished by informants has grown
from 25 in 1977 to 72 in 1979, and the number of cases
opened because of information supplied by informants has
grown from 64 in 1977 to 187 in 1979. Because of procedures
developed to protect the identity of informants, the extent
of the use of informants to investigate offshore cases
cannot be disclosed. However, there are no restrictions on

8/ § 7623.

9/ Treas. Reg. §301.7623-1 (c).

10/ See IRM 9772.

11/ See IRM 9372.2.

12/ IRM 9373.1.

the development of offshore informants, at least if they are
controlled in the U.S. In fact, the recent training film
dealing with developing informants, while not specifically
discussing developing offshore informants, does use as a
example a case involving laundering of money through an
offshore jurisdiction.

The IRS has also been involved in undercover operations,
both alone and in conjunction with other agencies. Where
necessary, the IRS has made funds available to use in those
operations.

In one case reported in the Dallas Morning News, Miami
Herald, and the Cayman Compus, the IRS cooperated with the
Drug Enforcement Administration (DEA) in laundering $50,000
of IRS money through a Cayman Island bank. According to the
press reports, DEA agents posed as drug dealers and approached
a Dallas businessman who told them that he could supply them
with cocaine and hashish and could advise them of a "fool
proof scheme to legitimize the illegal profits and make them
tax exempt at the same time". The businessman introduced
the agents to a Dallas attorney who formed a U.S. company
for them, took them to the Cayman Islands to a phony loan
company, deposited their $50,000 in a bank and then withdrew
$46,222, keeping a six percent service charge and a small
Cayman Islands tax. A check in the amount of $46,222 was
drawn on the phony loan company and made payable to the
U.S. company. The attorney then brought the check back into
the United States. Once back in the United States, according
to the newspapers, the attorney made out phony records to
show that the amount of the check was a loan to the U.S.
company from the Cayman company at six percent interest.
According to the paper, the undercover agents were told to
pay themselves liberal salaries, expense reimbursements, and
annual bonuses, and to drive company owned cars and deduct
the loan interest from their federal income taxes.

The DEA and IRS agents then followed the businessman to
Miami where he was eventually arrested and "charged with
smuggling currency and with possession of cocaine with
intent to distribute." The attorney was also arrested and
charged with smuggling currency out of the country. According
to an article which appeared on December 20, 1977, in the
Cayman Compus the phony loan company was under the management of a Cayman company.

E. Analysis

The IRS and the Department of Justice encounter significant problems when trying to investigate or prosecute cases involving tax haven transactions.

It is difficult, if not impossible, to obtain admissible evidence connecting the U.S. taxpayer with an income item in such cases. For example, in the Canadian loan case described above, there is circumstantial evidence which might tie the taxpayer to the money. However, there is no admissible evidence directly tying the taxpayer to the funds. Often, ownership of an entity cannot be proven. For example, in a number of the schemes described above, there are transactions which go through an offshore entity which appears to be accumulating a significant amount of money. While the money may accumulate for the benefit of a U.S. person or be used by him in some way, there is no available evidence to connect him with ownership of the entity. General information gathering problems and options for dealing with them are discussed in Chapter IX.

There are also administrative problems. The level of coordination of offshore cases is unclear. In at least one case, promoters of a scheme were being independently investigated in two separate districts. Problems of coordination are discussed in Chapter X.

Another problem is the identification of cases for investigation. Many offshore cases are technically difficult from a legal perspective, and the facts are difficult to sort out. A number of cases which were thoroughly investigated, after the expenditure of signficant time and money, turned out to involve lawful business arrangements, although legal issues such as pricing or allocation of expenses may be present. This problem, and the possibility of providing legal assistance to the agents during the course of an investigation, are addressed in Chapter X.

Options are presented in Chapter VII for technical changes, both administrative and legislative, which might help rationalize the taxation of tax haven transactions and accordingly might limit some fraudulent use.

VII. Options for Change in Substantive Rules

Many of the transactions described in Chapter V are perfectly legitimate and reflect Congressional policies as to United States taxing jurisdiction. In many cases, decisions to change those policies should not be made without thorough economic analysis; such analysis is beyond the scope of this report. Nevertheless, there are both administrative and legislative changes which can be made which might help to curtail some of the tax haven use and ease the government's administrative burdens in this area. Options dealing with tax haven income tax treaties, with information gathering problems, and with internal IRS structure are dealt with in Chapters VIII, IX and X, respectively.

The transactions described in Chapter VI are fraudulent, and, in general, will not be prevented by changes in substantial rules. However, better administrative efforts and more rational tax rules might discourage some fraudulent use, and might make fraudulent use easier to detect.

A. Options Which Can be Accomplished Administratively

While it may be advisable to make some legislative changes, decisions to change the Code should be made only after thorough analysis. Additional rules generally bring more complexity, and may make the process more difficult for both taxpayers and tax administrators. The options discussed below could be pursued without changes in legislation.

1. Burden of Proof

Many of the cases described above involve a U.S. person taking a deduction for an amount paid to a tax haven (e.g., shelter transactions). Agents often spend significant time attempting to determine whether the taxpayer has in fact incurred an expense, or whether an offshore piece of property is correctly valued. The same problem occurs in pricing cases where taxpayers fail to establish that the price which they charge is the proper price, or with allocation of deduction issues where foreign taxpayers refuse to produce home office books adequate to establish the proper allocation of home office expenses to the U.S.

The burden of proof to establish the tax consequences of a transaction is on the taxpayer. IRS agents should be given clear direction that they should deny deductions where a taxpayer has not established entitlement to the deduction, or where valuations or proper pricing have not been established. A series of rulings advising taxpayers that the IRS will take this position should be published. An initial step in this direction was taken in Rev. Rul. 80-324.1/

2. Section 482 Regulations

Consideration should be given to establishing a regulations project to analyze the §482 regulations, with a view toward amending them to ease some of the administrative burdens placed on taxpayers and the IRS, and to achieve greater certainty in pricing international transactions.

Section 482 is one of the most important provisions available to the IRS to deal with tax haven transactions. The regulations take the position that transactions between related parties are to be conducted at arm's length. If they are not, and taxable incomes are thereby understated, the IRS can make allocations to determine the true taxable income of each member of an affiliated group.[2] The regulations set forth rules for determining taxable income in five specific situations.[3] In each, the method to be used is a price which would have been charged an unrelated person. In a transaction involving a sale of goods, for example, this is referred to as the "comparable uncontrolled price".[4]

Taxpayers and IRS agents have had difficulty in dealing with the §482 regulations, in part because of the dependence upon comparable uncontrolled prices, which often are difficult to find, and in part because of the subjective judgments which need to be made. Some believe that in a number of cases IRS agents disregard the ordering rules in the regulations for determining the method to be used, and instead go to some more general method sooner than they should.[5] The Internal Revenue Manual directs the agents to perform a "functional analysis" to determine the relative values of the respective functions performed by the two related entities involved in a transaction.[6]

2/   Treas. Reg. §1.482-2 (e) (2).

3/   Treas. Reg. §1.482-2.

4/   Treas. Reg. §1.482-2 (e) (2).

5/   See, J. Burns, "How IRS Applies the Inter-Company Pricing Rules of Section 482: A Corporate Survey", 52 J. of Tax. 308 (May 1980).

6/   IRM 4233, Text 623.

The inconsistency between the two approaches, and the
problems caused both taxpayers and the IRS, can be seen by
contrasting the approach taken by the courts in the Du Pont
case[7] and the U.S. Steel case.[8]   In Du Pont the court
seemed to be saying that the IRS failure to use a pricing
approach set forth in the regulations was permissible, but
the taxpayer was obligated to prove its case under the
regulations.[9]   In U.S. Steel the court seemed to be saying
that the regulations as drafted required the IRS to use
comparables when they exist, even if they are not precisely
comparable.[10]   These cases, and the cited articles, point
out significant problems which deserve attention. In both
cases, tax havens were involved.

While the §482 provisions are extremely important
in dealing with tax haven problems, and while the cases
cited above involved tax havens, it is beyond the scope of
this report to recommend particular solutions, because these
regulations present major issues involving all international
transactions, most of which occur with countries which are
not tax havens. Instead, a major study should be undertaken
to identify problems and recommend solutions. Any such
study should involve the outside business community, which
will be greatly affected by changes in the §482 regulations.
The General Accounting Office has completed a study of the
administration of §482; its report should be published in
early 1981. Also, the IRS National Office Examination
Division is in the midst of a two year study of the administration of §482. In any event, the issues need to be debated
and resolved.

7/ E.I. Du Pont de Nemours and Company, 608 F. 2nd 445
    (Ct. Cls. 1979).

8/ United States Steel Corp. v. Commissioner, 617 F.2d
    942 (2nd Cir. 1980).

9/ See, Fuller, "Problems in Applying the §482 Inter-
    Company Pricing Regulations, Accentuated by Dupont
    Case", 52 J. of Tax. 10 (January, 1980).

10/ See, Decelles and Raedel, "Use of Comparability
    Test in Inter-Company Pricing Strengthed by U.S.
    Steel Case", 52 J. of Tax. 102 (August, 1980).

In the course of any such study certain approaches might be considered. For example, a profit splitting approach has been recommended.[11] Under this approach the IRS would look to functions performed by each of the related entities involved in a transaction and would attempt to split the profits between them. In effect, this was in part the approach which the court in the Du Pont case seemed to accept. Whether such an approach is feasible, and if so, whether it should be an alternative to an arm's length standard or should be applied only if an arm's length price cannot be found is something that needs to be considered. A disadvantage to this approach is the need to make subjective judgements and to apply significant audit time in performing a functional analysis. The IRS has particular problems today doing this, especially where a taxpayer refuses to cooperate.

In addition, some commentators suggesting a profit splitting approach assume that intercompany pricing really involves which country gets to tax which portion of the profits from a transaction, and that accordingly profit splitting is the issue. Where a tax haven is involved, however, this may not be the case, instead the issue may be whether the profits are taxed at all. It may be decided that a profit splitting approach is not adequate where a tax haven is involved and that special rules should apply to tax haven transactions.

Another problem with adopting new §482 rules which depart radically from the present rules is that the OECD has recently published a report which describes generally accepted practices to determine transfer prices.[12] The practices set forth are very similiar to the present §482 regulations. The hope was that the report would encourage geater uniformity among OECD countries in transfer pricing, and accordingly would reduce conflicts. Changes in the regulations would retard this process.

Another approach is a unitary or formula system, which is used by a few of the states. However, such a system would completely violate the separate accounting concept under which many multinational companies operate. It is contrary to the way most other OECD countries approach transfer pricing, and contrary to the taxation by the U.S. of other transfer payments such as those imposed on fixed or determinable income.

11/ See, for example, Fuller, supra at 11.

12/ OECD, Transfer Pricing and Multinational Enterprises, Report of the OECD Committee on Fiscal Affairs (1979).

A sense has developed that foreign multinational companies are competing against U.S. businesses in the U.S. and using tax havens to do this. They are often at a competitive advantage because the §482 regulations were not drafted with foreign investors in mind. We have seen cases where it is even unclear that a U.S. company owned by a foreign person is dealing with a related party in a tax haven, because it is often difficult to develop the facts to indicate affiliation.

Obviously, if a decision is made to revise the §482 regulations, the goal would be to develop workable rules which would enable a true and accurate allocation of income to be made.

Problems with income from the performance of services might also be dealt with through changes in the §482 regulations, even if a complete revision were not undertaken. Many of the service income cases involve a potential §482 adjustment, but the subjective judgments which must be made under the regulations are difficult and time consuming. Also, the treatment of the transfer of intangibles in the service business context is not clearly addressed.

It may well be that the service income situation can be best remedied by statutory enactment. However, in addition to, or as an alternative to, legislative changes, a regulations project could be established to determine whether the §482 regulations could be revised to develop clearer standards, particularly for allocating income attributable to "know how" and other intangibles used by a tax haven subsidiary performing services abroad.

3. Subpart F Regulations

The subpart F regulations should be reviewed with a view toward eliminating, where possible, the need for subjective judgments. The subpart F regulations, as in the case of the §482 regulations, often require that subjective judgments be made to determine whether a transaction falls within the ambit of subpart F. This is particularly true of the regulations which interpret the foreign base company service income provisions. For example, the regulations require that in order for foreign base company service income to be generated, substantial assistance contributing to performance of services by a controlled foreign corporation must be furnished by a related person or persons. The determination of whether substantial assistance is furnished is based on a mathematical formula, or on a facts and circumstances test. The facts and circumstances test, which it appears that revenue agents most often have to rely on, is unclear, and few guidelines are given in the regulations. It would be useful to at least provide additional guidelines as to when substantial assistance is deemed to occur.

4. Application of §269 and the Accumulated Earnings Tax

The IRS should determine the extent to which §269 and the accumulated earnings tax can be applied to tax haven transactions, and should publish a series of rulings showing cases in which §269 or the accumulated earnings tax will be applied to tax haven transactions.

The foreign taxation area is extremely difficult to administer. The audit of some of the more abusive transactions, or transactions which threaten the U.S. tax base, might require that a new approach be tried. One of these would be to apply §269 more vigorously. The extent to which §269 would apply in the foreign area has not been adequately explored. For example, in Chapter V there is described a promotion involving an offshore commodity company which has an offshore parent, the stock of which is owned by U.S. persons. The subsidiary distributes its earnings to its parent in order to avoid the accumulated earnings tax. This transaction might be attacked by applying §269 to disregard the subsidiary. Then, unless the parent distributed its income to its shareholders, the accumulated earnings tax would apply to the U.S. source income of the parent. Other instances abound where these provisions might be applied.

Arguably, both provisions are ideally suited to deal with tax haven transactions. Section 269 on its face is intended to apply where the principal purpose of an acquisition is avoidance of U.S. tax. By definition, tax haven entities are often formed for just such a purpose.

5. Review Rev. Rul. 54-140

Revenue Ruling 54-140[13] held, in effect, that a distribution of stock in a subsidiary corporation was a dividend, and established a brother-sister relationship between the two corporations. This result has been applied in the case of pairing of stock in Rev. Rul. 80-213.[14] Accordingly, abusive decontrol of foreign corporations can take place. (See discussion at chapter V.D. re "paired" or "stapled" stock.)

---

[13] 1954-1 C.B. 116.

[14] 1980-28 I.R.B. 7.

The IRS should reevaluate its position in Rev. Rul. 54-116. Although the IRS has stated its position, the cases are not clear[15], and the result of the ruling in the foreign area has been some avoidance of U.S. anti-abuse provisions.

6. Revocation of Acquiescence in CCA, Inc.

The IRS should consider revoking its acquiescence in CCA, Inc. v. Commissioner[16], in which the Tax Court held that a foreign corporation, fifty percent of the voting rights of which were held by U.S. shareholders and fifty percent of the voting rights of which were held by non-U.S. shareholders, was not a controlled foreign corporation. It is questionable whether the powers held by the foreign persons in this case were significantly different than the powers of the foreign shareholders in the cases that the IRS won in this area. Considering the potential for abuse, the acquiescence should be revoked.

7. Captive Insurance Companies

The IRS has published a ruling and won a Tax Court case on this issue. Nevertheless, there is significant activity. Taxpayers are attempting to have their captives write small amounts of unrelated risk to avoid "captive" status.

The IRS might consider publishing a ruling stating that a captive can be fragmented for purposes of determining whether premiums are deductible. Under this approach, there would be no shifting or spreading of risk, and hence premiums would not be deductible, if the premiums paid to the captive by affiliates exceeded a certain percentage of gross premiums received by the captive during a year.

8. Income of Foreign Banks

As described in Chapter V, foreign banks doing business in the U.S. can avoid U.S. tax by booking loans at a tax haven branch.

15/ See DeCoppet v. Helvering, 108 F. 2d 787 (2d Cir. 1940), Wilkinson v. Commissioner, 29 T.C. 421 (1957), nonacq. 1960-1 C.B. 7. Cf. Spreckels-Rosekrans Investment Co. v. Lewis, 146 F. 2d 982 (9th Cir. 1945).

16/ 64 T.C. 137 (1975), acq. 1976-2 C.B. 1.

The problem can be viewed as a regulatory problem, as a treaty problem, or as an audit problem. The regulations could be amended to provide that income from a loan negotiated in the U.S. will be effectively connected regardless of where booked. In the alternative, the Code could be amended to give the taxpayer an irrevocable election to treat the income as effectively connected or not. If the taxpayer treats the income as not effectively connected with a U.S. business, it would also have to waive any treaty benefit otherwise applicable to the interest payment. The audit problem is one of access to books and records. This could in part be solved by restructuring transactions in cases where taxpayers do not supply the necessary records, and putting the banks to their burden of proof.

B. Options Requiring Legislation

The study has shown a significant and growing level of tax haven use. Transactions which are attempts to evade U.S. taxes, including transactions to hide narcotics earnings, appear to be important elements, although legal use is probably much greater. The legal use, particularly use by multinational corporations, includes many transactions which involve drains on what would otherwise be U.S. source income. The IRS has great difficulty in administering the current rules. The levels of use and the potential for eroding the U.S. tax base, as well as the administrative problems caused by current law, are significant enough to warrant consideration of changes in the way in which the U.S. taxes tax haven income.

1. Expansion of Subpart F to Target it on Tax Haven Entities

Subpart F could be amended by adding a provision which would tax all of the tax haven income of a controlled foreign corporation. This could be accomplished by providing that subpart F income would include the income of a controlled foreign corporation formed in a tax haven, resident in a tax haven, or managed and controlled in a tax haven. In the alternative, the provision could be drafted to treat as subpart F income that income of a controlled foreign corporation which is not taxed above some minimal level by the country where the corporation is formed.

The addition of a targeted approach would be an improvement over the present system from an administrative point of view. It would provide a clearer focus than the current law and would eliminate many of difficult technical issues encountered in tax haven transactions, and accordingly might discourage some abusive tax haven use.

A targeted approach would require that the term "tax haven" be defined. The Secretary of the Treasury could be authorized to designate the countries considered tax havens. In general, a tax haven might be defined as any country in which the tax burden on all income or on particular categories of income is substantially lower than the U.S. tax rate on that income. Countries designated as tax havens would thus include countries (1) with low tax rates on all income; (2) with low tax rates on income from foreign sources; (3) with low tax rates on income from specific types of business; or (4) which grant low rates of taxation to companies engaged in "offshore business". A country with a low tax rate would generally be one which imposes a rate of tax which is one half or less than one half of the U.S. corporate tax rate. While targeting jurisdictions can present some difficult problems, Japan, France, and Australia have done so.

Some flexibility could be given to the Secretary by making the standards "guidelines," rather than fixed objective classification rules. Thus, the Secretary could take into account such factors as the existence of a tax treaty between the U.S. and the other country in determining whether or not to classify the country as a tax haven. The availability or nonavailability of commercial or bank information, however, should not be a factor, as this system would focus more on legal use than on determinations as to whether a country is an abusive tax haven.

An exclusion from U.S. taxation could be provided for income earned by a corporation: (1) that has a physical facility in its country of residence which is necessary for its business activities in that country; (2) that is managed and controlled locally, and which is engaged in its principal business activity, principally with unrelated parties, in the country of residence; and (3) that does not receive greater than a fixed percentage of its gross revenues in the form of holding company type income (say five percent).

While this option could subject some high taxed non-tax haven income to U.S. tax, a foreign tax credit would be available to offset any U.S. tax imposed on that income.

This option does not address the so called "runaway plants", which are manufacturing operations established by U.S. companies in countries offering tax incentives to attract labor intensive investment. Those cases present issues not addressed by this report.

As an alternative to amending subpart F to add a new category of subpart F income as described above, subpart F could be changed by narrowing its scope so that it would be targeted exclusively on tax havens. A problem with this approach is that non-tax havens can, at times, be used in ways similar to tax havens. Thus, it might be wiser to expand subpart F rather than simply to replace it with a narrower provision.

If a decision is made to target subpart F, the issue must be addressed of whether to permit taxes paid high tax countries to offset U.S. tax on tax haven income. Under present rules, the foreign tax credit limitation prevents U.S. taxpayers from crediting foreign taxes against U.S. taxes imposed on U.S. source income. The limitation is generally computed on an overall worldwide basis, with separate "baskets", however, for certain kinds of income, including oil-related income and certain interest income. Excess credits from one country can be used to offset U.S. tax imposed on income from another country. At times, taxpayers attempt to convert U.S. source income to subpart F income (which changes its source to foreign) in order to absorb excess tax credits. This leaves some continued incentive to use tax havens. If subpart F is amended to include a provision targeted at tax havens, without any change in the foreign tax credit limitation, the same planning opportunities would be available.

One alternative is to adopt a per-country limitation on the foreign tax credit, under which taxes paid to each country are in separate baskets. This method has been used before, and at one time was an optional alternative to the overall limitation. It is, however, difficult to administer Transfer pricing and allocation of deductions between all foreign affiliates, not only between the U.S. and foreign affiliates, would have to be scrutinized.

An alternative would be to create two baskets for foreign taxes, a high tax basket and a low tax basket. Taxes paid to all high tax countries would be averaged together, and taxes paid to all low tax countries would be averaged together. Therefore, the excess credits from high tax countries would not offset U.S. tax on tax haven income. While some administrative problems would exist because of the need to allocate income and deductions between the two baskets, the problems would be fewer than those involved with a per-country limitation.

2. Adoption of a Management and Control Test for Asserting United States Taxing Jurisdiction Over Foreign Corporations

Consideration should be given to expanding U.S. taxing jurisdiction over corporations to include foreign corporations which are managed and controlled in the United States. Today, the United States asserts worldwide taxing jurisdiction over a domestic corporation, which is defined as a corporation created or organized in the United States.[17] A foreign corporation is taxed only on its U.S. source income and foreign source income which is effectively connected with a U.S. business.

Often, tax haven corporations conduct substantial business overseas but are in reality managed in the United States. That is, all significant policy decisions, as well as some day-to-day management decisions, are made by employees of the U.S. parent corporation. Significant administrative support may also be provided. In some cases, the tax haven corporation has, at most, a few clerical support employees located in the tax haven.

In some cases, existing law would permit the United States to tax at least a portion of the earnings of the foreign corporation. For example, at times the IRS may argue that the foreign corporation is doing business in the United States. In other cases, it may be possible for the IRS to apply §482 to allocate income from the tax haven corporation to the U.S. Neither of these approaches is completely adequate. Prevailing in the trade or business argument only subjects the corporation's U.S. source income and its foreign source effectively connected income to United States tax, whereas U.S. source income would generally be taxed by the United States in any event. Section 482 can be extremely difficult to apply from an administrative point of view. Developing the necessary facts can be time consuming, particularly when the foreign corporation is located in a tax haven which restricts access to books and records.

The management and control test for asserting taxing jurisdiction over a corporation is used in many countries, including the United Kingdom and its former colonies. This

---

[17] §7701 (a)(4); Treas. Reg. §301.7701-5.

test does have limitations as the sole test of taxing jurisdiction because of the subjective judgments which often must be made. As an addition to the present rule, however, it would provide the IRS with an additional means of scrutinizing many tax haven operations. At times it would be easier to apply than § 482.

Canada applies a dual test (having adopted the incorporation test as an addition to the management and control test), and has found it useful in dealing with international taxation problems.

3. Change in Control Test

A number of cases involve attempts to decontrol tax haven corporations to avoid subpart F and U.S. reporting obligations. While case law supports the view that actual control, even without actual stock ownership control, leads to controlled status, it can be very difficult for the IRS to establish the fact of control, particularly where the corporation and the other owners are in a tax haven. At times, side agreements are suspected but their existence is difficult, if not impossible, to prove. There are other control problems, including pairing of stock, which could become significant if action is not taken. Furthermore, the 10 percent threshhold requirement for U.S. shareholder status permits distortions and unequitable treatment of taxpayers in some cases.

Consideration might be given to reducing the percentage ownership test for controlled foreign corporations status to a 50 percent test, and to adding a value test as an alternative test, as well as to reducing to one percent the level of stock ownership for determining when a U.S. person is a U.S. shareholder.[18/] Adoption of these rules would permit U.S. taxation of the growing number of 50/50 joint ventures, and would eliminate avoidance of U.S. tax through the pairing of stock. It would also provide some equity as between U.S. persons who own 10 percent of the stock and those who do not. Consideration might also be given to dropping the controlled threshhold down to 25 percent, as was done in the case of U.S. insurance of U.S. risks for subpart F purposes, and as the French have done in their tax haven legislation. A drop in the threshhold could apply only to corporations formed in tax havens.

18/ The Senate version of the Tax Reduction Act of 1975 contained a provision which would have redefined the term "U.S. shareholder" to include a U.S. person holding a one percent or greater interest in a foreign corporation See H. Rep. No. 94-120, 94th Cong., 1st Sess. 69-70 1975-1 C.B. 631.

At the very least, the "paired" or "stapled" stock problems should be addressed. One option is to amend the Code to treat stock of a corporation which is paired with stock of a second corporation as owned by the second corporation. Such a provision would also curtail avoidance of the anti-boycott and DISC provisions through pairing.

4. Service and Construction Income

The service and construction industries are significant users of tax havens, and present the IRS with unique problems. Many of the problems appear to involve the transfer of a U.S. business to an offshore subsidiary, and include the transfer of know-how or goodwill from the U.S. parent to the tax haven affiliate. There also seem to be significant situations involving, for example, the negotiation of contracts in the U.S., their signature by officers of the foreign affiliate who may also be officers or employees of the U.S. parent follow by the transfer of know-how without any compensation. Many of these cases might result in subpart F income or §482 allocations to the parent if identified and fully developed by the IRS. Considering the limitations of resources, however, identifying these cases and fully developing them is extremely difficult. Moreover, the foreign subsidiaries are routinely established in tax havens having commercial secrecy, which present the IRS with additional books and records problems.

A narrow approach to dealing solely with services income would be to add a branch rule to the foreign base company services income provisions. A branch rule (which is contained in the subpart F sales provisions) could provide that foreign base company services income would include the income attributable to the carrying on of service activities of a branch of the controlled foreign corporation, by treating the income as derived by a wholly owned subsidiary of the controlled foreign corporation. Thus, if a tax haven company is performing services in a third country through a branch, and the direction for or support of those services is provided by the tax haven company's home office, or by employees of that office, the income would be foreign base company services income. An alternative approach, and one which would be far simpler to administer, would be to treat all income from the performance of services outside of the country of incorporation of the controlled foreign corporation as subpart F income.

Two serious issues which must be addressed in the service and construction cases are whether the tax treatment of these businesses should be left alone for competitive reasons and whether we can afford to continue to export this kind of technology without exacting a U.S. tax.

5. Merger of the Foreign Personal Holding Company Provisions into Subpart F

Consideration should be given to eliminating the foreign personal holding company provisions and incorporating their substance into subpart F.

Today, foreign personal holding company income may be taxed under either the foreign personal holding company provisions[19] or under subpart F. If both provisions apply to a particular foreign corporation, then the foreign personal holding company provisions will apply and not subpart F.[20] Accordingly, it may be possible to avoid the investment in U.S. property rules[21] of subpart F by causing a foreign corporation to be a foreign personal holding company and to earn a small amount of foreign personal holding company income in a year in which a significant investment in U.S. property is made.[22]

Further, the foreign personal holding company attribution rules have never been rationalized. The provisions contain technical problems. For example, the foreign personal holding company attribution rules provide for attribution of stock ownership between siblings. In addition, they require attribution from a foreign individual to a U.S. individual. Accordingly, the acquisition by a U.S. person of a small amount of stock of a foreign corporation, in which his sister (who is a foreign resident) owns 50 percent of the stock, could make that corporation a foreign personal holding company and subject that person to tax. Attribution occurs even without actual ownership of stock by the individual. A U.S. person may thus have a technical obligation to file a

---

19/ §§551 through 558.

20/ §951(d).

21/ §956.

22/ See Estate of Lovett, 1980-1 USTC 9432; contra. Estate of Whitlock v. Commissioner, 494 F.2d 1297 (10th Cir. 1974), rev'g 59 T.C. 501 (1972), cert. denied, 419 U.S. 839 (1974), reh'g denied 419 U.S. 1041 (1974).

return with respect to the foreign company, even though he owns no stock and may not be able to get any of the details needed to complete a return. The IRS has lost a case on this issue.[23/]

Moreover, the foreign personal holding company provisions do not contain proper anti-double counting rules similar to those in §959.

Finally, it appears that few foreign personal holding company returns are audited. If foreign personal holding company issues are raised, they generally will be addressed by agents who are not trained in those issues. Because international examiners concentrate on large cases, they have not developed practical audit experience in the foreign personal holding company area.

The structure of taxing foreign corporations controlled by U.S. persons would be simplified by repealing the foreign personal holding company provisions, and incorporating their substance into subpart F. Some technical changes, including a change in the subpart F stock ownership test, might be made.

In the alternative, §951(d) could be amended to override the Lovett case. This could be accomplished by providing that a U.S. shareholder who is subject to tax under §551(b) on income of a controlled foreign corporation for his taxable year, which is also a controlled foreign corporation, will be required to include in gross income, for that taxable year, any amount with respect to that controlled foreign corporation invested in U.S. property, to the extent of its earnings and profits, but the amount so included will be reduced by the amount included under §551. The foreign personal holding company attribution rules could be amended to incorporate the §958 rules.

These changes would at least eliminate the loophole created by the Lovett case, and would rationalize the foreign personal holding company provisions somewhat. They would, however, still maintain two parallel and possibly overlapping systems with all of the attendant administrative problems.

23/ See Estate of Nettie S. Miller v. Commissioner, 43 T.C. 760 (1965), non acq. 1966-2 C.B. 8.

6. Captive Insurance

Despite IRS rulings and a successful court case, captive insurance companies continue to proliferate in the tax havens. In fact, aggressive planning is attempting to avoid the case law.[24] One legislative approach might be to amend subpart F to extend its coverage to include the premiums received by a controlled foreign corporation for insuring foreign risks of related persons. This approach would be consistent with the base company concept found in the foreign base company sales and services income provisions. Another approach might be to clarify the application of the foreign base company services income provisions to insurance of risks of related parties.

7. Shipping Income

The use of tax havens to shelter income from shipping has been considered by the Congress. As originally provided, shipping income was excluded from subpart F. In 1975, subpart F was amended to include shipping income, but earnings reinvested in the shipping business were excluded. The IRS has had little audit experience with these provisions to date, but they are technically complex and may require some on-site audits, which as a practical matter may be impossible to do. For administrative reasons, consideration might be given to taxing shipping income directly.

8. De minimis Exclusion from Foreign Base Company Income

The de minimis exclusion from foreign base company income could be amended to add an alternative dollar limitation

Today, if foreign base company income of a controlled foreign corporation is less than 10 percent of its gross income, none of its gross income is taxable as foreign base company income. By using this exception, larger companies can shelter significant amounts of passive income.[25] This shelter could be removed by adding an alternative dollar limitation, so that the exception would not apply if the controlled foreign corporation's foreign base company income exceeds a fixed dollar amount.

9. Commodity Shelters

One solution to the use of tax havens as situs for alleged commodity shelter transactions would be to deal directly on a technical basis with tax straddles. The Code

---

24/ See discussion at Chapter V. C.6.

25/ See discussion at Chapter V. C.2.

could be amended by adopting a provision which would (1) postpone recognition of losses from certain straddle positions during the period in which the taxpayer holds offsetting positions plus the following 30 days, and (2) suspend the running of the holding periods (of the assets comprising the offsetting positions) during the balance, plus the following 30 days. In addition, §1221(5) (denying capital asset treatment to certain government obligations) could be repealed.

Tax straddles are a significant and growing problem. They are motivated solely by tax considerations, and offer no opportunity for meaningful economic return. As explained in Chapter V, a tax haven situs is often used as the alleged situs for the transaction in order to obfuscate the audit trail. Significant amounts of audit time, as well as crowded court calendars, can make it difficult to deal with these cases under current law. Tax straddles are an even more significant problem domestically.

Most often the straddle shelters are used to defer income by producing paper losses in one year while deferring the offsetting gains to a later year. They may also be used in an attempt to convert short term gain into long term gain or capital losses into ordinary losses. These straddles have been structured primarily in commodities, including metals, and in government securities.

The above proposal would deal directly with the problem by denying the benefits of the tax straddle. While it could be developed solely in terms of tax haven transactions, the scope of the problem would require that any legislation considered should also cover domestic tax straddle transactions

10. Tax Haven Deductions

Another more general approach to tax haven related shelters, and to the overall problem of phoney tax haven related deductions, would be to amend the Code to specifically disallow a deduction for amounts paid or accrued to a tax haven person or entity, unless the taxpayer establishes by clear and convincing evidence that the underlying trans- action occurred and that the amount of the deduction is reasonable. While this in essence is the current law, a clear rule targeted at tax havens would help to speed up the administration of the law. A similar rule, requiring a taxpayer to produce documentary evidence as to the value of offshore property, would also be useful. This would require that the taxpayer give to the IRS written material which IRS engineers can evaluate without having to visit the property.

Additional reporting of tax haven transactions would also be helpful. A major problem today is identifying haven transactions so that they can be audited. Consideration should be given to reporting of any transaction with a foreign person, as well as any investment in foreign property. In addition to the existing criminal and civil penalties for non-filing which would apply in this case, the penalty for failure to provide the information could include denying any deductions relating to the unreported foreign transaction.

11. No Fault Penalty

Consideration should be given to adopting a no fault penalty on the order of 50 percent of a substantial tax haven related tax deficiency.

Today, taxpayers often enter into questionable tax haven transactions, taking the calculated risk that they will not be identified. Even if the taxpayer is identified, a number of years can pass before the tax plus interest is actually paid. During this time the taxpayer has the use of the money, the effect being a loan from the Treasury.

A no fault penalty would place the taxpayer under some risk and would go a long way toward curbing abusive shelter and other deduction generating transactions.

12. Foreign Trusts

Most non-fraudulent use of foreign trusts by U.S. persons appears to have been eliminated. However, some schemes have developed to take advantage of perceived loopholes For example, the sale or exchange exception from §679 is allegedly being abused. To curb this abuse, the exception could be eliminated. In the alternative, the provision could be eliminated only in the case of transactions with a trust which has as a party in interest a person related to the transferor. The sale or exchange exception is often met, by a long-term installment sale. This scheme could be eliminated either by eliminating the sale or exchange exception or by providing that an installment sale will not be considered a sale or exchange to a foreign trust if the note runs for more than a set period of years, such as five years.

The use of foreign trusts by foreign persons who later become U.S. residents could be minimized by providing that a tranferor will be taxed on the income from property transferred to a foreign trust if the transfer takes place within a fixed period of time before the transferor becomes a U.S. resident. This is a jurisdictional problem and any change requires a major policy decision as to the point at which the U.S. should assert taxing jurisdiction.

The foreign trust rules do not apply to a transfer by reason of the death of the transferor. To limit the estate planning opportunities exceptions for testamentary transfers could be removed. The income would have to be taxed to the beneficiaries, however. Technical changes, such as eliminating §679 from the scope of a §1057 election, and changing the definition of a U.S. beneficiary so that a foreign corporation is considered a U.S. beneficiary if more than 10 percent of its stock is owned directly or indirectly by foreign persons, could be made.

13. Expatriation

U.S. persons who seek to expatriate often expatriate to a tax haven. The current rules covering expatriates are complicated and at times difficult to administer. They could be improved and made easier to administer by subjecting the expatriate to tax on the difference between the fair market value of his property at the date of expatriation and his basis in the property. In this way the tax, including the tax on foreign property, would be paid upon expatriation and the expatriate could then be treated as any other non-resident alien person. Canada has a similar system. A similar rule could be adopted for the departure of resident aliens, although such a change would represent a greater deviation from present policy than the change suggested for expatriates.

14. Residence

A clear objective rule for determining when an alien becomes a U.S. resident might be adopted. Today, the rules as to when an alien becomes a resident are subjective and are difficult to administer. It might be better to adopt a clear rule for determining residence, for example, 183 days in the U.S. during a year. While such a rule is subject to manipulation, so is the present rule, and certainty might be preferable.

VIII. Treaties With Tax Havens

Tax treaties modify domestic tax law to reduce tax
otherwise imposed on foreign investment in the treaty countries.
Treaties with tax havens are often used by residents of non-
treaty countries to achieve a reduction in United States taxes.
Although most of this use is not fraudulent, some is abusive
and inconsistent with present United States tax policy. The
low rates of tax coupled with the anonymity afforded by tax
havens do, however, give rise to some fraudulent use.

United States taxpayers, particularly multinational
corporations, may also use the United States treaty network
and tax havens to advantage. The most widely known use is
that of Netherlands Antilles finance subsidiaries to achieve
zero rates of tax on interest paid on foreign borrowings.
Often, the advantages which can be achieved through tax
haven treaties can also be achieved through treaties with
non-tax havens.

A. Basic Principles

Tax treaties are often referred to as conventions to
eliminate double taxation and avoid fiscal evasion. Double
taxation can arise in the case of a United States taxpayer,
because the income earned by him may be taxed by both the
United States and, if earned in another country, by that
country as well. The United States unilaterally attempts to
mitigate this double taxation by permitting a tax credit for
income taxes paid to foreign countries. However, because of
differences in source rules between the United States and
the other country, and because of problems of defining when
a foreign tax is an income tax for purposes of the United States
foreign tax credit, there may still be some cases of significant
double taxation.1/

1/ It can be argued that the real impact of treaties
   is to eliminate excess taxation. The unilateral relief
   afforded by the United States probably works well in most
   cases. However, rates of tax in the other country may
   exceed United States rates, particularly when withholding
   taxes on distributions are taken into account. Reduction
   of these taxes leads to elimination of excess taxation
   rather than double taxation.

Under United States law, passive income paid to foreigners not doing business in the United States is taxed at a rate of 30 percent of the gross amount of the income.[2] United States income tax treaties reduce this rate of tax in the case of payments to residents of a treaty country. The United States position, as reflected in the United States Model Income Tax Treaty, is that the rate of tax on dividends should be reduced to five percent in the case of direct investment (ownership of 10 percent or more of the stock of the payor corporation) and to 15 percent in the case of portfolio investment. Interest and royalties should be exempt from tax at source. The OECD Model contains similar rules for dividends and royalties, but permits a 10 percent tax on interest at source.

While treaty benefits are theoretically intended to inure to residents of each of the treaty countries, third country residents often seek to take advantage of them. At times, this use by third country residents may coincide with perceived United States interests; at other times, however, this use may be abusive. The treaties therefore generally contain some provisions designed to limit the benefits of the treaty to residents of either of the two contracting countries. However, "resident" is broadly defined as any person who under the laws of a country is liable for tax by reason of his domicile, residence, citizenship, place of management, place of incorporation, or other criterion of a similar nature. Persons taxable in a country only on income from sources in that country or on capital situated in that country are not residents.[3] Interest and royalties are covered at source only if both "derived and beneficially owned by" a resident of the other country.

The United States Model and some of the treaties in force contain an anti-holding company provision which denies the reduced rate of tax on dividends, interest, and royalties (1) if the recipient corporation is a resident of the other country which is at least 25 percent owned, directly or indirectly, by individual residents of a country other than the country of residence of the corporation, and (2) if special tax measures apply in the country of residence which

_____

2/ §§871 and 881.

3/ Article 4, U.S. and OECD Models.

reduce, substantially below the generally applicable corporate tax rates, that country's tax imposed on dividends, interest, and royalty income from sources outside that country.[4]

Variations on the Model article are found in other treaties. In the proposed Cyprus treaty, denial of reduction of tax at source is applicable if either (1) the tax burden in the country of residence of the corporation on the income is substantially less than the tax generally applied in that country on corporate profits, or (2) 25 percent or more of the stock of the recipient corporation is owned by individuals not resident in that country.

B. Tax Haven Treaty Network

The United States has over thirty income tax treaties in force. Most are with developed countries which are significant trading partners. However, the United States does have treaties in force with at least 15 jurisdictions generally considered to be tax havens to some degree. In addition, the United States has an income tax treaty with the Netherlands, generally considered a tax haven by reason of its treaty network and its special holding company legislation. For purposes of this chapter, the Netherlands will be considered to be a tax haven.

Most tax haven treaties are in force as a result of the extension of the old 1945 United States-United Kingdom Income Tax Treaty to the former United Kingdom colonies. That treaty provided for its extension to overseas territories of the United Kingdom. The United Kingdom requested that extension, and the Senate gave advice and consent to ratification of the extensions in 1958. The extensions became fully effective in 1959.

Likewise, the treaty with the Netherlands Antilles is in force as a result of the extension of the United States-Netherlands Income Tax Treaty of 1948, as amended. The treaty provided for extension to overseas territories of the Netherlands. This extension was effective to the Netherlands Antilles in 1955. The Netherlands Antilles adjusted its internal law to take advantage of the treaty by providing

---

4/ Article 4, United States and OECD Models. Similar provisions are contained in United States treaties with Finland, Iceland, Korea, Luxembourg, Norway, Trinidad and Tobago, and the United Kingdom. A limited anti-avoidance provision applicable only to direct investment dividends is contained in the Netherlands Antilles treaty.

for special tax regimes for certain local holding companies.
Generally, such companies were taxed at rates ranging between
2.4 and 3.0 percent. This made the Netherlands Antilles an
attractive vehicle to residents of third countries who
wanted to invest in the United States. A 1963 protocol,
effective in 1967, reduced or eliminated some of the benefits
of the Antilles treaty which were formerly available, but
other benefits remained.

The United States also has tax haven treaties which
were directly negotiated with Luxembourg, the Netherlands,
and Switzerland. The Luxembourg treaty was signed in 1962
and came into force in 1964. The Swiss treaty was signed in
1951 and entered into force in that year. The treaty with
the Netherlands was originally entered into in 1948, and has
been amended from time to time, most recently by a 1965
protocol which became fully effective in 1967. The United
States has recently signed an income tax treaty with Cyprus,
a recognized tax haven.—5/

There does not seem to have been much, if any, consideration of either potential abuse in the negotiation of the
existing tax haven treaties, or of whether to permit extension
of treaties to the territories of our treaty partners.
Currently, efforts are under way to deal with the problems
created by the Swiss and Netherlands treaties, as well as
the Netherlands Antilles and British Virgin Islands treaties.
In addition, abuse of treaties was addressed in the Cyprus
treaty, which contains a number of anti-avoidance provisions.

The data in tables 1 and 2, to this chapter, indicate
that there is significant use of treaty countries in general,
and tax haven treaties in particular for investment in the
United States. Much of this use must be by nonresidents of
the treaty country, because the volume of investment does
not bear any relationship to the indigenous populations of
those countries. In 1978, $3.9 billion out of a total of
$4.5 billion, or 89 percent, of gross income paid to nonresidents
of the United States was paid to treaty countries. Of that
amount, $1.8 billion out of the total $4.5 billion of gross
income paid to nonresidents of the United States went to
treaty countries which are also tax havens. In that same
year, $309 million or 31 percent of the interest paid to
nonresidents went to tax haven treaty countries, and $1.4

5/ M. Langer, Practical International Tax Planning, 278, 279
    (2d ed. 1979) B. Spitz, Tax Havens Encyclopaedia, (1975).

billion or 48 percent of the dividends paid went to tax
haven treaty countries. On a country by country basis,
Switzerland is clearly the most widely used. In 1978, over
one-third of the dividends ($985 million) paid to nonresidents
of the United States, and 14 percent ($135 million) of the
interest, went to Switzerland. The Netherlands and the
Netherlands Antilles also received significant amounts of
passive income from the United States. In 1978, residents
of the Netherlands received 12 percent ($331.7 million) of
the dividends, and 3.6 percent ($35.5 million) of the interest
paid to nonresidents. Residents of the Antilles, a country
with a population of only 230,000, received four percent of
the total United States payments to foreigners, comprised of
13 percent of the interest and almost two percent of the
dividends. These three countries together accounted for
approximately 40 percent of all payments made to foreigners;
more than 48 percent of the dividends and 30 percent of the
interest. None of the other tax havens is significant in
gross terms, although total payments to "residents" of the
British Virgin Islands have grown from approximately $1
million in 1975 to $8 million in 1978, with about two-thirds of
the gross payment in 1978 consisting of dividends.

It is interesting to note that the number of British
Virgin Island companies in which United States persons have
an interest grew from 53 in 1970 to 678 in 1979. The number
of BVI companies in which United States persons own more
than 95 percent of the stock increased over the same period
from 40 to 316.

Despite the obvious abuse of the treaties, a large and
growing network of treaties, and an aggressive treaty negotiation program, existing treaties are not reviewed on any
systematic regular basis, and the United States has shown
little inclination to terminate them. Consequently, treaties
which perhaps can be abused or which no longer serve a
legitimate economic purpose are still in effect. Further,
the United States has been slow to take action to deal with
changes in the domestic laws of its treaty partners.

Barbados amended its tax laws some years ago to provide
for favorable tax treatment for international business
companies.[6] The United Kingdom quickly dealt with the
problem by insisting that the United Kingdom-Barbados Income
Tax Treaty be revised to exclude international business

6/ Barbados International Companies Act of 1965 (No. 50 of
    1965, as amended by No. 60 of 1977).

companies.[7/] The United States has never taken steps to
deal with Barbados. Another of our treaty partners, St.
Vincent, has become a center for "captive banks," that have
been used to perpetrate some significant frauds upon United
States banks and that allegedly have been used by aggressive
tax planners in an attempt to avoid subpart F.[8/] The efforts
of the British Virgin Islands to adapt its law to the United
States-British Virgin Islands Income Tax Treaty are set out
in a detailed article in the Tax Law Review.[9/]

C. Third Country Resident Use of United States Tax Treaties
    with Tax Havens

Most of the transactions described below are permitted
by the literal language of the Code and the treaties. These
transactions are permissible because of a conflict between
two inconsistent policy objectives:

(1) Encouraging foreign investment in the United States
and the free flow of international trade and capital;

(2) Not treating foreign investment in the United States
differently from investment by United States persons,
and not providing incentives to foreign investment by
United States companies.

Any attempt to tax some of the transactions must also
attempt to reconcile this conflict. In addition, foreign
policy considerations as well as international trade policy
considerations must be taken into account.

1. Forms of Third Country Use

Each of the following hypothetical transactions is
based on a number of actual cases that either have been
described to us or have been the subject of a ruling or a
court case. Many of these transactions are permitted by the
treaty language. Some reflect policy decisions of the

7/ See Article XXIII U.K.-Barbados Income Tax Convention.
    See M. Edwards-Ker, The International Tax Treaties Service,
    Article 4, page 46.

8/ See Chapter V.C.2.

9/ Vogel, Bernstein, and Nitsche, "Inward Investment in
    Securities and Direct Operations Through the British
    Virgin Islands: How Serious a Rival to the Netherlands
    Antilles Island of Paradise?", 34 Tax L. Rev. 321 (1979).

treaty negotiators. The tax consequences of some transactions would be changed if detected, however, detection is difficult, often depending upon the cooperation of the treaty partner.

a. Foreign borrowing. A borrowing by a United States person is arranged through a treaty jurisdiction to take advantage of the reduced rate of tax (zero in most cases) on interest. There are two patterns of borrowing: (1) a conduit which a United States borrower or foreign lender forms as an entity in a treaty country for the specific purpose of funneling a specific loan through it; (2) a finance company situation in which a United States company forms a subsidiary in a treaty country and the subsidiary then sells its obligations to the public overseas.

An abusive example of the conduit case is described in Aiken Industries, Inc.[10] A United States corporation borrowed money from its Bahamian parent and issued a promissory note to the parent. A Honduran company was then formed and the parent transferred the United States corporation's note to the Honduran company in exchange for its demand notes bearing the same rate of interest as the United States corporation's note. The United States corporation claimed exemption from its withholding obligation under the then effective United States-Honduras income tax convention, which exempted interest received by a Honduran corporation from a United States corporation from United States withholding tax. Although not stated in the case, presumably interest payments by the Honduran company to its Bahamian parent were not taxed by Honduras.

The court held that the exemption did not apply because the treaty language exempted interest from United States sources "received by" a Honduran corporation. Under the facts presented the interest was not received by a Honduran corporation. The Tax Court interpreted the words "received by" to mean something more than merely obtaining physical possession of the funds coupled with an obligation to pass it on to a third party.

b. Finance companies. Without a treaty, a United States company which borrows abroad must withhold the statutory 30 percent tax imposed on the interest paid with respect to the debt. The cost of this tax is born, at least in part, by the United States borrower in the form of an increased interest payment to cover the United States tax on the interest. In an attempt to avoid imposition of this tax, many borrowers, particularly multinational companies, establish a subsidiary in the Netherlands Antilles. The subsidiary then borrows overseas (usually in the eurodollar market), and relends the borrowed funds to the parent. The

10/ 56 T.C. 925 (1971).

position taken by the borrower is that the interest paid by the parent to the subsidiary is deductible for United States tax purposes and is exempt from United States withholding tax. The payment of interest by the subsidiary to the foreign lender is also exempt. The Antilles company would be taxable by the Antilles on the interest it receives, but the interest it pays out to the ultimate lenders is deductible Accordingly, the only tax on the interest payment is the Antilles tax on the difference between the interest received and the interest paid out, usually a small amount. That tax might be a creditable tax for United States purposes. The Antilles will not impose a withholding tax on the interest paid by the Antilles company. (Similar results, sometimes through different arrangements, might be achieved under other treaties, e.g., British Virgin Islands, Luxembourg, and the Netherlands.)11/

c. <u>Holding companies</u>. Another use of tax haven treaties involves establishing a holding company in a tax haven with which the United States has a treaty and then arranging to have the income received from the United States paid out in a deductible form. One use of a holding company is for so-called back-to-back or pass through royalties. A foreign person licensing a patent for use in the United States is subject to a United States tax of 30 percent of any royalty received. This tax can be reduced (in some cases to zero) by forming a Netherlands corporation and licensing the patent to that corporation. The Dutch corporation would then license the patent to the United States licensee. The royalty would be paid to the Dutch company, which will, in turn, pay it to the owner of the patent in a deductible form either as a royalty or as interest.

Article IX of the United States-Netherlands income tax treaty exempts from United States tax "royalties paid to a resident or corporation of one of the contracting states . . . Accordingly, taxpayers take the position that the payment of the patent royalty to the Netherlands company will not incur any United States tax. The Netherlands company can deduct the royalty (or interest) paid to its shareholder and the Netherlands does not impose a tax on a royalty payment. Thus, the royalties will be paid out to the Netherlands

---

11/ <u>See</u>, however, Lederman, "The Offshore Finance Subsidiary: An Analysis of the Current Benefits and Problems," <u>J. of Tax</u>. 86, (1979), discussing various possible approaches which the IRS could consider to deal with finance companies. <u>See</u>, Joint Committee on Taxation Pamphlet, <u>Description of H.S. 7553 Relating to Exemptions from U.S. tax for Interest Paid to Foreign Persons</u> (June 18, 1980).

company free of United States tax, the Netherlands company will incur little or no tax, and the patent owner will pay no tax (assuming, of course, that he is resident in a country which does not tax the income, or he has the royalties paid to a nominee in a second zero tax jurisdiction).

The Netherlands treaty does not have any anti-treaty shopping provision applicable to this structure. Even if the treaty contained a provision similar to Article 16 of the United States Model, the abuse would not be prevented because, in order for Article 16 to apply to deny treaty benefits, the income of the Netherlands company must be subject to a special rate of tax by the Netherlands. Instead of subjecting the corporation to a special rate of tax, the regular corporate rates may be applicable, but because the payment by the Netherlands company is deductible by it, and because it almost equals the royalty received, there would be little or no tax due.

The payment of the royalty from the Netherlands company to the ultimate owner is United States source income subject to the 30 percent United States tax, because the royalty is paid for the use of patents in the U.S.[12] A taxpayer might attempt to avoid this result by having the Netherlands company pay the royalties in another deductible form such as interest.

Direct investment in the United States can also be structured through a holding company. For example, a foreign company can establish a Netherlands holding company which in turn forms a wholly owned subsidiary in the United States. Under the treaty with the Netherlands, dividends paid by the United States subsidiary (assuming it conducts an active business) may be taxed by the United States at the rate of five percent rather than the 30 percent statutory rate.[13] With proper planning, the Netherlands corporate tax may not be imposed. Furthermore, if the Dutch company is a subsidiary of an Antilles company, the Dutch company can then pay dividends to the Antilles free of tax. The same result is available by having a corporation resident in the British Virgin Islands own all of the stock of the United States corporation.

12/ §861(a)(4). See Rev. Rul. 80-362, 1980-52 I.R.B. 14.

13/ Article VII, United States-Netherlands Income Tax Convention.

156

d. Active business. A foreign person can engage in an
active United States business by forming a company in an
appropriate tax haven treaty country and having that company
conduct the business. Some treaties waive the tax imposed
on dividends and interest paid by a foreign corporation
which earns most of its income in the United States.[14]
Article XII of the United States-Netherlands Income Tax
treaty as extended to the Antilles (the United States-Antilles
treaty), for example, provides that dividends and interest
paid by an Antilles corporation are exempt from United
States tax except where the recipient is a United States
person. The Antilles does not impose a tax on dividends
paid by an Antilles company. Accordingly, if an Antilles
company earns most of its income in the United States no tax
would be paid on its dividend distributions (or payments of
interest by it). A resident of a non-treaty country can,
therefore, establish a corporation in the Antilles to
directly engage in an active business in the United States,
and avoid the 30 percent tax on dividends which would otherwise
be imposed. The same result can be achieved under the
Netherlands treaty by structuring the investment so that the
stock of the Netherlands company is held by an Antilles
company.[15]

e. Real estate investment. Another form of tax haven
treaty investment in the United States is the use of a
company formed in the treaty country to invest in United
States real estate. The tax advantage of using a tax haven
for real estate investment has been limited by recently
enacted legislation. This legislation will override existing
treaties, but not until 1985. A non-resident alien individual
or foreign person not engaged in trade or business in the
United States is taxable on the gross amount of rents from
real property at the 30 percent or lower treaty rate.
Before the new legislation is effective for treaty countries,
gain from the sale of the property is not taxed. The
investor could elect to tax the income on a "net basis"
rather than a gross basis. The election applied to gain
from the sale of the property, as well as to rental income
from it. The election could not be revoked except with
consent of the IRS. Under the United States-Antilles treaty,
however, an individual or corporation resident in the
Antilles could make an annual election to have the

14/ See §861(a)(1)(D) and §861(a)(2)(B) providing
     that dividends and interest paid by corporations are
     United States source income.

15/ The second withholding tax is also waived in United
     States treaties with Finland, Iceland, Korea, Luxembourg,
     Norway, Trinidad and Tobago, and the United Kingdom.

157

income from United States real estate taxed on a net basis.
Accordingly, a foreign investor who purchased real estate
through an Antilles company would usually make the net
election in the years he holds the property in order to be
able to use the deductions generated by it. Then, in the
year he wishes to sell, he could simply not elect to be
taxed on a net basis and avoid United States capital gain
taxes on any gain realized on the sale. Furthermore, amounts
could be paid on the property free of United States tax to
the Antilles company or by the Antilles company to other
foreign persons. The use of an Antilles company by non-
residents of the Antilles to take advantage of this provision
had become standard practice.

    f. Personal service companies--artists and athletes. The
provider of an entertainment service enters into an employment contract with a company formed in a tax haven. The
contract generally provides that the artist will work exclusively
for that company which will have the sole right to contract
his services. In addition, the company has the right to the
proceeds from the sale of artistic works, such as phonograph records. The entertainer receives a fixed salary from
the company. The company then enters into a contract with a
promoter who arranges a United States tour for the entertainer.
The entertainer takes the position that the income from the
tour is income of the company. The company does not have a
fixed place of business in the United States and therefore
there is no United States tax. The entertainer's salary may
not be taxed because of the operation of a treaty. Further,
the proceeds from the sale of the phonograph records will be
paid to the tax haven company, and the zero treaty rate of
tax on royalties will be claimed. In some cases, the IRS may
argue that the entertainer has a permanent establishment in
the United States, that the profits from the sale of the
record are effectively connected with it, and that they are
therefore subject to United States tax.

    Under Article 17 of the new United States-United Kingdom
treaty and under the United States Model, the income from
the performance of the services would be subject to United
States tax. However, in most cases the expenses related to
a tour are high and thus taxable income is low. The real
purpose of the tours is often to promote records, and the
income from the sales of records can be high. The payments,
however, may be exempt from tax as royalties. They will not
be taxed in the tax haven.

2. Analysis of Third Country Use

    The problem created by treaties are third country use,
or treaty shopping, and administration of the treaties.

Successful treaty shopping generally consists of three elements: (1) a reduction of source country taxation; (2) a low or zero effective rate of tax in the payee treaty country; and (3) a low or zero rate of tax on payments from the payee treaty country to the taxpayer. Many of these elements exist with respect to non-tax haven treaties as well as tax haven treaties. For example, some non-tax haven countries with which we have treaties do not impose a withholding tax on payments of interest or dividends, and accordingly can be used as the Netherlands or the Antilles is used.

The first element is provided by the treaty reduction of United States tax on United States source fixed or determinable income, by the limitation on business income subject to tax, and by certain exemptions from tax for capital gains and transportation income.

The second element is provided by a tax haven which may impose a low rate of tax on income of "residents", or which may provide a special tax regime for holding companies. It is also provided by a back-to-back pattern in which the amounts received by the company in the treaty country are paid out in a deductible form.

The third element is provided by tax havens, by some non-tax havens which do not tax distributions, and by treaties between the payee country and third countries. It is also provided by United States treaties which eliminate the second withholding tax imposed by the United States.

The above cases, as well as IRS data, indicate significant third country use of United States treaties. The data indicate that our treaties are a substantial funnel for foreign investment in the United States, particularly through tax haven countries with whom we have treaties.

The tax burden on a third country treaty user can be less than that on a non-user, a United States investor or a resident of the treaty country. This is because in most cases the United States investor will pay a United States tax on his return on investment, and the true resident of a treaty country will pay tax to his home country, while in the case of a third country user who is avoiding his home country tax or whose home country does not impose a tax, no tax will be paid.

Accordingly, our tax haven treaties probably do place United States businesses in a competitive position to attract foreign capital. As the above transactions demonstrate, however, this incentive is often accomplished at the expense of simplicity and overall equity, by economic structures and business transactions which cannot be justified on business grounds. In addition, a substantial part of the investment through tax haven treaties may not be incremental at all. It may merely be shifted to the most favorable structure from a tax planning point of view.

In relying on treaties with tax havens to encourage foreign investment in the United States we also encourage the use of transactions which have little or no economic substance. This, in turn, has a negative effect on the taxpayer's respect for the system. For example, a Netherlands holding company that licenses patents to United States persons, or a Barbados international business corporation which invests in U.S. securities, have little business purpose other than utilization of the treaties (and perhaps avoiding local exchange controls). While the United States arguably benefits in some way by the investment, it does so at the cost of allowing taxpayers to play fast and loose with the system, with adverse consequences for overall tax administration.

The first inquiry therefore is whether, in fact, we wish to curtail some or all of the above described transactions. Such a decision requires basic policy analysis and decisions which are beyond the scope of this report. However, it should be pointed out that much of what we say we are doing through treaty policy, that is, encouraging inward invest- ment, could be done unilaterally through the Code. What would be lost would be the reciprocal benefits which we can negotiate; what would be gained would be a clearer, more rational tax system. Also, the existence of treaty shopping potential discounts the value of high withholding taxes as a bargaining chip in treaty negotiations. As long as the treaty shopping potential exists, there is less pressure on other treaty countries whose residents invest in the United States through treaty countries to negotiate with the United States.

D. Use of Treaty Network by Earners of Illegal Income or for Evasion of United States Tax

It is not possible to determine the extent of use of the United States treaty network by earners of illegal income, or by persons who have moved money from the United States for tax evasion purposes. There is, however, evidence of such use.

Treaty oriented tax evasion includes: (a) recycling funds earned (legally or illegally) in the U.S. or abroad back into the United States through a treaty country after it has first been laundered in a non-treaty tax haven jurisdiction; (b) fraudulent use by United States persons to remove income from the United States at reduced rates of tax by masquerading as foreign taxpayers; and (c) fraudulent use by foreigners to obtain benefits of treaty rates.

1. Methods of Use

A United States person who has earned illegal income from, for example, narcotics trafficking, might carry that income in cash to the Cayman Islands. In the Caymans, the money would be placed in a trust account with a small private bank. Those funds could then be used to capitalize an Antilles bearer share company. The Antilles company could in turn invest in United States real estate, taking advantage of the treaty benefits. Because of the exchange of information provision in the Antilles treaty, it is unlikely that the money would be carried directly to the Antilles. However, the Antilles government cannot determine who the true owner of an Antilles bearer share company is, nor could it determine the true owner of any other Antilles company if its shares are held by a nominee located in a second tax haven jurisdiction.

Fraudulent use of treaties by United States persons to remove passive income from the United States could be accomplished by forming a corporation in a non-treaty country, having that corporation in turn establish a second corporation in a treaty country, and then running passive income (such as royalties) from the United States to the treaty country and through it to the second country. Under the treaty, the payment would be taxed at a reduced rate by the United States. Because the second company may be in a haven or a commercial secrecy jurisdiction, the true owners remain anonymous.

This latter case has allegedly arisen under the Antilles treaty. Under that treaty, an Antilles corporation owned by a Dutch corporation is entitled to receive royalties free of United States tax. The United States payee can pay the royalties, without withholding, _if_ certification of Dutch ownership by the Antilles government is provided by the Antilles company. (Certification is indicated on a "VS-4" certificate.) The Antilles government does little checking to see who owns the Netherlands company. They also do not check, in all cases, to see whether the Antilles company is filing a tax return. Because the VS-4 is good for three years, three years can go by before anybody realizes that the Antilles company is not paying tax. By that time, whatever fraud was planned may have been completed.[16]

16/ Where the Antilles entity is not owned by a Dutch resident, certification of entitlement to treaty benefits is given by a VS-3 which is good for only one year. Similar problems have apparently arisen for payments covered by a VS-3.

Another fraudulent use of treaties by foreigners has allegedly arisen under the Antilles treaty. That treaty provides for a zero rate of tax on interest payments from the United States to an Antilles resident who does not take advantage of the special low rate of tax accorded Antilles investment companies. A third country resident wishing to lend funds into the United States can establish an Antilles company, capitalize it, and have the company lend the money into the United States. The interest payments from the United States to the Antilles company are free of United States tax. If, however, the interest is paid to the controlling shareholders of the Antilles company, the Antilles company may not be permitted to deduct that interest. Accordingly, the regular corporate rate (30 percent) will be applied to the interest received.

To avoid this tax, and the necessity of establishing an Antilles company, a foreigner can deposit, in an Antilles bank, an amount equal to the amount of the loan he wishes to make. The Antilles bank then lends the proceeds to the United States person. The Antilles bank will receive interest from the United States person, subject to the zero rate of tax under the treaty. The interest, and eventually the principal, are then remitted to the nonresident, with the bank retaining a small fee.

Under this scheme, the bank would insist upon security for the loan, which would be documents signed by the foreign person. This scheme is fraudulent because, if the IRS agent knew all of the facts (the existence of some kind of security agreement between the nonresident and the bank), the loan would clearly be considered a direct loan by the foreign person to the United States person, which does not qualify under the treaty because the foreign person is not a resident of the Antilles.

At times, back-to-back arrangements might also be considered fraudulent. For example, the use of a Dutch holding company to sublicense patents into the United States would be tax fraud if the recipient of royalties paid by the Dutch company did not pay the United States tax on those royalties known to be subject to United States tax.

2. Analysis of Illegal Use

As in any other case of tax fraud, the problems in dealing with fraudulent use of treaties are of detection, investigative techniques, and the ability to gather evidence which can be used in a criminal prosecution. The schemes described above depend, to a large extent, on the anonymity afforded by a tax haven country. For example, the use of an Antilles bearer share company makes it difficult to identify the true owners of the company. Likewise, bank secrecy policies make it difficult to identify the relationship of a bank depositor and a bank loan. Layering of entities in treaty and non-treaty countries makes detection even more difficult. As in many other areas, complexity plus information gathering difficulties makes it hard to identify the improper or fraudulent transactions.

E. Administration of Tax Treaty Network

Treaty issues involving foreign investment in the United States and treaty issues involving foreign persons doing business in the United States are generally under the jurisdiction of the IRS Office of International Operations (OIO). Treaty issues involving United States investment overseas are under the jurisdiction of the Examination Division, and are most often addressed by agents in its International Examination Program.

Procedural treaty matters such as exchanges of information and competent authority cases are generally handled by OIO. Certain exchanges of information pursuant to the simultaneous examination program, and spontaneous exchanges of information, are handled by the Examination Division. Tax treaties are negotiated by the Office of the Assistant Secretary of the Treasury for Tax Policy, specifically the Office of International Tax Affairs. That Office also gives policy guidance in the interpretation of the treaties.

Tax haven treaty issues most often involve the question of whether a payment of passive income to a tax haven qualifies for an exemption or reduced rate of tax under a treaty. One of the most important administrative tools available to the IRS is the withholding of tax on payments to foreigners.[17] Present regulations require withholding of the statutory 30 percent tax on United States source gross income when the income is paid to a foreign person.[18] An "address" system is used for dividend income under which withholding is at the reduced treaty rate, if the address of the dividend recipient is in a treaty country. With respect to other income, a self-certification system is in effect under which

---

17/ §§1441 and 1442.

18/ Treas. Reg. §1.1441-1.

the recipient of the income can claim a treaty reduction or
exemption by filing a Form 1001 with the withholding agent.
Once claimed, an exemption is valid for three years. Under
this system, a foreign trustee or an officer of a corporation
resident in a treaty country can file the Form 1001 and
achieve the treaty reduction. The withholding agent is
under no obligation to look behind the claim and the IRS is
not notified of the claim before payments are made. Accordingly,
there is no practical opportunity for the IRS to determine
qualification for exemption before a payment is made.

For example, a Dutch company licenses a patent to a
United States manufacturer. The Dutch company supplies the
manufacturer with a Form 1001 claiming the benefits of the
United States-Netherlands income tax convention, which
provides that industrial royalties paid to a Dutch resident
are exempt from the 30 percent United States tax. The IRS
may, however, wish to independently determine whether the
Dutch company is entitled to the exemption. For example,
the IRS may wish to determine whether the Dutch company is,
in reality, an agent of a resident of a third country, or if
the Dutch company itself is paying out the royalties to a
resident of a non-treaty country, in which case the royalties
are United States source income and subject to tax by the
United States. To make these determinations, the IRS would
want the records of the Dutch company to determine whether
it is the effective owner of the patent. IRS may wish to
know the owners of the company, and it may wish to know
whether the Dutch company is making payments (such as interest)
in lieu of royalty payments. Much of this information could
be obtained under the exchange of information provision of
the treaty, but this takes time. In addition, the information
sought might be protected by the secrecy laws of the treaty
partners. If some of the information is not available, then
it may be necessary to audit the books of the company or
talk to its personnel. All of this is time consuming, and
some tax havens might not permit it. Furthermore, by the
time the IRS can gather the necessary facts, all of the
income may have been paid out; the tax may have become un-
collectable.

Effective administration of tax treaties and the anti-
abuse provisions contained in them are limited for at least
three reasons. First, because effective administration
depends upon the full and willing cooperation of the treaty
partner's tax administration. This involves a commitment of
their resources and the availability of the necessary
expertise.

The anti-abuse provisions of the treaty operate when a nonresident of a treaty country seeks to take improper advantage of the treaty, usually through a holding company or a trust or nominee account in the treaty country. Information as to ownership of an entity and the residence of the owner is in the hands of persons within the jurisdiction of the treaty partner. Therefore, any application of the anti-abuse rules requires an inquiry by the tax administrators of the treaty partner into the residence of the owners of the entity. The IRS can do very little to adequately administer these provisions without the full cooperation of the treaty partner.

For example, the holding company anti-abuse rules in the proposed Cyprus treaty apply to deny certain benefits if a Cyprus company is owned "directly or indirectly" by non-residents of Cyprus. The only way the IRS can tell whether a Cyprus company is owned by non-residents is by being able to look behind any required documentation. If the stock is owned by a Cypriot individual, the only way to determine if he is the true owner, rather than a nominee, is to investigate him, which may involve interviewing him. The IRS does not have the resources to conduct this kind of examination on a wide scale, nor can we expect our treaty partners to permit it.

It is not clear that most of our present or prospective tax haven treaty partners have the resources or expertise to make the inquiries on a regular basis. Many promote themselves as tax havens, and it may not be in the best interest of the tax haven to vigorously administer the anti-abuse provisions.

Second, proper administration of the treaties depends, to a great extent, on a meaningful exchange of information, which in turn depends upon the scope of the information which can be provided under the exchange of information article. The articles in the existing tax haven treaties do not override local commercial secrecy laws or customs. They also do not obligate our tax haven treaty partner to obtain any more for the United States then they obtain for themselves. Accordingly, the IRS cannot always expect to get the information needed to determine whether third country residents are improperly using the treaties. In the existing Model treaty, the exchange of information article does follow the OECD article, and we can anticipate negotiation problems if we deviate from it. Nevertheless, the article does contain gaps when dealing with a jurisdiction which has commercial secrecy.

Third, administration at a level which can prevent abuse of the treaty would require a much greater committment of resources than are presently available. The IRS has limited resources which it can devote to administering tax treaties. In 1979 only about 75 Form 1042's (the form which must be filed by a United States person making a payment to a foreign person) were audited. Despite a growing treaty network, the Congress has not made available additional resources necessary to administer the treaties. The IRS simply is not in a position to audit tax haven holding or insurance companies claiming treaty benefits to determine if they are eligible for those benefits.

Furthermore, there are practical limitations. Effective administration of anti-abuse provisions most likely involves auditing tax haven entitites. This infringes on the sovereignty of the tax haven. It is unlikely that a tax haven would permit any large scale activity of this kind.

IRS rulings policy has not always kept up with developments in the use of tax haven treaties. IRS rulings show an inconsistent policy toward treaty shopping, which reflects equally inconsistent Treasury and Congressional policies.

The IRS has attempted to deal with some of the most obvious abuse cases while at the same time permiting some treaty shopping. For example, Revenue Ruling 79-65[19] held that dividends paid by a United States subsidiary to its Netherlands Antilles parent company were not eligible for the five percent withholding rate provided by the United States-Antilles treaty, because the United States subsidiary had not provided the information, when requested by the IRS, to establish that the relationship between it and its Antilles parent was not "arranged or maintained" primarily to secure the five percent rate. The sole shareholder of the Antilles company was an individual who was not a United States person, or a citizen or resident of the Netherlands, the Antilles, or any other country having a treaty with the United States.

While the ruling denies the five percent rate, it does so under the "arranged or maintained" language in the treaty (which is not in the United States Model and is found only in a few of our older treaties), and indicates that the dividend may qualify for the 15 percent rate allowed under the treaty if the recipient is a resident of or a corporation of the Antilles. Even the 15 percent rate places a premium on treaty shopping. See also Revenue Ruling 75-23[20] and

---

19/   1979-1 C.B. 458.

20/   1975-1 C.B. 290.

Revenue Ruling 75-118[21]/ which indicate approval of the use
of the Antilles and the Netherlands, respectively, by persons
who are not resident in either country.

The United Kingdom treaty extensions (the BVI, etc.)
provide for a 15 percent rate of United States tax on dividends
derived from a United States corporation by a resident of a
former United Kingdom territory who is subject to tax by
that former territory on the dividend. The rate is five percent
if the corporate parent controls 95 percent of the voting
power of the payor, and if the passive income limitation is
met. The reduction to five percent does not apply "if the
relationship of the two corporations has been arranged or is
maintained primarily with the intention of securing such a
reduced rate."[22]/ The dividend article contains a provision
permitting either party to terminate the article under
notice to the other party.

The "arranged or maintained" language in the context of
the United Kingdom extensions has not been interpreted.
There are no published IRS positions, and the issues do not
seem to have been raised on audit.

Another problem in tax treaty administration is the
lack of adequate coordination between Treasury's Office of
International Tax Counsel (ITC) and IRS, and lack of coordination with the Tax Division of the Department of Justice
(Tax Division) on exchange of information problems. Today,
coordination appears to be on an ad hoc basis. Only if ITC
has a problem, do they coordinate. As a result, it is
possible that inadequate attention is given to tax administration
concerns in formulating treaty policy.

F. Options for Tax Haven Treaties

Tax haven treaties present special problems because the
combination of low rates of tax imposed by the other country
and the reduction in United States tax rates by reason of
the treaty attracts third country residents to use the
treaty to invest in the United States. Accordingly, when
attempting to deal with tax haven treaty problems, we are
attempting to limit treaty shopping. This could be done by
administrative, legislative, or treaty policy changes. The
best approach, of course, is not to have treaties with tax
havens. Other factors, however, often make that goal unattainable

21/ 1975-1 C.B. 390.

22/ Article VI United States-United Kingdom Income Tax
     Convention of July 25, 1946, as extended to the United
     Kingdom territories.

1. Administrative Options

     Many of the investment patterns described above are
permitted by the literal language of the treaties. There
are, however, some which are not, and administrative actions
might be taken which might help in dealing with some of the
problems.

     Consideration should be given to the following options
for curtailing tax haven treaty abuse.

     a. Refund system of withholding. The present system
of withholding could be changed to a refund system. Many of
the schemes involve the use of a treaty to obtain a reduced
rate of tax at source. In order to qualify, all that the
foreign taxpayer need do is submit a form or letter to the
withholding agent once every three years.

     Under a full refund system, withholding would be at
the statutory rate, and the reduced rates accorded by the
treaties would be available only upon application for a
refund by the affected foreign investor. The application
would include a certification from the treaty partner that
the investor is entitled to the benefits of the treaty. The
United States certifies for Belgium, France, Luxembourg, and
the United Kingdom. A refund system would at least force
the foreign investor to submit a claim with the government,
which could in itself curtail some of the more abusive use.
It would also give the IRS a better opportunity to identify
cases for audit.

     A refund system, however, can be expensive to administer
Moreover, those who can afford competent tax advice can
often get around it. It can be argued that what is created
is really just a loan to the United States Government without
any meaningful reduction in abuse.

     As an alternative, a "certification system" could be
adopted under which withholding would be at the statutory
rate, unless the investor submitted a certification from the
treaty partner that he was entitled to the reduced treaty
rate. A combination of the two is also possible. Under
this system, withholding would be at the statutory rate for
the first year in which a payment is made. The investor
would then file for a refund and include a certification of
eligibility from the treaty partner. Thereafter (or for a
fixed period of years), withholding would be at the reduced
treaty rate.

b. <u>Increase audit coverage of treaty issues</u>. Consideration should be given to expanding the audit coverage of foreign investors claiming treaty benefits. One possibility is to use the tables which list the tax haven payees who receive income (the 1042 tables) in an attempt to identify quality cases.

Clearer directions could be given to examining agents in the finance company area, and better training in the treaty area could be provided. There is an ambivalence in the law and in IRS rulings policy which in the past has been reflected in agents generally not auditing many finance company cases. Some agents appear to avoid finance subsidiary issues on the theory that they had subpart F income in any event. This analysis shows a need for better understanding of the treaty issues involved. The IRS should develop a clear policy toward finance subsidiaries, and make that policy known to the examining agents.

c. <u>Periodic review of treaties</u>. Treasury should consider subjecting treaties to a regular periodic review. Jurisdictions that have treaties in effect that are abused, or are not in the best interest of the United States, would be notified of termination. Priority renegotiation would then be instituted. In this way, the pressure to renegotiate would be placed on the treaty partner. Congress might pass legislation requiring that results of this review be made available to the public and subject to Congressional scrutiny.

In order to facilitate this option, a change could be made in the termination clauses of the treaties. Under most of the existing treaties, notice of termination must be given at least 6 months before the termination date. The treaty then terminates as of the first day of January next following the expiration of the 6 month period. Accordingly, the Treasury would have at most one year to negotiate a treaty and have it approved by the Senate. This is not enough time. This problem could be solved by making it clear that the notice of termination can be effective the first of a designated January which is at least 6 months in the future. Thus, more than one year could be allowed for renegotiation, but with a fixed termination date.

Adoption of this option would require that additional resources be made available to the Treasury.

d. <u>Exchange of information article overriding bank secrecy</u>. The exchange of information article in U.S. tax treaties with tax havens could be strengthened to override local bank and commercial secrecy. This issue and a possible approach is discussed in Chapter IX.

e. <u>Improve the quality of routine information received.</u>
Attempts should be made to improve the quality of the
information which we get from our tax haven treaty partners.
In many cases, the information which we receive from our
treaty partners is not in usable form. Often, details
necessary to identify a United States taxpayer receiving
income are not available. This makes it difficult to identify
United States persons who may be receiving income from a tax
haven and not reporting it. Furthermore, the IRS does not
get information which is useful in dealing with treaty
shopping. Moreover, the exchange of information articles in
the treaties do not override bank secrecy, which means that
important information is often not available.

f. <u>Rulings</u>. IRS rulings policy has at times appeared
ambivalent with respect to the use of tax haven treaties by
treaty shoppers. At times taxpayers get the impression that
the IRS condones such use. To dispel this impression, the
IRS could attempt to challenge the back-to-back royalty
situation, by taking the position that amounts paid by a
corporation in a treaty country are United States source
income and are not exempted by the language of the treaty.
For example, as described above, patents may be licenses
into the United States through a company established in the
Netherlands. The United States-Netherlands treaty provides
that royalties paid to a corporation of one of the contracting
countries are exempt from tax by the other contracting
country. Accordingly, royalties paid by the United States licensee
to the Netherlands company are exempt. The IRS could argue,
however, that royalties paid by the Netherlands company to a
third country national are royalties for the use of a patent
in the United States and accordingly are United States source
income[23/], and that the Netherlands company is a withholding
agent required to withhold the United States tax of 30
percent of the gross amount paid. While it would be difficult
for the IRS to enforce the withholding obligation of the
Dutch company, the payments to the Dutch company could be
attached.

The IRS could also publish a ruling stating that any
United States investment through a former United Kingdom territory
will be closely scrutinized, with a view toward determining
whether the "arranged or maintained" language is applicable
to deny the five percent rate. A procedure could be adopted
under which the reduced rate will not be granted, unless a
prior ruling is obtained that the arrangement between a United
States corporation and a corporation resident in the treaty
partner has not been and will not be aranged primarily with
the intention of securing the reduced rate.

23/ See §861(a)(4).

g. Coordination with ITC. ITC should consider coordinating with IRS and the Tax Division on a more regular basis when formulating treaty policy. This would enable ITC to be better aware of the administrative and law enforcement problems faced by the administrators who will have to deal with the treaties. It might also give tax administration considerations more weight in formulating treaty policy. Efforts to improve coordination within the IRS would make coordination with ITC easier.24/

2. Changes in Treaty Policy

The options set forth below are intended to apply to treaties with tax havens, and are intended to help limit the use of tax haven treaties by third country residents. It is this use of treaties by third country residents which creates whatever problems are caused by treaties.

a. Treaty network. The most direct attack on tax haven treaty problems would be not to have treaties with tax havens. Solely from a tax administration perspective, the United States should not have standard treaties with tax havens.

The United States should consider terminating its existing tax haven treaties, particularly those with the Netherlands Antilles and the former United Kingdom territories. The United Kingdom extensions are an affront to sound tax administration, existing only to be abused. The Antilles treaty has also been regularly abused. The IRS has not had much success in enforcing the anti-abuse rules.

It is recognized that for non-tax considerations, it may be necessary to enter into tax treaties with tax havens. Such treaties should be as limited as possible, and should focus on the specific policy objectives for negotiating the treaty. They should contain a strong exchange of information provision which overrides secrecy laws and practices.25/

In order to prevent some of the smaller Western Hemisphere jurisdictions (and perhaps jurisdictions in other areas) from becoming aggressive tax havens, we might consider entering into limited income tax treaties with them. These treaties could provide for competent autority procedures to deal with transfer pricing and allocation problems. They

24/ See discussion in Chapter X, supra.

25/ See Chapter IX for suggested model exchange of information article.

could contain a non-discrimination provision. They should
also contain a strong exchange of information provision,
similar to that discussed in Chapter IX. They might also
obligate the United States to provide technical assistance
for tax administration. Further, the termination Article should
contain a provision providing that either party can terminate
the treaty, if either determines that the other party is not
able to administer the anti-abuse provisions of the treaty
or is not meeting its obligations under the treaty.

      b. <u>Source country taxation</u>. Present treaty policy,
which is consistent with the OECD approach, is to give
primacy to tax to the country of residence of the earner of
income, except in the case of business income and income
from real property. Even in the case of business income,
the treaty approach is more restrictive of the source country's
jurisdiction than is the Internal Revenue Code. This policy
should be reconsidered with respect to tax havens or jurisdictions which have the potential to become tax havens.

      One solution to the tax haven treaty shopping problem,
which is reflected generally in the approach of the developing
countries[26], would be to adopt a policy of giving the
source country the primary right to tax income. The reductions
in tax on the gross amount of passive income (dividends,
interest and royalties) would be limited, some significant
United States tax on the investments would be preserved, and
the incentive to shop for the best possible return would be
limited. Further, the categories of income considered to be
business profits could be restricted, and more categories
could be subjected to gross tax.

      c. <u>Anti-holding company or anti-conduit approaches</u>.
Article 16 of the United States Model and similar provisions
in a number of existing treaties attempt to limit the use
of the treaties by third country residents through an investment
or holding company. There are also other anti-abuse provisions
contained in the treaties. These provisions do not appear
to be effective in preventing treaty abuse.

      One or more of the following approaches could be adopted
to deal with tax haven treaty shopping, the goal being to
eliminate third country use of these treaties. In general,
treaties with countries that are or that have particular
potential to become tax havens should contain as many useful
anti-avoidance provisions as possible.

26/   <u>Manual for the Negotiation of Bilateral Tax Treaties
Between Developed and Developing Countries</u>, United
Nations Publication ST/ESA/94 (1979), discussion of
interest guidelines at 66-73.

(i) Article 16 of the Model could be expanded to con-
form to the proposed Cyprus treaty[27]/, to deny reduced rates
of tax in the case of payments to a company (1) that is
owned 25 percent or more by non-residents of the treaty
partner, or (2) whose income is subject to tax in the other
state at a rate substantially less than the normally applicable
corporate rate. In dealing with potential tax havens, this
approach would be an improvement over the existing provision.
It does, however, contain the same administrative difficulties.

(ii) Article 16 could be expanded to deny treaty benefits
to a company if more than a stated percentage of its gross
income is passive income. A payment to a holding company
would not be eligible for reduced withholding taxes, regardless of the ownership or tax burden borne by that company in
the home country. In the alternative, the passive income
test could be combined with the ownership test in (i) above,
or with the ownership and reduced rates of tax test. The
reduced rates of tax would be denied to a company which
receives a substantial amount of passive income, and which
is subject to a reduced rate of tax in the home country,
even though it is owned exclusively by residents of the
treaty country.

(iii) The holding company test could be abandoned in
favor of a more direct approach. For example, the reduced
rate of tax on interest could be denied with respect to a
debt obligation that is created or assigned mainly for the
purpose of taking advantage of the reduced rate of tax, and
not for bona fide commercial reasons. A similar provision
for royalties could be included, under which the reduced
rate of tax would not be available if the right or property
giving rise to the royalty was created or assigned mainly
for the purpose of taking advantage of the reduced rate of
tax, and not for bona fide commercial reasons.[28]/

d. Expansion of anti-abuse provisions to active business.
The Article 16 approach could be expanded to cover all
treaty rules. Article 16, and most anti-treaty shopping
provisions, apply to dividends, interest and royalties.
They do not apply to a corporation established by a third

27/ Article 26.

28/ See Articles 12 and 13 of the Netherlands-United Kingdom
Income Tax Treaty, as amended by protocol entering
into force on October 19, 1977.

country resident to conduct an active business in the United States. Accordingly, a third country resident wishing to conduct an active business in the United States can form a resident corporation in a treaty country, and take advantage of the benefits accorded by the permanent establishment rules and any other benefits given by the convention. This use of treaties could be curtailed by extending the anti-holding company rules to all activity carried on by a corporation owned by third-country residents.

e. <u>Second withholding tax</u>. The second withholding tax should not be waived when the treaty partner does not impose a tax on payments out. The waiver of the United States tax imposed upon payment of dividends and interest by a foreign corporation is an important element in successful treaty shopping. This waiver permits the income to be paid from the treaty country to the owner of the income free of tax. By insisting on retaining the second withholding tax, this element is removed. See 3.c. below for a legislative suggestion dealing with replacing the second withholding tax with a branch profits tax.

f. <u>The insurance premium exemption</u>. The United States imposes an excise tax on insurance or reinsurance premiums paid to foreign insurers.[29] The rate is four percent of the premium, or one percent in the case of reinsurance. The United States-United Kingdom treaty gives up the tax on payments of insurance or reinsurance premiums to a United Kingdom enterprise.[30]

The exemption has allegedly been abused, and some of the premiums may be flowing through insurance companies resident in a treaty partner (particularly in the United Kingdom) to insurance companies or reinsurers located in tax havens such as Bermuda. In some cases, the tax haven company may be owned by the United States company, but this relationship is hidden. Further, if the foreign company is not paying a significant rate of tax in its real country of residence, it has a competitive advantage over United States insurers. While, in theory, a tax is due when the treaty country insurer lays off the risk to a foreign company, in fact, any procedures to collect such a tax would be unenforceable.

29/ §4371.

30/ Article 7 (6A).

(i) The broad exemption from the excise tax imposed on insurance or reinsurance premiums paid to foreign insurance companies could be eliminated.

(ii) The IRS could adopt, generally, the position taken in the French protocol, under which the exemption is applicable only "to the extent that the foreign insurer does not reinsure such risks with a person not entitled to exemption from such tax under this or another convention."[31] This approach has the administrative problems of any anti-treaty abuse provision: dependence upon our treaty partner to enforce a provision it may be unable to enforce or which it may have no interest in enforcing. An additional administrative problem is that, generally, pools of risk, not single risks, are reinsured. This makes any anti-abuse provision difficult to administer, even with a fully cooperative treaty partner. The taxpayer could be put to his burden of proof that the premiums were not passed through, if problems are suspected.

g. Personal service companies--artists and athletes. The United States Model contains an article which deals with the so-called lend-a-star problem, by permitting the country in which services are performed by an artist or an athlete to tax the income from performance of the services where the income in respect of the service accrued to another.[32] The model provision is based on Article 17 of the United Kingdom treaty.

As explained above, the provision does not deal clearly with amounts paid for works created by the artist. The real problem with taxing the income from record sales, for example, is defining what that income is, i.e., income from the performance of services or royalties. If the income is service income then arguably it should be taxed where the services are performed, which is where the record is recorded.[33] If the compensation is royalty income the result may be different. This conflict could be handled in the treaties by further defining what the income is and how it will be taxed. In the alternative, it could be dealt with by amending the Code to establish clear source rules.

---

[31] Art. 1(a) United States-France Income Tax Convention.

[32] United States Model, Art. 17.

[33] See Ingram v. Bowers, 47 F. 2d 925 (S.D.N.Y. 1931); aff'd, 57 F. 2d 65 (2d Cir. 1932).

An alternative is to treat the compensation from the
use of any copyright of literary or artistic work as business
profits, and attributable to a permanent establishment or
fixed place of business in the country where entertainment
activities are performed, if the royalties are earned
within a fixed period of time after the artist has performed
in the United States. Under this system, the amounts from
the sale of the records would be taxed on a net basis when
paid to the tax haven company. Another alternative is to
clearly define the income as royalties, and not have a zero
rate of tax on royalties, at least in tax haven treaties.

3. Legislative Approaches

The best approach to dealing with treaty problems is to
handle them through the negotiation process. Some of the
problems can, in part, be dealt with through administrative
changes. There are, however, some legislative options which
should be considered for dealing with tax haven oriented
treaty problems. As with any other treaty legislation
directed at tax havens, a decision would have to be made
whether any legislative approaches would apply generally, or
would apply solely to tax haven transactions.

a. Reduction of the rate of tax on fixed or determinable
income. One possible approach is to reduce the 30 percent
tax which the United States currently imposes on fixed or
determinable income paid to foreigners. Many claim that our
current rates are high. For example, when imposed on interest
paid to a bank, they can exceed the net income of that bank.
Treaties are the mechanism by which we bring our rates down
to a more reasonable level. In lieu of the treaty approach,
we could rationalize our rates of tax legislatively. If the
rates are set at a rate which is higher than current treaty
rates, the legislation could override the treaties, or, in
the alternative, the legislation could provide a maximum
rate with the treaties continuing to take precedence.
Legislation to eliminate the tax on portfolio interest has
been proposed, but to date the Congress has failed to act on
that proposal.

As an anti-haven measure, the present 30 percent
statutory rate could be continued for payments to designated
tax havens, or an even higher rate could be imposed.

b. <u>Anti-treaty abuse rule</u>. Another possibility is to place an anti-treaty abuse provision in the Code. The Code could be amended to deny treaty benefits to a foreign person who is not a contemplated beneficiary of treaty benefits, or if a substantial part of the treaty relief benefits persons not entitled to the benefits of a convention. This provision would give the IRS the authority to deny treaty benefits in abusive cases which might come within the literal language of the treaties, but which were not anticipated by the treaty negotiators. The provisions could be drafted by simply referring to a person who is not a contemplated beneficiary, leaving the IRS with broad authority to develop guidelines. An objective standard could be included to deny treaty benefits in the case of payments to a foreign entity if (1) more than a fixed percentage of income for which the treaty benefit is claimed is paid to a person not entitled to the benefits of the treaty, (2) the income is not reported as taxable income to the treaty partner, or (3) the debt to equity ratio of the recipient company exceeds a designated level.

In the alternative, or in addition, an anti-holding company provision similar to that contained in the United States Model or the more extensive provision contained in the proposed Cyprus treaty could be added to the Code. Such a provision might be applicable only with respect to designated tax havens.

c. <u>Branch profits tax</u>. The second withholding tax problem may also be handled through legislation. As discussed above, some countries, particularly tax havens, do not impose a tax on payments from their domestic corporations to non-residents of the tax haven. The United States, however, imposes a tax on dividends and interest of foreign corporations which earn a certain percentage of their income in the United States. Some treaties waive this second withholding tax, and even when not waived it can be difficult to collect because the withholding agent is the foreign corporation. An alternative, used by numerous countries, is to impose a branch profits tax on the income of a United States branch of a foreign corporation. Under this approach, a tax equal to the withholding tax imposed on fixed and determinable United States source income would be imposed on the branch when it remits income to its foreign office. This removes the collection problem and is a somewhat more rational system. This tax could be waived in appropriate treaties, but not in treaties with tax havens.

Table 1
U.S. Gross Income Paid to Nonresident Aliens
and Foreign Corporations in Tax Havens and Other Jurisdictions
Within and Without the U.S. Treaty Network, by Type of Income, 1978
(In Thousands of Dollars)

	Total Gross Income	Dividends	Interest	Other
All countries, total	4,451,059	2,867,596	990,949	592,514
Treaty countries, total	3,947,926	2,595,741	826,882	525,304
Tax haven treaty countries, total	1,797,378	1,388,314	308,553	100,511
Antigua	2,808	3	2,798	7
Barbados	496	300	121	75
Belize	108	87	1	20
British Virgin Islands	8,195	5,423	1,716	1,056
Dominica	30	15	*	15
Falkland Islands	122	1	–	121
Grenada	2	1	1	–
Luxembourg	21,066	14,195	5,968	904
Montserrat	4	4	–	1
Netherlands	415,266	331,680	35,499	48,087
Netherlands Antilles	190,759	51,207	127,021	12,531
St. Christopher-Nevis-Anguilla	396	392	1	4
St. Lucia	7	6	–	*
St. Vincent	1	1	–	*
Seychelles	10	9	1	*
Switzerland	1,158,108	984,991	135,426	37,690
Non-tax haven treaty countries, total	2,150,548	1,207,427	518,329	424,793
Australia[1]	28,431	6,011	1,265	21,155
Austria	7,358	4,542	1,437	1,380
Belgium	105,421	54,408	37,868	13,146
Burundi	31	2	20	9
Canada	591,695	282,727	187,426	121,542
Denmark	4,678	2,289	308	2,080
Finland	949	166	128	654
France[2]	308,492	213,735	51,520	43,237
Gambia	2	*	–	2
Germany, Federal Republic of	177,536	124,459	18,882	34,196
Greece	5,337	3,167	714	1,455
Iceland	181	94	*	87
Ireland	5,589	4,093	532	964
Italy	42,982	8,631	11,333	23,017
Jamaica	693	83	5	604
Japan	207,410	63,279	97,216	46,915
Malawi	16	16	*	–

[1] Includes Norfolk Island and Papua New Guinea.
[2] Includes French Guiana, Guadeloupe, Martinique and Reunion.

178

U.S. Gross Income Paid to Nonresident Aliens
and Foreign Corporations in Tax Haven and Other Jurisdictions
Within and Without the U.S. Treaty Network, by Type of Income, 1978

(In Thousands of Dollars)

	Total Gross Income	Dividends	Interest	Other
New Zealand[3/]	3,563	1,811	640	1,112
Nigeria	253	80	*	173
Norway	5,398	3,816	480	1,102
Pakistan	673	47	12	614
Poland	883	206	88	589
Romania	130	26	29	75
Rwanda	2	2	*	–
Sierra Leone	20	5	2	13
South Africa	2,627	1,314	392	921
Sweden	28,568	18,696	5,309	4,563
Trinidad and Tobago	209	81	13	115
U.S.S.R.	510	43	63	404
United Kingdom	620,822	413,527	102,643	104,653
Zaire	32	20	*	12
Zambia	57	53	3	2
Non-treaty countries, total	503,133	271,855	164,067	67,211
Tax haven countries	97,475	67,536	15,061	14,879
Non-tax haven countries	405,658	204,319	149,006	52,332

[3/] Includes Cook Islands and Niue.

*Less than $500.

Note: Detail may not add to totals due to rounding.

Source: Statistics Division, Internal Revenue Service, unpublished tabulations on "Nonresident Alien Income and Tax Withheld as Reported on Forms 1042s" for Calendar Year 1978.

Table 2

U.S. Gross Income Paid to Nonresident Aliens
and Foreign Corporations in Tax Haven Countries
Within and Without the U.S. Treaty Network, 1978

(Amounts in Million Dollars)

	Amount	Percent of all countries
Treaty countries, total	3,947.9	88.7
Tax havens	1,797.4	40.4
Other	2,150.5	48.3
Nontreaty countries, total	503.1	11.3
Tax havens	97.5	2.2
Other	405.7	9.1
All countries, total	4,451.1	100.0

Sum of components may not add to totals due to rounding.

Source: Statistics Division, Internal Revenue Service, unpublished tabulations on "Nonresident Alien Income and Tax Withheld as Reported on Forms 1042s" for Calendar Year 1978.

IX. Information Gathering

The Secretary of the Treasury has broad authority to require taxpayers to file tax returns and to keep records necessary to determine tax liability.[1] The Secretary is empowered to examine any books, papers, records, or other data that may be relevant, or material to verify the correctness of any return or to compute any tax liability.[2] The Secretary's powers, which are delegated to the IRS, and the IRS' ability to enforce them are essential to effective administration of the Internal Revenue Code. In the international sector, these powers frequently are insufficient for the task.

International transactions in general, and tax haven-related transactions in particular, present special problems to the tax administrator. To begin with, U.S. tax laws governing international transactions are among the most complex in the Internal Revenue Code. In addition, the acquisition of information necessary to verify a return or establish tax liability where such transactions are involved is always difficult, often impossible. Investigative efforts are logistically complicated by distance or language differences. Such efforts are procedurally complicated by internal laws and practices of other sovereigns. The ultimate stumbling block is political--the U.S. investigative need often clashes with a foreign interest. When a tax haven is involved, conflicts with foreign laws and practices result in more than merely complex and time-consuming procedures.

A. Reporting

The foundation of the U.S. self-assessment system is the reporting of income and income-producing transactions by taxpayers. Reliance on taxpayer-supplied information applies to international as well as domestic transactions. In both areas, that reliance gives rise to the following questions: (1) What information should be reported? (2) Is IRS asking for it? (3) Is IRS asking for it in a manner that does not place an undue burden on the taxpayer? (4) Is IRS obtaining what it is asking for? (5) Is IRS using the information it gathers?

1/ §6001.

2/ §7602(1).

1. IRS Forms

The primary source of taxpayer-supplied information is the IRS forms filed by taxpayers. Some forms are used to compute tax liability. Others report data or the occurence of certain transactions which do not necessarily reflect the reporter's tax liability. The IRS forms required of a U.S. taxpayer to report international transactions are as follows:

Form 959 (acquisition or disposition of an interest in a foreign corporation);

Forms 926 and 3520 (transfer of property to a foreign entity);

Forms 958 and 2952 (transactions of a controlled foreign corporation);

Form 3520-A (income of a foreign trust in which the taxpayer has an interest);

Forms 957, 958, and 3646 (receipt of income from a foreign corporation);

Forms 1042 and 1042S (payment of certain fixed or determinable income to a foreign person);

Forms 1120NR (corporation) and 1040NR (individual) (receipt of U.S. income or foreign effectively connected income by a resident or non-resident foreign corporation, and a nonresident alien individual, respectively).

The time and place for filing these forms vary. The time is often controlled by the event to be reported (e.g., Form 959). Some are filed with the taxpayer's return (e.g., Form 2952), others are filed separately but at the same service center where the taxpayer files his return (e.g., Form 926), while still others are filed at the Philadelphia Service Center (e.g., Form 957).

a. Analysis

Problems associated with reporting include: (1) inadequacy of the information requested from taxpayers, (2) poor quality of information supplied by taxpayers, (3) overlap among forms requesting information, (4) ambiguity in filing requirements for these forms, and (5) IRS processing difficulties.

With respect to the first problem, there are several significant reporting gaps.

A U.S. person doing business overseas is not required to report the nature of his transactions. Thus, loans from foreign entities, a primary method of repatriating funds laundered through tax havens, need not be reported. As a result, the IRS is unable to identify returns where audit would be appropriate.

In addition, there is a gap in the Form 959 filing requirements. Today, a Form 959 must be filed by certain U.S. persons with respect to an acquisition of stock in a foreign corporation if the acquisition results in a U.S. person owning five percent or more of the value of the stock of the corporation.[3] Stock owned directly or indirectly by a person will be taken into account.[4] The regulations provide for attribution of stock owned by a foreign corporation or a foreign partnership to its shareholders or partners.[5] They do not provide for attribution from a foreign trust.

Accordingly, under the regulations, if a foreign trust for the benefit of a U.S. person acquires stock in a foreign corporation, the fact of that acquisition does not have to be reported. If the foreign trust which acquires the stock is a grantor trust with a U.S. grantor or is a §679 trust, then the grantor or U.S. person taxable under §679 as the owner of the property would have to file, because that person is considered to be the owner of the stock. This rule is not explicitly set forth in the regulations.

A fiduciary of a foreign trust that has U.S. source income or that is engaged in a trade or business in the U.S. must file a Form 1040NR. However, the form does not require that the fiduciary identify the principal of the trust, specify whether the trust entity has a U.S. business, or clarify his relationship to the entity (i.e., trustee, nominee). As a result, information which the IRS might use to classify a return is not readily available.

A U.S. beneficiary of a foreign trust which was established by a foreign person does not have to report his interest in the trust. As a result, it can be difficult for the IRS to identify income paid to such a person from the trust.

3/ §6046.

4/ §6046(c).

5/ Treas. Reg. §1.6046-1(i)(1).

A U.S. partnership is required to report its income and deduction items on Form 1065, as well as each partner's distributive share of the partnership income and expenses on Schedule K of the form. The partnership advises each partner of his distributive share on Schedule K-1, which the partner then reports on his return. A foreign partnership has a duty to file Form 1065 only if it is engaged in a trade or business in the U.S. A U.S. partner in a foreign partnership not so engaged in business in the U.S. is required to report his distributive share of the income and deductible items of that partnership. However, because the partnership does not file a Form 1065, the IRS is without details regarding the nature of partnership income and deductions. As a result, it is difficult to identify partners of foreign partnerships for audit.

A U.S. subsidiary of a foreign parent is required, as a U.S. corporation, to file a Form 1120. It need not submit information concerning its foreign affiliates. Thus the U.S. subsidiary may engage in transactions with foreign affiliates without the IRS being aware of the relationship. As a result, the IRS may not scrutinize the arms-length nature of such transactions.

With respect to the second problem, any number of factors (e.g., placement of questions on forms, clarity of questions, lack of follow-up by the IRS where responses are inadequate) come into play, all of which are correctible.

With respect to the third problem, overlap among the forms certainly exists. Although Form 3646 is used to compute tax liability (income attributable to certain U.S. shareholders), and Form 2952 is an information return, both require much the same information. Likewise, Form 957 and 958 often overlap and may overlap with Forms 2952 and 3646 if the foreign corporation is both a foreign personal holding company and a controlled foreign corporation. Form 959 may also require information similar to that required on these other forms. To the extent that overlaping does not serve a useful tax administration purpose, it places an unnecessary burden on taxpayers.

With respect to the fourth problem, the multiplicity of forms, and ambiguity in designating "who should file what", creates confusion. Not only is it difficult for individuals to know precisely what form they are supposed to be filing, it also appears that the IRS also has difficulty in determining the manner in which to deal with these forms, as discussed below.

184

With respect to the fifth problem, some required IRS forms that are filed never get into the regular audit stream and, consequently, are rarely audited. Until recently, some required information returns (e.g., foreign trust forms) were neither associated with relevant individual or corporate income tax returns nor otherwise used.$^{6/}$ For example, Forms 957 (United States Information Return by an Officer, Director, or U.S. Shareholder of a Foreign Personal Holding Company) and 958 (U.S. Annual Information Return by an Officer or Director of a Foreign Personal Holding Company) are filed with the Philadelphia Service Center, but not forwarded to the district offices. Thus they are rarely audited or associated with the U.S. taxpayer's return. In fact, during extensive field visits with international examiners, only one examiner was found who had audited a foreign personal holding company return.

The IRS has taken steps to associate Forms 3520 and 3520-A with the relevant income tax returns. The Philadelphia Service Center now posts the fact that a related 3520 or 3520-A has been filed in the taxpayer's computerized tax file (module) in Martinsburg, West Virginia. The existence of a related 3520 or 3520-A will be noted on the return. Whether this will prove to be of value has yet to be determined, since very few Forms 3520 and 3520-A are filed.

b. Options

For taxpayer-supplied information to remain a solid foundation of the U.S. self-assessment system where international transactions are involved, change is required. The above analysis suggests a number of possibilities, both legislative and administrative.

(i) One possibility is to streamline and improve existing forms by combining them into fewer forms. If no other action with respect to IRS forms is taken, the IRS should reevaluate all existing forms for reporting foreign-related items and, to the extent possible, combine them into a single clear and concise form. For example, Forms 957 and 958 covering foreign personal holding companies, and Forms 2952 and 3646 covering controlled foreign corporations, can be combined into a single form. The IRS has already prepared draft Form 5741 to replace the above-mentioned forms and

6/ GAO report, "Better Use of Currency and Foreign Accounts Report by Treasury and IRS Needed for Law Enforcement Purposes" (April 6, 1979).

Form 958 as well. Prior to disseminating the draft form, it needs to be updated to reflect changes made to subpart F by the Tax Reduction Act of 1975, the Tax Reform Act of 1976, and the Revenue Act of 1978. In addition, it might be expanded to include the information currently combined on Form 959. At least two legislative changes are necessary. The filing date for Form 959 must be changed to require filing within a fixed period of time after the taxable year in which the reportable event took place, instead of within 90 days after the event. Also, §6035 must be amended so that returns relating to a foreign personal holding company can be filed on an annual basis with the return of the U.S. filer.

(ii) As an alternative to option (i), the IRS could create a new all-encompassing IRS "international" form. IRS could devise one form to be filed by any taxpayer engaged in any international transaction or having any interest in a foreign account or entity. Taxpayers could be clearly and directly advised of the obligation to complete this form by a reference on Form 1040.

(iii) Consideration should be given to imposing additional reporting requirements, such as, for example, the following:

(a) Requiring an individual engaged in any international transaction to submit a balance sheet identifying assets held overseas. The requirement could be limited to individuals with total positive income above a certain level.

(b) Requiring an individual engaged in any international transaction with a foreign entity to report that transaction (e.g., where a loan is obtained from a foreign entity, whether or not the taxpayer has an interest in or association with that entity). An exemption for transactions under a minimum amount (e.g., $1,000) might be appropriate.

(c) Requiring a U.S. partner in a foreign partnership to report the income, deductions, and assets of the partnership in a form similar to that used by U.S. shareholders of a controlled foreign corporation. Where the partnership has more than one U.S. partner, permit one to report on behalf of the others, provided that each U.S. partner refers to ownership of the partnership interest on his individual return.

(d) Amending Treasury Regulation §1.6046-1(i)(1) to provide that for purposes of determining liability for filing a Form 959 stock owned directly or indirectly by a foreign trust will be considered as being owned proportionately by its beneficiaries or grantors. It should be made clear that a grantor or transferor to a foreign trust who is otherwise considered to be the owner of the stock of the foreign corporation will continue to have the obligation to file a Form 959 with respect to the acquisition of stock of a foreign corporation.

(e) Placing an additional block on Form 1040NR to be checked by a fiduciary of any foreign trust engaged in a trade or business in the United States. Further, the fiduciary should be required to clearly state the capacity in which he is acting as a fiduciary, and to list any U.S. beneficiaries of the entity.

(f) Deleting the "ordinary course of a trade or business" exemption referred to in question 12 of Form 2952 (Information Return with Respect to Controlled Foreign Corporations). This would provide additional information on transactions between brother-sister corporations when a U.S. person is the parent of both.

(iv) IRS should encourage better taxpayer information reporting. The IRS should work with the Tax Executive Institute, the American Institute of Certified Public Accountants, and other interested groups to develop methods for improving the quality of reports now filed.

2. Bank Secrecy Act Forms

In 1970 Congress, recognizing the ". . . serious and widespread use of foreign financial facilities located in secrecy jurisdictions for the purpose of violating American law"[7] enacted the Bank Secrecy Act of 1970[8] which authorized the Secretary of the Treasury to require reporting of (1) transactions with domestic financial institutions, (2) transport of currency into and out of the United States, and (3) relationships with foreign financial institutions. Congress intended to enable law enforcement agencies to secure information which might provide leads to earners of illegal income. In fact, the Act does provide IRS with a secondary source of taxpayer-supplied information concerning assets which may or may not have tax consequences.

a. Transactions with financial institutions

A financial institution covered by the Act is required to report each deposit, withdrawal, exchange of currency, payment, or any transfer by, through, or to such financial

_____

7/ H. Rep. No. 91-975, 91st Cong., 2d Sess., 1(1970).

8/ Bank Secrecy Act, 31 C.F.R. §103.22(a) (1970).

institution, on Treasury Form 4789 (Currency Transaction Report, or "CTR"), if it involves a transaction in currency of more than $10,000.[9] Exceptions are provided.[10] Prior to July, 1980, transfers or transactions with or originated by financial institutions or foreign banks were not required to be reported; nor were transfers between banks and certain established customers maintaining a fixed deposit relationship with the bank, provided the bank determined that the amounts involved were commensurate with the customary conduct of the customer's business.

In July, 1980, Treasury published new regulations[11] which expand the scope of reporting to (1) require the reporting of large currency transactions by securities dealers, foreign banks, and miscellaneous financial institutions, such as dealers in foreign exchange, persons in the business of transferring funds for others, and money-order issuers; (2) require more complete identification of a person dealing in large amounts of currency; and, (3) restrict the ability of financial institutions to exempt customers from the reporting requirements.

Transactions with an established customer maintaining a deposit relationship have always been exempt from the reporting requirement. The recent amendment limits this exemption to certain domestic businesses and requires that the location and nature of the business be identified in a report of exempt customers which must be furnished to Treasury. These changes were made necessary when it became clear that certain banks were abusing the existing exemption rules, exempting foreign nationals, boat dealers and others whose only common trait was that they frequently deposited large amounts of cash.

A CTR must be filed within 15 days of the qualifying transaction with the Ogden, Utah, Service Center. The financial institution must retain a copy of the report for five years. The original is processed in the Ogden Service Center. Information on the form is entered into the Treasury Enforcement Communications System (TECS). The fact that a CTR has been filed is recorded in several IRS taxpayer files, so that if a return is audited, the auditor can use TECS to retrieve the CTR information. The existence of a CTR is also noted in the IRS' "non-filer check."

9/ 31 C.F.R. §103.

10/ Id.

11/ 45 Fed. Reg. 37, 818 (1980) (to be codified in 31 C.F.R. §103).

b.   Transport of currency

Each person who transports, mails, ships, or causes to be physically transported, mailed, or shipped, more than $5,000 in currency or any other bearer instrument into or out of the United States, must report the transaction on Treasury Form 4790 (Report of the International Transportation of Currency or other Monetary Instruments, or "CMIR"). The form must be filed with the U.S. Customs Service at the time of entry into or departure, mailing, or shipping from the United States. A recipient of currency must file the form with the Commissioner of Customs within 30 days of receipt. The information contained on the form is entered into TECS, and is thereby made available to IRS agents through that system

Form 4790 is rarely used by the IRS. The identifying information on the form is generally incomplete, and most filers appear to be non-resident aliens.

c.   Foreign bank account

In accordance with the authority granted by Title II of the Bank Secrecy Act, the IRS requires a taxpayer who files Form 1040 to answer the question whether ". . . at any time during the taxable year, [that person] had an interest in or signature authority over a bank, securities, or other financial account in a foreign country." If the answer is "yes" and the amount involved is over $1,000 at anytime during the year, the taxpayer is required to report that account by filing Treasury Form 90-22.1 with the Treasury Department on or before June 30 of the following year. Form 90-22.1, formerly IRS Form 4683, was removed from IRS jurisdiction in October, 1977, to give freer access to the information contained on the form to other agencies.[12]/

Upon receipt, Treasury enters onto TECS the name, social security number, and reference to a microfiche where a copy of the form can be located. An IRS agent then can have access to the information contained on the form.

d.   TECS

The Treasury Department operates a computerized information storage and retrieval system which makes information available to Federal Government personnel in carrying out law enforcement functions. The system is the Treasury

12/ See §6103.

Enforcement Communication System (TECS). TECS is controlled
by Customs, which places the information into the system.
Information from CTRs, CMIRs, and the Foreign Bank Account
reporting forms is entered on TECS. IRS civil and criminal
investigating agents then have access to the information
through TECS.

e.   Analysis

     In April, 1979, GAO released its study captioned "Better
Use of Currency and Foreign Account Reports by Treasury and
IRS Needed for Law Enforcement Purposes", highlighting areas
in which return information was poorly utilized. Current
processing of CTRs and foreign bank account forms reflects
an attempt to adopt GAO suggestions. Additional processing
changes are planned and will be implemented. For example,
IRS will begin corresponding with reporting financial
institutions when incomplete CTRs are received.

     The IRS has become more aggressive in this area. A
recent notice to all agents reminds them that they are
required "to pursue, in all field and office examinations,
the Foreign Accounts and Foreign Trust questions appearing
on tax returns." Examiners have also been directed to
verify whether the taxpayer filed correctly any required
foreign trust, bank account, or currency reports. A forthcoming
Manual Supplement will make it mandatory for the agent to
attempt to determine the correctness of the answer to the
bank account question, and will re-emphasize the directive
to pursue the above mentioned forms.

     The GAO study did not analyze the effectiveness of the
various forms; their utility for tax administration purposes
is still uncertain. Form 4789 probably has the greatest
potential, because it is prepared and filed by an impartial
third party (the financial institution). Just how useful
this form can become may depend upon Treasury's success in
securing better quality reporting from financial institutions.
The information received is still of poor quality, and in
many cases the CTRs are incomplete. It has, however, already
proved useful. For example, CID has found cases of CTRs
filed for transactions by persons for whom there is no
record of income tax returns being filed. CTRs have provided
leads for investigations, and have resulted in referrals to
the IRS civil tax auditors for civil investigation. CTR
portraits have lead to the discovery that banks in a particular
state were generally not filing CTRs.

     Skepticism exists as to whether Form 4790 can be useful.
The information secured is of poor quality, probably because
it is filled out by the transporter under hurried conditions,
i.e., at the airport. The limited authority of Customs to

enforce the reporting requirement further inhibits the production of quality information. For example, although it is illegal to export or import currency without filing the required form, an argument can be made that it is not illegal to attempt to do so. Accordingly, a person passing through a boarding gate without reporting possession of more than $5,000 has not necessarily committed a criminal act, because he has not yet left the country and, thus, not yet exported the currency.

The usefulness of the foreign bank account question has yet to be established. There have been few criminal prosecutions for failure to answer the question, and civil penalties are generally not imposed. However, taxpayers have been prosecuted and, in at least two instances, convicted for answering the question falsely. In addition, a false response can be used in the prosecution's case as evidence of willfulness, even though the taxpayer is not specifically charged with answering the question falsely.

Most taxpayers do not answer the foreign bank account question. Placement of the question on the Form 1040 does appear to affect the response rate. For tax year 1970, when the question was at the top of page 2 of Form 1040, 66 percent of the returns filed contained no answer. In 1971 and 1972, when the question was on the bottom of page 1 of Form 1040 just above the signature line, returns containing no answer were 4 percent and 6 percent respectively. In 1973 and 1974 when the question was moved to the bottom of page 2 of Form 1040, the "no-response" rose to 62 percent and 64 percent respectively. Since 1976 when the question was moved to Schedule B, the "no-response" rate has ranged from 20 to 33 percent. It should be noted that TCMP data for 1973 suggest that only 300,000 taxpayers had foreign bank accounts. Preliminary TCMP data for 1976 suggests that perhaps 345,000 taxpayers had foreign bank accounts. This is a relatively small number of accounts when compared to the Form 1040 filing population of over 52,000,000. However, there was more than a four-fold increase in the number of audit adjustments due to transactions involving foreign bank accounts, from 7,005 adjustments in 1973, to 31,810 in 1976.

It may be that those taxpayers who do not file a Schedule B, but do have a foreign bank account, also do not file a Form 90-22.1. Even if Schedule B is filed with "yes" checked for the foreign bank account question, there is no routine verification made that the taxpayer filed the Form 90-22.1 with Treasury (the form is not to be filed with IRS).

The reporting requirement is not comprehensive. Reporting is required only if the taxpayer has a financial interest in or signature authority over an account in a foreign country. It does not cover a U.S. account with a foreign nominee acting for a U.S. person, or control over other foreign assets. Nor does it cover an account held by a corporation, trust or partnership unless the individual has more than a 50 percent interest in the entity. This may exclude accounts owned by a foreign corporation in which a husband and wife each own 50 percent of the stock.

The IRS seems to have made substantial progress in utilizing information currently on TECS. It would seem, however, that TECS could be put to additional uses in tax administration, and aid in coordinating investigations involving two or more agencies, as well as in coordinating IRS investigations. Actions along these lines are being taken.

f. Options

The Bank Secrecy Act reports have proved useful at times. Their utility increases as more experience is gained. Some options to be considered for further improvement are presented below.

(i) Recent amendments to the Treasury Regulation regarding Form 4789 should improve the quality of the information provided; the IRS is taking positive steps to improve processing of that information. More work, however, is required. With respect to tax haven cases, some attempt to verify addresses should be undertaken. Other recent recommendations, such as increased use of CTR printouts with additional information on those printouts, should be pursued. Furthermore, additional attempts should be made to obtain the assistance of the Controller of the Currency in improving reporting.

(ii) More work is required with respect to Form 4790. To improve the quality of information on that form, legislative changes may be required. Initially, Congress should amend the Bank Secrecy Act to make it illegal to attempt to export or import currency and to give Customs greater authority to conduct border searches with respect to currency transportation. H.R. 5961, introduced during 1980, contained amendments which would have accomplished this.

(iii) With respect to the bank account question, the following suggestions should be considered.

(a) Consideration should be given to improving the existing placement of the question on the income tax return. It could, for example, either be returned to page one of Form 1040 or, at a minimum, placed on side A rather than side B of Schedule A-B.

(b) The information presently requested could be supplemented by requiring a taxpayer to report beneficial ownership of assets acquired or managed by a foreign inter-mediary (e.g., ownership of U.S. assets managed by a foreign nominee).

(c) IRS could encourage better taxpayer information reporting by, for example, sending a follow-up to taxpayers who fail to respond to the question. This follow-up could be limited to those who both failed to check either box and have a total positive income of over a certain amount (e.g., $50,000). In addition, tax return preparers' penalties might be imposed for failing to answer the question on returns they prepare.

3. Penalties for Failure to File or Adequately Complete Forms

a. IRS forms

The Internal Revenue Code provides civil penalties for failure to file or for filing inaccurate income tax forms and returns. Criminal penalties are provided for willful failure to file and for tax evasion. Most civil penalties are not viewed as severe, and we are not certain how aggressively they are enforced. For example, §6038 of the Code requires a U.S. person who controls a foreign corporation to file Form 2952. Section 6038(b) provides that the penalty for failure to file is reduction of the foreign tax credit. Despite complaints by IRS agents that taxpayers do not properly complete the form, this penalty is rarely, if ever, imposed. In part, this may be because the penalty itself is mechanically complicated. Or, the IRS may have determined that this particular penalty is too severe. Some agents have stated that they hesitate even to recommend imposition of the penalty, because it makes the taxpayer more antagonistic and, if imposed, will be abated anyway.

b. Bank secrecy act forms

Willful violations of the Bank Secrecy Act may con-stitute either a felony or a misdemeanor. Fines of up to $500,000 and imprisonment for up to five years are provided in cases of long-term patterns of substantial violation, and violations committed in furtherance of certain other Federal crimes. It is also a felony for any person to make a false or fraudulent statement in any required report. Any currency or monetary instruments being transported without the required report having been filed, or as to which the report omits material facts or contains misstatements, may be seized and forfeited to the United States. The Act also provides for assessing a civil penalty, which may range from $1,000 up to the amount of currency or monetary instruments seized, less any amount forfeited.

c.   Options

Civil penalties are essential to the enforcement of filing requirements. As a general proposition, such penalties should be significant in amount so as to be meaningful, sufficiently easy to impose so as to be readily available, and flexible in application so as to be useful toward the goal of securing taxpayer compliance. The IRS might re-examine existing penalty provisions and procedures related thereto, with an eye toward the following:

(i) Seeking legislative changes where the penalties are inadequate. For example, where a taxpayer fails to file a properly completed Form 2952, reduction of the foreign tax credit may be an appropriate secondary penalty to be applied in flagrant cases. Where a taxpayer required to furnish information under §6039(a) of the Code fails to do so in a timely and complete manner, §6038(b) could be amended to provide a minimum mandatory penalty (e.g., $25,000). The IRS should also have the option to reduce the foreign tax credit in gross cases.

(ii) Providing clearer direction to the field regarding the imposition of penalties. Field personnel must be made aware that voluntary compliance is promoted through the exercise of good judgment in assessing penalties. A policy of imposing penalties in all cases of poorly completed IRS forms serves only to increase tensions with taxpayers and clog the administrative and judicial systems. On the other hand, failure to impose the penalty when merited has a detrimental impact on voluntary compliance.

B.   Books and Records -- Foreign Transactions -- In General

Many of the tax and information returns previously discussed give IRS the basic information with which to begin investigations involving international (or domestic) transactions Thereafter, a meaningful audit or investigation of a taxpayer's

return may require access to books and records of the taxpayer
or third parties, irrespective of whether such books and
records were used in preparation of the return being scrutinized

1. **General Requirements for Maintenance of Adequate Books
    and Records**

Every person who is liable for any income or excise tax
must keep such records, render such statements, make such
returns, and comply with such rules and regulations as the
Secretary of the Treasury prescribes.[13] The Secretary has
promulgated regulations which require a taxpayer to maintain
books and records adequate to establish his tax liability or
other matters required to be shown on a return.[14] These
records must be kept at a convenient location and must be
accessible to IRS employees.[15] Similar recordkeeping
requirements are specifically directed to a U.S. shareholder
of a controlled foreign corporation "as necessary to carry
out the provisions of subparts F and G."[16] The Secretary,
by regulation, permits such records to be maintained in a
foreign country, but requires their production within a
reasonable time after demand.[17] The records required to be
produced are, in general, those necessary to verify the
amounts reported under subpart F or G.[18]

2. **Penalties for Failure to Maintain Adequate Books and
    Records**

The Internal Revenue Code authorizes a civil penalty of
five percent of any underpayment due to negligence or intentional disregard of rules and regulations.[19] This penalty
can be imposed for failure to maintain books and records
adequate to establish items of income and deduction.[20]

13/ §6001.

14/ Treas. Reg. §6001-1(a).

15/ Treas. Reg. §31.6001-1(e).

16/ §964(c)(1).

17/ Treas. Reg. §1.964-3(a).

18/ Treas. Reg. §1.964-3(b).

19/ §6653(a).

20/ R. Simkins Estate, 37 T.C.M. 1388, DEC 35, 368 (M) T.C.
    Memo 1978-338, affd., D.C. Cir. (Apr. 28, 1980), unpub-
    lished opinion.

3.   Powers to Compel Production of Books and Records

While the Internal Revenue Code gives the IRS the right
of access to taxpayer books and records, taxpayers do not
always willingly cooperate. To deal with these situations,
the IRS is given broad authority to compel the production of
books and records (and testimony) believed to be relevant.

Section 7602 of the Code provides that the IRS may
examine any books, papers, records, or other data which may
be relevant or material to determine tax liability, and may
summon or command the person liable for the tax or an officer
of the taxpayer to produce the above and to give testimony
under oath as may be relevant or material to computation of
the tax liability. Section 7602 further authorizes the IRS
to command production of books and records in the hands of a
third-party recordkeeper. A summons may be enforced by a
United States district court.[21] Failure to comply with a
summons can result in a contempt citation.[22]

4.   Analysis

Although the IRS is statutorily granted broad access to
relevant information, significant legal and practical problems
restrict that access.

a.   Legal

A taxpayer may assert legal defenses against an IRS
demand for books and records. If the taxpayer believes that
an investigation may lead to a criminal charge, he may
exercise his Constitutional privilege against self-incrimination. If the books and records are in the hands of an
agent, the taxpayer may assert that they are protected by
the attorney-client privilege. The limits of these defenses
are fairly well established by case law. A taxpayer may
claim that the material summoned is irrelevant to his tax
liability, or that production of the material would be
unduly burdensome. A taxpayer may stay compliance of the
summons and intervene in a summons enforcement proceeding to
contest the production of books and records in the hands of
third-party recordkeepers.[23]

21/ §7604(b).

22/ Id.

23/ §7609.

A few taxpayers have apparently taken the position that
production of books and records of their foreign subsidiary
is not required unless a subpart F issue is raised.24/
Thus, if the issue raised by the agent deals with §482,
these taxpayers argue that they are not required to produce
the records. Section 6001 does not specifically refer to
books and records of a foreign affiliate.

b. Administrative

The IRS is often subject to administrative constraints,
self-imposed and otherwise. Perceived time pressures often
encourage the closing of cases at the agent level before
access has been gained to all accountable books. Limited
resources produce a similar result.

c. Tactical

Taxpayers aware of IRS administrative constraints often
employ delaying tactics. Legal claims may be asserted for
dilatory purposes only. Because a taxpayer can stay compliance with a third party summons without reason, such is
often the practice. Intervention does toll the statute of
limitations, but only from the time a Government petition in
response to a stay of compliance is filed with the district
court. Significant time lags occur between IRS receipt of a
stay of compliance and filing of a petition in response.
The IRS and Justice internal review processes are partially
responsible. Also, there are significant delays after a
proceeding is brought in a district court.

Taxpayers may employ more devious delaying tactics.
In some cases, deadlines agreed to between IRS agents and
taxpayers pass without receipt of requested and promised
information. In some cases this is due to taxpayer administrative
difficulties in complying with a request, but in others it
appears due to malice or benign neglect on the part of the
taxpayer, who believes that procrastination will cause the
IRS to lose interest in the case or to propose only poorly
developed adjustments. A survey of all International Examiners
in conjunction with this study identified a significant
number of cases where the agent believed, and appeared to
have reason to believe, that a taxpayer unnecessarily delayed
the production of requested material. A number of cases
appeared clearly abusive.

_____

24/ In which case production is required under §964(c).

On the other hand, it was not our impression that most
taxpayers procrastinated. As industry groups have pointed
out, it is both time consuming and expensive for a company
to delay the conclusion of an examination. There is also
the problem of imprecise requests for information from IRS
agents. Industry groups have alleged that, in some instances,
requests for information are "nothing more than fishing
expeditions." Overly broad requests, such as requests for
"all sales invoices of a particular foreign subsidiary" or
"all communications between the foreign subsidiary and the
parent company", have been cited. There is a great deal of
reluctance to respond to such broad based inquiries, particularly
when the materials are in a foreign country and in a foreign
language.

Furthermore, in some cases cited by International
Examiners as abusive delays, a criminal investigation had
been commenced. It is unrealistic to expect that the subject
of a criminal investigation will cooperate in an investigation
which could lead to a criminal prosecution.

C.   Information Gathering Abroad

Except in the case of a United States shareholder of
a controlled foreign corporation, the Internal Revenue Code
does not specifically require that books and records relevant
to tax liability of a U.S. taxpayer be maintained in the
United States.25/ Of course, the Code cannot mandate maintenance
of books and records of third parties who are not U.S.
taxpayers, citizens, or residents. When information necessary
for an audit or investigation is unavailable in this country,
it must be sought abroad.

Information may be sought abroad unilaterally or through
bilateral or multilateral conventions to which the United
States is a party. In either case, success in obtaining
information is dependent on a number of factors. Initially,
the IRS must be aware that the information does or may
exist. While the tax and information returns previously
discussed may be useful, a taxpayer seeking to avoid or
evade tax, or to hide assets, may either fail to file the
relevant return or file a false return. A second major
factor is gaining access to the information; this depends to
a great degree on resolving conflicts between U.S. and

_____

25/ §964(c).

foreign law and on the willingness of the foreign jurisdiction to cooperate. An additional factor, of primary
importance in criminal cases, is that the information must
be secured in a form admissible in a United States court of
law.

1.   Unilateral Means

The United States does not have income tax treaties or
other exchange of information agreements with most tax havens.
Those in force often do not override local secrecy laws and
practices. Therefore, unilateral means to gain access to
information must be used.

a.   Public Information

The extent to which useful public information is available
depends upon the country involved. In some jurisdictions
public information concerning commercial or corporate affairs
is extensive, while in others such information is extremely
limited. In jurisdictions maintaining extensive public
records, an "impartial observer" seeking, for example,
information concerning the business and financial affairs of
a foreign corporation, might expect to find a copy of a
corporate charter, corporate financial statements, a statement
of corporate business affairs, corporate earnings statements,
and perhaps even the identify of the corporate board of
directors or similar body, and principal officers and shareholders
However, even where useful information is publicly available,
some jurisdictions view access to it in the course of an
official IRS examination as a breach of sovereignty which
requires permission of the foreign government before information
gathering may commence. As part of this study, the Office
of International Operations (OIO) compiled a description of
publicly available information in over 30 tax haven jurisdictions.

Even where public records are available and the local
government does not unduly restrict IRS activities in obtaining
them, the legal use of nominees or bearer shares which
conceal the identity of persons involved with the corporation
will close off investigative leads. OIO advises that use of
nominees is common in tax haven countries such as the Bahamas,
the Cayman Islands, and Panama.

An example of a tax haven country maintaining extensive
public records is Switzerland. Switzerland requires that
corporations publish extensive corporate and finanacial
data. Under Swiss law, every business enterprise is required
to file certain basic information in the register of commerce

located in the Canton where its principal place of business
is situated. Information required to be filed includes: a
copy of the statute (charter) of the enterprise, including
its name, purpose and address of registered seat; the names
and nationalities of directors or managers; the names of the
founder or partners, and the extent of their contributions,
liabilities and preferential rights; the amount of authorized
and paid-in share capital; the names and powers of persons
authorized to sign on behalf of the enterprise; and the way
in which official notices are to be published. Changes with
respect to any of the required information must also be
published.

Notwithstanding the extensive amount of information
required to be made public, the identity of owners of a
Swiss entity can easily be hidden. It is common practice
for those wishing to conceal their business affairs to use
either nominees or bearer shares to do so. In addition,
holding companies may appoint the office of a local bank, a
lawyer, or a chartered accountant as their local office in
order to further conceal corporate affairs.

Information gathering in Switzerland is severely restricted by both Swiss law and Swiss Government policy.
Swiss approval must be obtained before any information
gathering is conducted in Switzerland. Several articles of
the Swiss Penal Code, the violation of which would subject
an IRS agent to imprisonment, apply to unauthorized information
gathering in Switzerland, even for an official IRS investigation.

In contrast to Switzerland, the Cayman Islands government
prohibits extensive public records with respect to corporations.
The Confidential Relationships (Preservation) Law prohibits
the disclosure of any corporate information other than the
name of the corporation, date of incorporation, and registered
office for the corporation. The registered office is usually
the office of a law firm or trust company, which also is
prohibited by the law from disclosing information. No
commercial register is maintained on the Cayman Islands, and
disclosure of court records is prohibited to the extent that
they involve matters covered by the confidentiality laws. A
limited procedure for obtaining some information subject to
the confidentiality laws is available, in the case of crimes
occuring within the United States involving financial transactions
in the Cayman Islands.

Even this limited exception does not apply in the case
of tax crimes. Moreover, any information gathered in the
Cayman Islands, including public information, is subject to
clearance by the United States Consul and permission of the
Cayman Government.

Even in those instances where useful public information can be obtained, practical problems may arise which render such information useless for tax purposes. For example, in conducting a net worth investigation of a taxpayer, a special agent may discover that the taxpayer is secreting money into the Cayman Islands to purchase real estate there. Although the Cayman Islands maintains public records of real estate transactions, this information is not indexed in an alphabetical file. To obtain land records, it is necessary to know the legal description of the property. In those cases where such information is not available, and where the taxpayer refuses to cooperate or exercises his right against self-incrimination, it is impossible to confirm ownership absent an independent source.

b. Overseas Examination

If, during an audit or investigation, it becomes necessary to examine the taxpayer's books and records located outside the territorial jurisdiction of the United States, the IRS may request the taxpayer's permission to conduct an overseas audit or on-site examination. In criminal cases taxpayers obviously will not cooperate. If permission is granted, the IRS may have one of its overseas Revenue Service Representatives (RSRs) perform the task. In the alternative, the agent assigned to the case in the United States may be authorized to travel abroad. Either alternative has drawbacks. Travel funds and time involved in sending a U.S. based agent abroad can be substantial. Use of an RSR can limit the cost, and the RSRs have been very helpful in obtaining specific information. The RSR may not, however, have the background in the matter to know when to follow up on specific requests.

In many instances an on-site examination may not be the most efficient use of resources. For example, if the IRS is trying to corroborate a deduction, the records might be more appropriately produced here or the deduction denied.

Where an on-site examination appears desirable, the IRS is generally required to secure permission of the local government before proceeding.[26] Governmental permission is likewise generally needed prior to interviewing a person in a foreign country relative to an IRS investigation. The necessity for obtaining both taxpayer and local government permission to make an on-site examination severely limits its utility. The IRS has experienced situations in which an on-site audit was successful in one year, and permission was then denied in the next year, either by the taxpayer or the local government.

26/ See infra at C.1.a. of this Chapter re Switzerland.

c. Compulsory Process

If the taxpayer is unwilling to permit an on-site examination of books and records located outside the United States, or if the books and records are those of a third party, the IRS may resort to compulsory process. This can take the form of an administrative summons, a judicial subpoena, or, when requesting that a foreign juridiction exercise its compulsory process for the benefit of the IRS, letters rogatory.

(i) Administrative summons. The IRS has been successful in obtaining access to books and records, physically located in a foreign jurisdiction, through the issuance of an administrative summons, at least where those documents are under the custody or control of an entity or person controlled by a U.S. person. In addition to the defenses (discussed in B.4.a. of this chapter) which a taxpayer or third party record keeper has to the production of books and records in response to an administrative summons, the defense often encountered here is that a foreign law or rule of law imposing civil or criminal liability prohibits the taxpayer or third party from producing the documents requested. By definition, this will generally be the case where the documents to be produced are located in a tax haven jurisdiction.

As a general proposition, the courts of this country will not require a person to perform an act in this country which would violate foreign law.[27] Some courts have balanced the IRS interest in obtaining the documents or testimony requested against the foreign government's interests in maintaining its rule of law.[28] Thus, cases are decided on an ad hoc basis, the outcome depending on the unique facts involved in each (e.g., the type of foreign law involved, the identity of the person being requested to produce). Some relevant factors are illustrated by the following hypothetical examples, based, in part, on actual cases.

In an investigation of a United States-based multinational corporation, a special agent believes that a Swiss bank account, maintained by a wholly owned subsidiary of the U.S. parent, was used by the foreign subsidiary to make an illegal

---

27/ United States v. First National City Bank, 396 F. 2d 897 (2d Cir. 1968).

28/ In re Westinghouse Electric Corporation Uranium Contracts Litigation, 563 F. 2d 992 (10th Cir. 1977); Restatement (Second) of the Foreign Relations Law of the United States, §§39 and 40 (1965).

payment to a foreign official to effectuate a sales agreement between the U.S. parent and the foreign official's government. The agent further believes the payment was incorrectly characterized and deducted on the corporate tax return. The agent has served an administrative summons on the U.S. parent commanding production of the subsidiary's records of the Swiss Bank account, including copies of deposited items to the account and checks written on the account. Upon advice of counsel, the U.S. parent refuses to produce these records on the basis that (a) the records are located in Switzerland and hence not subject to the summons power, and (b) the production of these records would violate the Swiss bank secrecy law.

Standing alone, the fact that records are located overseas will not deprive a United States district court of jurisdiction to compel their production in proceedings to enforce an IRS administrative summons.[29] Similarly, the argument that the U.S. parent could not produce the records since it does not have control over them would be unavailing because the U.S. parent is the sole shareholder of the Swiss subsidiary and, in that capacity, would be able to exercise its authority as shareholder to force the subsidiary to have the records produced.[30]

A different question is presented with respect to the violation of the Swiss Bank Secrecy law. While it is generally true that the United States courts will hesitate to require a person to do an act in this country which would violate foreign law, under the facts of this example a violation of the Swiss bank secrecy law is not involved. Under that law the customer is "the master of the secret."[31] In the summons enforcement proceeding, the court would require the U.S. parent to exercise its control with respect to the requested records.[32]

29/ Societe Internationalee Pour Participations Industries v. Rogers, 357 U.S. 197 (1958).

30/ Societe, supra; First National City Bank v. Internal Revenue Service, 271 F. 2d 616, 618 (2d Cir. 1959), cert. denied, 361 U.S. 948 (1960).

31/ Trade Development Bank v. Continental Insurance Capital, 469 F. 2d 35, 41 at n. 3 (2d Cir. 1972).

32/ Securities and Exchange Commission v. Minas de Artemisa, S.A., 159 F. 2d 215 (9th Cir. 1945).

In another case, a revenue agent is examining the
income tax return of a nonresident alien, a foreign entertainer
who has earned substantial sums of money, on a concert tour
in the United States, which the entertainer claims are
exempt from U.S. income taxes by reason of an income tax
treaty. To determine the entertainer's U.S. tax liability,
the revenue agent must see several employment and royalty
agreements between the entertainer and a Grand Cayman Islands
corporation, copies of which are in the physical possession
of the Grand Caymans branch of a large international accounting
firm whose headquarters are in New York. The revenue agent
served an administrative summons on the head office of the
accounting firm in New York to obtain copies of these agreements.
Upon advice of counsel, the accounting firm refuses to turn
over the records, citing as its reason that production of
the records would violate the criminal laws of the Cayman
Islands.

Based on the authorities discussed above, the accounting
firm would be required, at a minimum, to exercise good faith
efforts to obtain the consent of the entertainer to produce
the agreements. Failing in that, it is unclear whether the
accounting firm would still be required to produce the records.33/

In another case, a special agent has under investigation
a taxpayer who is a sole shareholder of a corporation in the
manufacturing business. The special agent believes that the
taxpayer has omitted substantial amounts of income from the
corporate tax return, by deducting payments to a Bahamian
corporation for goods allegedly used in the manufacturing
process. The special agent believes that, in reality, the
Bahamian corporation is owned by the taxpayer, and that the
payments made to it are not for items purchased but are merely
a diversion of corporate receipts to a numbered bank account
in the Bahamas owned and maintained by the taxpayer. A check
of the public records in the Bahamas indicates that the
Bahamian corporation is incorporated and has its office at the
offices of an attorney in the Bahamas. In response to a
summons issued to him, the taxpayer has refused to answer any
of the special agent's questions regarding this transaction,
citing his right against self-incrimination under the Fifth
Amendment.

33/ Application of Chase Manhattan Bank, 297 F. 2d 611 (2d
    Cir. 1962); United States v. First National City Bank,
    396 F. 2d 897 (2d Cir. 1962); United States v. Field,
    532 F. 2d 404 (5th Cir. 1976); cert. denied, 429 U.S.
    940 (1976); Arthur Andersen Company v. Finesilver, 546
    F. 2d 338 (10th Cir. 1976), cert. denied, 429 U.S. 1096
    (1977).

Under the facts of this example, the agent will be unable
to gain access to either the bank or corporate records needed
to complete the investigation, since there is no person subject
to the personal jurisdiction of the United States courts who
can be forced to produce these records. Thus, absent evidence
of other violations by this taxpayer, or evidence provided by
an independent source, this case cannot be forwarded for
prosecution. However, in the event that a person became subject
to the jurisdiction of the United States courts to be required
to testify, the taxpayer would be unable at trial to block such
testimony based upon the assertion of the bank secrecy law of
the Bahamas.[34]

Use of process has other limitations. If a United States
citizen is outside the United States, an administrative
summons apparently can be directed to him. However, IRS may
not be able to enforce that summons, since the law neglects
to specifically confer venue except when a person "resides
or may be found" in a judicial district of the United States.[35]
A summons cannot be served on a foreign person not present
in the United States. Accordingly, as indicated in the last
example, an administrative summons cannot be used to compel
the testimony of a Cayman bank official not present in the
United States.

(ii) Judicial subpoena. Where IRS has determined that
a particular matter should be pursued criminally, it may
seek authorization to place the investigation in the hands
of a grand jury. A grand jury investigation has the advantage
of the subpoena power, which is much faster than an administrative
summons in compelling the production of books and records
relevant to an investigation. Moreover, when IRS personnel
are assigned to assist the grand jury, they are able to
coordinate closely with law enforcement personnel from other
agencies, a practice otherwise restricted by statute.[36] On
the negative side, the procedures which the IRS must follow
to obtain grand jury authorization have been cumbersome and
time-consuming. At one time, approval of a request through
both IRS and the Department of Justice, which approval is
required by law, could take six months, even if the request

34/ United States v. Frank, 494 F. 2d 145 (2d Cir. 1974).

35/ §§ 7402(b) and 7604(a). See United States v. Harkins,
581 F. 2d 431, 438 at n. 11 (5th Cir. 1978).

36/ See §6103.

was generated outside of the IRS. Steps have been taken to reduce this time lag[37] and, while it is too early to tell whether they will be effective, there are indications of improvement.

Grand jury proceedings are secret and an IRS employee privy to information obtained by the grand jury may not disclose it. Thus, information gathered by the grand jury may not be used to determine civil tax liabilities, absent a court order granted pursuant to Rule 6(e), Federal Rules of Criminal Procedure, unless the information becomes part of the public record. Information independently developed by the IRS is not so restricted and may be used for civil tax purposes. Should the IRS desire to secure grand jury material for civil tax purposes, a request for a Rule 6(e) order can be made only by a Justice Department attorney, not by an IRS (Chief Counsel) attorney. The IRS interest in civil enforcement can come into conflict with the Justice Department's overriding interest in the criminal justice system.

The ability of a subpoena to secure books and records physically located in a foreign jurisdiction is roughly equivalent to that of the administrative summons. The same legal principles apply. Unlike the summons, a subpoena directed to a U.S. citizen situated abroad is clearly enforcable in the United States district court from which it issues.

(iii) Letters rogatory. Where evidence located in a foreign jurisdiction is neither in the custody of nor controlled by a person subject to the jurisdiction of the United States court, the IRS may seek to obtain it through letters rogatory. In this case, letters rogatory represent the request of the United States court (in a civil or criminal matter) for the assistance of a foreign tribunal in obtaining evidence. The requested assistance can range from the effecting of service of process to the taking of testimony or the securing of books and records. The procedure is available only in a judicial proceeding.

Letters rogatory have been used infrequently in tax cases (civil or criminal). The decision to grant assistance is completely within the discretion of the foreign tribunal. Should that tribunal decide to execute the request, the "turn around" time is tremendous -- anywhere from three months to a year.

37/ See IRM 9267.2.

d. Tax Court

The United States Tax Court, at the trial stage, has
the authority to require a foreign petitioner to produce
books, records, documents or other evidence deemed necessary
to the proceeding.[38] If the petitioner fails or refuses to
comply after a reasonable time for compliance, the Tax
Court, upon motion, may strike the pleadings or parts thereof,
dismiss the proceeding or any part thereof, or render judgment
by default against the petitioner.[39]

These Tax Court powers are limited to those cases in
which the petitioner is a nonresident alien individual,
foreign trust or estate, or foreign corporation. Such
sanctions are not otherwise available and, therefore, cannot
be used to penalize, for example, a U.S. shareholder of a
controlled foreign corporation which fails to produce the
necessary corporate records.

e. Information Gathering Projects and Informants

The IRS has conducted information gathering projects.
Some were intended to develop institutional knowledge about
tax haven activities. Others were intended to identify tax
offenders or evaders. In criminal cases, informants have
proved valuable at times. These subjects are discussed in
Chapter VI.

2. Bilateral or Multilateral Means

Because unilateral means for obtaining information are
limited by the willingness of foreign governments to cooperate
on a case-by-case basis, and by the lack of established
channels for obtaining assistance, the United States has
entered into various bilateral and multilateral agreements
with other countries which provide both an agreement for
cooperation and a procedural framework for obtaining information
pursuant thereto. Unfortunately, with the exception of tax
treaties, these agreements have been of little use in tax administration.

38/ §7456(b).

39/ Id.

a. Tax treaties

Tax treaties, in addition to dealing with double taxation issues, are intended to prevent fiscal evasion.[40/] United States treaties in force contain an article obligating this country and its treaty partner to exchange information on matters related to tax administration. The United States Model Income Tax Convention and the OECD Model Income Tax Convention "exchange of information" articles provide for exchanges of information necessary to carry out the provisions of the convention or of the domestic laws of the respective contracting countries.[41/]

Both models contain identical limitations. The parties need not go beyond the internal laws or administrative practices of either party to obtain information for the requesting country. (The OECD commentary states that a country is obligated to make special investigations if similar investigations would be made for its own purposes.) Both parties must treat information received as confidential, to be used only in tax proceedings concerning taxes covered by the convention. A party may disseminate information only to those involved in the collection of taxes or the enforcement of tax laws.

The U.S. model is broader in scope than the OECD model. The U.S. model requires that information be provided in an authenticated form. However, a country is required to produce this quality of information only if permitted under its laws and practices. It also provides for collection of taxes if necessary to ensure that the tax benefits of the convention do not inure to persons not entitled to the relief provided. It further applies to taxes not covered by the convention.

The United States has interpreted most of its treaties as permitting three methods of providing information:

First, a routine or automatic transmittal of information, consisting generally of lists of names of U.S. resident tax-payers receiving passive income from sources within the treaty partner, and notifications of changes in foreign law.

_____

40/ The substantive provisions of income tax treaties are discussed in Chapter VIII.

41/ Article 26, U.S. Model Income Tax Convention; Article 26, OECD Model Income Tax Convention.

Second, requests for specific information, which generally are requests of the U.S. competent authority for information. Specific requests for information also result from simultaneous examinations of a single taxpayer coordinated with certain treaty partners. One criterion in selecting a taxpayer for simultaneous examination is the use of tax havens in its operations.

Third, spontaneous exchange of information at the discretion of the transmitting country. This exchange occurs when an examining agent in one country discovers information during a tax examination which suggests or establishes noncompliance with the tax laws of a treaty partner. This information may be provided without a specific request.

The utility of tax treaties is presently limited. The United States does not have tax treaties with the most important tax haven countries (e.g., Bahamas, Bermuda, Cayman Islands, Lichtenstein, Panama). Where the United States does have treaties, serious technical deficiencies with the exchange of information provisions restrict the value thereof. The tax haven treaty partner is obligated only to give such information as is obtainable under local law. Thus, if the jurisdiction has a bank secrecy law, bank account information will not be obtainable; if the jurisdiction has a commercial secrecy law, corporate ownership and business information will not be obtainable and, perhaps, even interviews with residents of the jurisdiction will be prohibited. In many tax haven jurisdictions, access to such information is not only limited to foreign jurisdictions, but also to the government of the jurisdiction itself.

A second deficiency with the exchange of information provision is that under a literal reading a requested country may not be obligated to perform actions which the requesting country could not perform under its laws. Thus, once the IRS has referred a matter to the Department of Justice for possible criminal prosecution, the United States cannot be certain that a treaty partner will secure information by administrative process to be provided pursuant to the exchange information provision, because the United States can no longer use an administrative summons internally. This is, admittedly, a literal reading of the treaty provision; however, it is one that has been adopted in some cases. A strict reciprocity approach contrasts sharply with the United States position in mutual assistance treaty negotiations, wherein this country has attempted to move away from direct reciprocity.

209

Even where secrecy laws are not a factor, the attitude
of the treaty partner can make a significant difference.
Some countries (e.g., Canada) are more cooperative in preventing
international tax evasion and avoidance and, accordingly,
take an expansive view of the exchange of information provisions.
Other countries (e.g., Switzerland) take a very restrictive
view of the scope of the exchange of information provisions.
Attitude may or may not affect the quality of information
received from a treaty partner. In any event, it is often
of poor quality. For example, IRS receives routine information
from many treaty partners which fails to identify the particular taxpayer involved or the year in which the significant
transaction took place. The United States does not have
leverage available to encourage a treaty partner to provide
quality information. Information is rarely produced in a
form which will allow it to be introduced in court.

IRS internal policies and procedures may have further
restricted treaty effectiveness. With respect to procedure,
those requests which are made pursuant to treaty take a
substantial amount of time, upwards of a year from the
agent's preparation of a routine request until the time he
gets the information requested. The IRS internal review
process may have been partially at fault. Prior to September,
1980, a request generated by an agent was reviewed by his
group manager, reviewed through the regional level, and sent
to the competent authority, the Assistant Commissiner (Compliance),
where it is forwarded to OIO for formal processing. The procedure
has been streamlined so that the final field review is now
at the district, rather than regional, level. The request
then goes directly to OIO with copies to appropriate managers.
Information received is sent by OIO directly to the district.
If problems develop, supplemental information must also
follow this same path. The request must then be prepared
and delivered to the competent authority of the requested
country. Thereafter, IRS is dependent upon the good will of
the treaty partner to get the information within a reasonable
period of time.

b. Mutual assistance treaties

The United States has only one mutual assistance treaty
in force -- with Switzerland.[42/] A second, with Turkey, is
awaiting ratification by the Turkish government. The
United States has initialed treaties with Columbia and the
Netherlands, and is currently negotiating similar treaties
with a number of other governments. None of those negotiations
is with an important tax haven country. Some agreement with

42/ 2 U.S.T. 2019, TIAS 8302 (1976).

the Commonwealth of the Bahama Islands may soon be possible.
At one time, the Bahamian government indicated its willingness
to discuss a mutual assistance treaty. In December, 1980, a
United States delegation went to the Bahamas on a fact-
finding mission, one purpose of which was to further explore
the possibility of negotiating such a treaty.

The usefulness of mutual assistance treaties with
respect to tax matters will depend on the scope of each
treaty. Experience with the Swiss treaty has not been
encouraging. First, the Swiss treaty is limited to criminal
matters. Second, it is applicable to "tax crimes" only if
the subject of the investigation is an organized crime
figure, the evidence available to the United States is
insufficient to prosecute the individual in connection with
his organized criminal activity, and the requested assistance
will substantially facilitate the successful prosecution and
imprisonment of that individual. Third, under Swiss imple-
menting legislation, the subject of the investigation can
contest the taking of authenticated testimony. If contested,
production of the testimony could be delayed for at least
one year. Understandably, the Swiss treaty has not been
useful in tax cases; the standards are too difficult to
meet.

Treaties negotiated or under negotiation since the
Swiss treaty are much broader in scope. Fiscal crimes in
general, and tax offenses in particular, are specifically
covered. Moreover, the United States negotiators have taken
the position, with a great deal of success, that criminal
tax offenses ought to be treated in a manner similar to any
other criminal offenses.

D. Options

Where books and records are not in the United States,
the IRS and the law enforcement community have special
problems. Some options to be considered to improve access
to books and records are presented below:

1. Unilateral Actions

The United States could change its regulations and laws
to make more information available, and to make it easier to
introduce evidence obtained. Some suggestions follow.

a. Asserting the taxpayer's burden of proof. In
civil cases, the burden of establishing the tax consequences
of a transaction is on the taxpayer. As discussed in Chapter
VII.A.1., this burden should be vigorously relied upon in
appropriate cases.

b. Requiring that books and records be maintained in the U.S. Consideration should be given to requiring that books and records relevant to tax liability in the United States be maintained within the territorial jurisdiction of this country, in appropriate cases. The regulations under §6001 could be amended to make clear the requirement that revelant books and records of foreign subsidiaries of U.S. persons must be made available to the IRS. The regulation could provide that if the requested records are not produced within some stated period of time (e.g., 90 days) the taxpayer would thereafter be required to maintain the records in the United States. In addition, records of a controlled foreign corporation formed in or doing business in a tax haven could be required to be kept in the United States, unless the U.S. shareholder and the controlled foreign corporation agree, in writing, to comply with the stated time rule and provide any necessary waivers of foreign law rights to withhold the records.

Similar record keeping requirements could be provided for U.S. persons who have control over a foreign trust or an interest in a foreign partnership. A regulations project dealing with these issues has been established.

c. Venue where a party summoned is outside the United States. Section 7604 could be amended to establish venue in a particular U.S. district (e.g., the District of Columbia) in those situations where the party summoned is subject to the summons jurisdiction of the IRS but resides or may be found outside the territorial jurisdiction of the United States.

d. Admissibility of foreign business records. Once access to books and records in a tax haven is secured, the materials must be obtained in a form admissible in court. Moreover, an authenticating witness is often required. Because, in dealing with foreign jurisdictions, either or both requirements often cannot be met, consideration should be given to amending Rules 803 and 902 of the Federal Rules of Evidence to provide that extrinsic evidence of authenticity as a condition precedent to admissibility is not required with respect to a foreign business record if (1) the record was obtained pursuant to a treaty of the United States, (2) authenticity of the record is attested to by the custodian, and (3) advance notice is given to the opposing party to provide a reasonable opportunity to investigate the authenticity of the document. Requiring the above procedures to be followed (including use of the treaty mechanism) should insure that documents will have a high degree of reliability.

e. IRS review process for mutual assistance. The IRS review process for exchange of information requests has been streamlined. It should be monitored to see that delays are not occurring. If they are, consideration might be given to further streamlining so that a group manager will have final field review. Problems of regional or district coordination could still be handled by providing copies of correspondence to an appropriate official.

2. Bilateral Approaches

Tax haven problems, by definition, involve a second sovereign jurisdiction, and, also by definition, conflict between the laws of that jurisdiction and the U.S. The best way to overcome these problems, particularly where a possible crime is under investigation, is to enter into bilateral agreements with the tax haven.

a. Mutual assistance treaties. The U.S. should consider expanding its effort to enter into mutual assistance treaties under which the U.S. and its treaty partner agree to provide assistance in criminal investigations. Every effort should be made to cover fiscal crimes in general, and tax offenses in particular. Tax offenses should be treated as any other criminal offense. The persons responsible for negotiating these treaties should coordinate with IRS, Treasury, and Tax Division in deciding which countries should receive priority.

b. Limited tax treaties. Mutual assistance treaties apply only to criminal matters. In addition to mutual assistance treaties the United States might attempt to negotiate limited tax treaties with tax haven jurisdictions, along the lines suggested in Chapter VIII. They would include an exchange of information article overriding bank and commercial secrecy laws. See draft Model Exchange of Information and Administrative Assistance, Paragraph 2, at Appendix A to this chapter. The exchange of information article would cover both civil and criminal tax information.

c. Bilateral exchange of information agreements. Congress could empower the President to enter into bilateral executive agreements with foreign jurisdictions for the exchange of tax information. Arguably, the Internal Revenue Code disclosure of information provision contained in §6103(k)(4) would permit such agreements, in spirit if not literally. Technical amendment to the disclosure provision is recommended for the sake of clarity. In addition, the summons provisions of the Code should be amended to permit the United States to assist a foreign jurisdiction which is a party to such an agreement.

d. Revise exchange of information article. The Treasury
Department should consider amending the model exchange of
information provision to better comport with the realities
of international evidence gathering among countries with
disparate internal legal systems. A contracting country should
be obligated to use its best efforts within the framework of
its internal system to supply information pursuant to a
treaty request. The model, by considering mutuality of
legal systems among treaty partners, inhibits this. The
model should require a requested country to use whatever
procedures it has, even if the requesting country does not
have or cannot use similar procedures. A draft model article
is attached as Appendix A to this chapter.

e. Steps to isolate abusive tax havens. While most
tax havens deny any interest in attracting tainted money,
the United States receives little or no cooperation in
penetrating bank and commercial secrecy laws for tax administration
purposes. As described in various portions of this report,
this unwillingness to cooperate creates significant, and at
times insurmountable, problems for United States tax administrators, as well as members of the law enforcement community.
At some point the United States may determine that tax
havens are a sufficiently serious problem to require drastic
steps directed towards gaining access to such information,
either through a tax convention or an executive agreement.
One such step might be to adopt legislation specifically
aimed at tax havens which do not provide information necessary
to enable the United States to administer its tax laws, as well
as its other relevant laws. Any country which refused to
provide information necessary to prove the substance of a
transaction in a United States court of law would be designated
a tax haven. Any such legislation would, of course, have to
contain appropriate relief provisions to permit U.S. taxpayers
to rearrange their affairs without adverse tax consequences.
United States taxpayers would be denied tax benefit of any
transactions with a country so designated. The purpose
would be to discourage U.S. business activity in the tax
haven.

(i) The tax imposed on amounts paid from the United
States to a foreign individual or corporation in a designated
tax haven would be increased from 30 perent to 50 percent.
This rate would be applied to interest on deposits in U.S.
banks.

(ii) The proceeds of a loan from a designated tax
haven to a U.S. person would be taxable to the recipient as
ordinary income, unless that person could prove to the
satisfaction of the Commissioner, that the loan is bona fide,
and that the borrower does not have an interest in the
lender.

(iii) For purposes of §902, a foreign corporation organized in a designated tax haven would not be deemed to have paid any foreign taxes. In addition, the income from a designated foreign tax haven would be considered U.S. source income, so that it would not increase the numerator of the foreign tax credit limitation. This would effectively prohibit excess credits from other countries to offset U.S. taxes otherwise imposed on income from designated tax havens, and would discourage U.S. business from establishing sub-sidiaries in tax havens.

(iv) No deduction would be allowed for an expense or a loss arising out of a transaction entered into, with, or by an entity located in a designated tax haven, unless the taxpayer could establish by clear and convincing evidence, including records in the hands of third parties, that the transaction had in fact taken place and did not involve a related party. Inability to produce third party records because of local law would preclude the deduction or other tax effect claimed by the taxpayer.

(v) United States airlines might be prohibited from flying to a designated tax haven, and direct flights from the United States to or from the haven would be prohibited.

(vi) U.S. banks might be prohibited from conducting business in a designated tax haven. In the alternative, they may either be prohibited from making wire transfers from the United States to a designated tax haven, or from designated tax havens to the United States, or they may be required to report all wire transfers between a designated tax haven and the United States.

The following inducements might also be provided to encourage tax havens to provide information:

(i) An exception from the foreign convention rules of §274(a).

(ii) Technical tax administrative assistance to smaller tax havens and potential tax havens willing to enter into limited tax treaties, exchange of information agreements, or mutual assistance treaties covering fiscal crimes, with the United States. Any treaty would have to contain a meaning-ful exchange of information article which overrides present or later-enacted secrecy laws.

215

Article 26

EXCHANGE OF INFORMATION AND ADMINISTRATIVE ASSISTANCE

1. The competent authorites of the Contracting States shall exchange such information as is necessary for carrying out the provisions of this Convention or of the domestic laws of the Contracting States concerning taxes covered by the Convention insofar as the taxation thereunder is not contrary to the convention. The exchange of information is not restricted by Article 1 (Personal Scope). Any information received by a Contracting State shall be treated as secret in the same manner as information obtained under the domestic laws of that State and shall be disclosed only to persons or authorities (including courts and administrative bodies) involved in the assessment or collection of, the enforcement or prosecution in respect of, or the determination of appeals in relation to, the taxes covered by the Convention. Such persons or authorities shall use the information only for such purposes. They may disclose the information in public court proceedings or in judicial decisions.

2. The provisions of paragraph 1 shall be construed so as to impose on a Contracting State the obligation to establish laws and administrative practices which permit disclosure to its own competent authority of such information as is necessary for the carrying out of the provisions of this Convention or of the domestic laws of the Contracting States concerning taxes covered by this Convention. The provisions of paragraph 1 shall not be construed so as to impose on a Contracting State the obligation:

(a) to carry out administrative measures at variance with its laws and administrative practices;

(b) to supply information which is obtainable under the laws or administrative practice of neither Contracting State;

(c) to supply information which would disclose any trade, business, industrial, commercial or professional secret or trade process, or information, the disclosure of which would be contrary to public policy.

3. The competent authority shall promptly comply with a request for information, or, when appropriate, shall transmit it to the authority having jurisdiction to do so. The competent judicial officials and other officials of the Cotracting State requested to provide information shall do everything in their power to execute the request.

4.   If information is requested by a Contracting State in accordance with this Article, the other Contracting State shall obain the information to which the request relates in the same manner and to the same extent as if the tax of the first-mentioned State were the tax of that other State and were being imposed by that other State. If specifically requested by the competent authority of a Contracting State, the competent authority of the other Contracting State shall provide information under the Article in the form of depositions of witnesses and authenticated copies of unedited original documents (including books, papers, statements, records, accounts, or writings), to the same extent such depositions and documents can be obtained under the laws and administrative practices of such other State with respect to its own taxes.

5.   Each of the Contracting States shall endeavor to collect on behalf of the other Contracting State such amounts as may be necessary to ensure that relief granted by the present Convention from taxation imposed by such other Contracting State does not enure to the benefit of persons not entitled thereto.

6.   Paragraph 5 of this Article shall not impose upon either of the Contracting States the obligation to carry out administrative measures which are of a different nature from those used in the collection of its own tax, or which would be contrary to its sovereignty, security, or public policy.

7.   For the purpose of this Article, this Convention shall apply to taxes of every kind imposed by a Contracting State.

X. Administration

International issues in general, and tax haven related
issues in particular, are diffused throughout IRS functions
and programs. In addition, responsibility for these issues
shifts, at the litigation stage, either to the Office of the
Chief Counsel or to the Tax Division of the Justice Department.
Moreover, other agencies may be investigating a taxpayer
with respect to the nontax aspects of a case. This is
particularly likely to occur in narcotics related investigations
and in tax shelter investigations.

A. In General

The IRS annually processes over 95 million income tax
returns, sends out more than 27 million computer notices
and conducts over two million examinations of tax returns. It
is a highly decentralized organization. In the last fiscal
year the IRS employed an average of approximately 87,000
people. Approximately 5,000 of these people work in the
National Office in Washington, D.C. The remainder are
spread throughout seven regions and 58 districts in more
than 850 offices across the country and in 15 posts abroad.

The National Office provides policy direction and
program guidance and has principal responsibility for
allocating available resources among IRS programs and among
the regions. The regional offices, under the direction of
the Regional Commissioners, perform supervisory oversight
functions with respect to the districts and service centers
within their respective regions. The District and Service
Center Directors are responsible for the conduct of the
IRS's various programs, including the audit of returns
having international and tax haven issues and the investigation
of criminal cases.

Legal assistance to the IRS is provided by the Office
of the Chief Counsel. The office is divided into Regional
and District Counsel Offices. In addition, the Tax Division
of the Department of Justice litigates tax cases, other than
in the U.S. Tax Court.

The two principal IRS functions that establish policy
and overall direction with respect to enforcement of the tax
laws as they relate to tax havens are the Examination Division,
and the Criminal Investigation Division (CID). The principal
IRS function with day-to-day involvement in the foreign
area, in support of programs developed at the policy level
is the Office of International Operations (OIO). A brief
description of each of these functions follows.

1. Examination Division

The National Office Examination Division provides policy direction and program guidance for the examination of returns. The General Program Branch has program responsibility for a wide range of returns, while the Special Programs Branch develops programs for handling special cases, including international issues. Generally, field agents of the Examination Division audit U.S. persons doing business abroad and foreign subsidiaries of U.S. corporations.

The Examination Division programs that may cover tax haven issues include the general program, the fraud program, the coordinated examination program (which handles large cases and includes an industrywide program), the tax shelter/partnership program, the illegal tax protesters program, the unreported income program and the drug and narcotics program. The International Enforcement Program (IEP) provides specialists to assist examination agents with the international aspects of a case.

The IEP was part of OIO and was removed from OIO in a reorganization in the 1960's. This program is deployed on a key district concept. Presently, there are approximately 200 international agents in 11 key districts and 17 groups. The international examiners are specialized agents who assist revenue agents in the General Program when a referral is submitted. Most of the international examiners are assigned to the examination of large multinational corporations. International examiners generally do not work on tax haven cases concerning individuals, trusts, partnerships or small corporations.

The IEP includes a simultaneous examination program, which coordinates joint audits of multinational companies with certain of our treaty partners. One criterion for selecting a taxpayer for simultaneous examination is involvement of a tax haven. There is also an industrywide program that gathers and exchanges information on particular industries.

2. Office of International Operations

OIO was established in 1955 as a division under the Baltimore District. On May 1, 1956, it was transferred to the Office of Assistant Commissioner (Operations), now Office of Assistant Commissioner (Compliance). Over the years some organizational changes have been made to better enable OIO to deal better with international tax matters under its jurisdiction.

OIO is a district type office that, because of its unique jurisdictional base and structure, is organized within the Office of the Assistant Commissioner (Compliance). As in a district office, OIO has an Examination Division, Collection Division, Criminal Investigation Division and Taxpayer Service Division. In addition to these functions, there are the Foreign Programs, and Tax Treaty and Technical Services Divisions.

OIO examination agents audit returns of U.S. citizens residing abroad, foreign taxpayers (individual and corporate) having U.S. source income and returns filed by persons required to withhold tax on income paid to foreign persons. It conducts coordinated examinations of large foreign corporations and, on request from the field, it conducts support examinations of overseas subsidiaries of U.S.-based multinational corporations. It also examines estate and gift tax returns of both nonresident U.S. citizens and aliens. Groups of field agents specialize in foreign entertainers, athletes, banks and insurance companies.

OIO operates as a service organization for all 58 districts in securing information from foreign countries to the extent that the districts bring these matters to the attention of OIO. The Foreign Programs Division assists in the performance of functions under tax treaties, principally involving specific requests under the exchange of information provisions. The Division also coordinates and controls foreign travel of IRS employees and generally assists employees in the execution of assigned duties performed overseas.

The IRS has 15 foreign posts organized under the Foreign Programs Division, including a post in the Bahamas. The foreign activities of OIO are carried out by Revenue Service Representatives (RSR's) located at the foreign posts. They perform examination and collection functions directly and also pursuant to collateral requests from other IRS offices. On request of a district, they may obtain information in connection with a district criminal investigation. They hold conferences abroad for the Appeals Office, and assist in settling administratively with foreign counterparts any international tax disputes that arise under Competent Authority provisions of tax treaties.

The Tax Treaty and Technical Services Division accumulates and analyzes information concerning foreign tax laws and U.S. tax treaties. It also has responsibility for the preparation and negotiation of Competent Authority cases.

3. Criminal Investigations

The Criminal Investigation Division (CID) generally deals with fraud investigations of U.S. residents and citizens, including citizens residing abroad and nonresident aliens that are subject to U.S. filing requirements. The National Office CID assists field CID offices in special inquiries and assists in securing available information from foreign countries and U.S. possessions relating to tax matters under joint investigation.

The Criminal Investigation Division oversees 2,800 special agents that enforce the criminal statutes applicable to the tax laws. Special agents receive specialized professional training at the Federal Law Enforcement Training Center operated by the Department of Treasury. The special agents investigate criminal violations of the tax laws in joint investigations with revenue agents. They also participate in joint investigations with other agencies, often in a grand jury. The tax crimes investigated include bribes, kickbacks, laundered money and hidden deposits.

Special agents are located in each of the 58 IRS district offices throughout the country. Within each district, a Criminal Investigation Division is responsible for investigations within its area. OIO also has a Criminal Investigation Division which may investigate alleged criminal violations by taxpayers under OIO jurisdiction. Seven Assistant Regional Commissioners (Criminal Investigation) work functionally with the Office of the Director of CID in the National Office.

The criminal narcotics effort of the IRS is undertaken by CID and is coordinated in the National Office in the Special Enforcement Program by the High Level Drug Dealers Project, which focuses on major drug traffickers. The IRS has investigated some 1,200 cases since the inception of the project in July of 1976 and currently has under active investigation over 400 alleged drug traffickers. The IRS is also currently participating in 14 strike forces, in connection with which it is investigating some 270 organized crime cases.

Few of these cases (less than 10) involve narcotics. IRS management intends to increase the narcotics-related effort. In fiscal year 1981, it is estimated that 15 percent of CID's direct investigation time will be devoted to narcotics-related investigations.

In order to develop high quality narcotics cases
efforts are being made to improve coordination with the
Department of Justice, particularly the Controlled Substances
Unit under the direction of the U.S. Attorneys, and the cash
flow projects. Further efforts at better coordination with the
Drug Enforcement Administration (DEA) are proceeding and
investigations of leads supplied by the DEA are being stepped-
up. It is too early to determine how many of these will
result in prosecutions that involve the use of offshore tax
havens.

The IRS is also increasing its efforts to identify
potential criminal investigation targets. Additional work
is being done to increase the utilization of the currency
transaction reports (Form 4790) in cooperation with the
Customs Service. The IRS has also placed one full-time
agent at the El Paso Intelligence Center (EPIC) run by DEA.
EPIC is a computerized data base with numerous participating
federal and state agencies of which DEA is the leading
agency. EPIC is used for the detection, interdiction and
investigation of narcotics trafficking and financing. It is
hoped that placing an agent there will help the IRS to
identify high level drug traffickers and those helping them
to conduct their finances.

4. Office of the Chief Counsel

The Office of the Chief Counsel is organized in regions
and districts parallel to the IRS field structure. In the
National Office there are various divisions, including a
Criminal Tax Division, a General Litigation Division, a Tax
Litigation Division, an Interpretative Division, a Legislation
and Regulations Division and a Disclosure Division. Much
of the attorney time is spent in preparing, reviewing and
assisting in the development of substantive and procedural
guidance, including tax regulations, revenue rulings and
decisions to litigate.

There are also seven Regional Counsel and 45 District
Counsel. Most of the attorneys in the District Counsel
offices are engaged in tax court litigation; others advise
Justice attorneys on various matters, including summons
enforcement. One of the District Counsel offices services
OIO.

B. Analysis

The international examiners and the OIO agents are the IRS's international tax audit experts. Therefore, the manner in which they are trained and deployed can impact on all international audit areas, including tax havens. The agents in the General Program are not prohibited from examining international issues, and, in fact, there appears to be significant international activity in the general program.

1. Coordination

One of the most significant problems in international enforcement lies in achieving effective coordination between functions. The volume of international transactions with which the IRS must deal continues to grow. Issues become continuously more complex. Despite the continued efforts of management to maintain close liason and coordination in the international area, there are delays and failures of communication These problems impact particularly on the ability to deal with tax haven transactions, where the law and the schemes change rapidly and where it is important that up-to-date information be disseminated to the field.

Because IRS is a diverse decentralized organization, international tax matters, as any others, arise in many of the functions. Within the Office of the Assistant Commissioner (Compliance), international issues arise in both the international program and the general program of the Examination Division, in OIO, in CID, and in Collection. There is an international group in Technical. In the Chief Counsel's office, international issues are addressed by the Legislation and Regulations Division, by the Interpretative Division, and by the Tax Litigation Division, as well as by District Counsel attorneys in the course of litigation. Furthermore, the Department of Justice Tax Division deals with international issues in its consideration of civil and criminal cases.

The central problem is that there is no one person below the Assistant Commissioner level with whom one can discuss international compliance problems. For example, if it is necessary to gather information concerning civil international activities, both OIO and the Examination Division must be contacted.

The lack of centralized control also makes it difficult to be certain that tax haven cases are being properly controlled. For example, it is possible for OIO to refer matters to the field without clearance from the Examination Division. Accordingly, cases which IEP is trying to coordinate can inadvertantly be sent to the field.

This also creates problems of dissemination of information to the field. For example, general information that is gathered by IEP and disseminated to its agents is not necessarily given to OIO and CID agents. The converse is also true.

In addition, there appears to be some problem in coordination between Treasury's Office of International Tax Counsel and IRS. There is some feeling that IRS is consulted only on an ad hoc basis, making coordination between the overall needs of international tax administration and current treaty policy difficult. In part, this may result because of the difficulty of finding the proper person with whom to coordinate in IRS.

Another problem of coordination that was raised numerous times during our discussions with field agents is a perceived lack of communication between the field and OIO. The feeling was expressed that the problems arose particularly where a tax haven was involved. Some agents believe that their requests were not always handled as quickly as the field agents would have liked and that, at times, information that may have been available was not developed and sent to the field. The same problem was raised by attorneys in the Tax Division.

In part, the problem may be a failure of communication. CID agents, Examination agents, and Justice attorneys do not fully understand the problems faced by RSRs in gathering requested information. In part, the problem may lie in the procedures for referrals from the field to OIO. This procedure has recently been streamlined and an option for further streamlining is presented in Chapter IX.

Questions have been raised as to the adequacy of coordination between the IRS and other federal agencies concerned with offshore transactions. There seems to be a high level of coordination with respect to individual requests involving specific active cases. We are uncertain whether there is adequate coordination at higher levels on other than an ad hoc basis. There does not appear to be much coordination in the way of exchange of information on offshore issues.

Most coordination takes place at the case investigation
level. The Examination Division, which handles civil cases,
has a central coordinator or liaison with responsibility for
funneling field agents' requests for information to other
agencies. Often, there is a liaison person at the requested
agency with whom the IRS liaison can speak. There is no
central IRS liaison for requests from other agencies. The
other agency writes to the director of the IRS district
that has audit jurisdiction over their target. The request
is then routed through that district's disclosure office to
determine whether it can be honored. There is no centralized
file of such requests.

Liaison with the Commodity Futures Trading Corporation
(CFTC) is handled separately. Commodity shelters, partic-
ularly so-called "tax straddles," have become a major problem,
and are of particular concern to the IRS and the CFTC. The
IRS has established a shelter coordinator to monitor IRS
shelter activity, including commodity shelters. Liaison
with the CFTC is maintained directly by that coordinator.
This liaison includes funneling IRS field requests to the
CFTC as well as arranging for some joint training with the
CFTC. A procedure has been established under which the
CFTC will advise IRS when it has completed an investigation,
thus IRS can conduct a tax investigation if warranted. The
CFTC, however, has rarely become involved in offshore transactions,
because it does not have jurisdiction unless the offshore
transactions are being conducted through a domestic broker.

CID has a liaison person in the National Office who
funnels requests from the field to other agencies. In CID,
however, much of the routine coordination occurs at the
field level. National office liaison is available to those
agencies that prefer to deal with the National Office. Most
agencies apparently prefer to deal directly with the field
and come to the National Office only if there is a liaison
problem. The general feeling is that the liaison works well
within the bounds set by the disclosure rules.

There are special coordination procedures with the Drug
Enforcement Administration (DEA) with respect to narcotics
investigations. CID has a separate DEA liaison person.
Most of the contact is at the local level where it can be
focused on ongoing investigations. The National Office
generally attempts to facilitate local level contacts and to
arrange for new methods of cooperation, should that be necessary. In addition, approximately 32 percent of the currently
active narcotics cases are before grand juries, coordinated
by the Assistant U.S. Attorney conducting the grand jury.
Most of these grand juries involve multiagency investigations.

With respect to ongoing investigations of major drug dealers and other major financial crimes, interagency coordination can best be achieved through the grand jury. There the U.S. Attorney can provide direction and coordinate the efforts of the various agencies involved. It also overcomes some of the coordination problems caused by the disclosure rules of §6103.

At the beginning of this study some agents in the IRS and other agencies expressed the opinion that it took too long for IRS to approve participation in a grand jury investigation Steps have been taken to speed up the review process for grand jury clearance, and most agents we talked with were hopeful that the problem had been minimized.

There is also an interagency narcotics-oriented group that meets to discuss general offshore problems and to share expertise involving offshore cases.

There appears to be little routine regular coordination at the managerial level, either in the civil cases involving the Examination Division or in the criminal cases involving CID.

2. <u>Coverage of Tax Haven Cases - Availability of Expertise</u>

Another significant problem is the lack of expert coverage of smaller tax haven cases. During 1980, the Tax Haven Study Group sent a questionnaire to 6,085 General Program agents. Two thousand five hundred responded that they had closed a case involving a foreign transaction during the preceding 12 months. A second questionnaire prepared in an attempt to get more detailed information on certain specific international transactions indicated that a significant number of these cases involved a tax haven. This survey of the General Program indicated that agents are raising international issues, but the survey did not attempt to evaluate the merit, quality or development of these issues. Nevertheless, we did note that General Program agents, particularly those who handled smaller cases, did not always seem to understand the international issues in general, and the special problems of tax havens in particular. Often, the agents did not distinguish between the IEP and OIO.

International Enforcement Agents deal primarily with large cases. In many districts, the international enforcement program does not have the resources to handle a significantly increased work load, which would likely result if more referrals from the General Program were made. Furthermore, because they have not had the opportunity to work the cases, agents in the International Program did not appear to be knowledgeable about tax haven-type entities commonly used by individuals, such as trusts and partnerships. As a result, tax haven issues often do not get adequate coverage.

In fact, the Internal Revenue Manual sets forth mandatory requirements for selecting for audit, domestic corporate returns having stated international characteristics.[1] However, there are no mandatory requirements for selecting domestic individual, partnership, and fiduciary returns indicating foreign business transactions or interest in foreign financial accounts.[2] Thus, the tendency would be for corporate rather than individual returns to be scrutinized.

During discussions with field personnel it has been stated that there is a reluctance to examine tax returns with international tax issues, and tax haven issues in particular, because of the difficulty of obtaining information, and because such cases were perceived as taking more time than domestic cases. This perception may have been due to a lack of understanding of the issues.

It is obvious that practitioners are aware of, and take advantage of, both the lack of coverage and the lack of coordination. It would appear that at least some tax planning using tax havens for smaller taxpayers results in transactions that are not receiving expert coverage; some of these are the most abusive transactions.

The staff resources devoted to international issues, and tax haven issues in particular, have not kept pace with the growth in international business. As indicated in Chapter III, data show that U.S. direct investment levels in foreign corporations almost tripled from 1968 to 1978, and that earnings increased four times. During the same period the number of international examiners only doubled, from 94 to 192. As of the end of 1980, there were 209 international examiners. A concomitant problem is that overall audit coverage has not increased since 1971, and in fact has declined since 1976. In 1976 2.59 percent of relevant returns were audited,

---

[1] IRM 4171.22.

[2] IRM 4171.21(1).

while in fiscal year 1980 only 2.12 percent were audited.
If current budget requests are not supplemented, it is
projected that coverage may drop to 1.86 percent in 1981.
This means that the IRS will not be able to do its job in
the tax haven area. More coverage is necessary and additional
resources are needed to provide that coverage.

3. Providing Technical and Legal Assistance to the Field

Adequate technical expertise is not available to the
field on a routine basis. In the course of an audit, an
agent can request technical assistance from the Assistant
Commissioner (Technical). This, however, is a formal procedure
that can require significant time. Accordingly, the
tendency is not to use it in many cases. The process is not
available to a CID agent and was never intended to be.
Furthermore, there is no central repository of knowledge on
tax haven problems. Accordingly, new developments in the
tax havens themselves, or in the use of tax havens by U.S.
persons, are not brought to the attention of agents or
others who can deal with them. Part of the problem is
coordination, which was addressed above.

Tax shelter cases that come to the attention of Technical's
tax shelter group are an exception. If needed, a ruling can
be prepared and issued on an expedited basis.

In CID, unless there is a local agent who has gained
some expertise on offshore cases, there is no ready source
of knowledge about tax haven problems to whom a special agent
can turn for guidance.

Examination and CID agents have only limited access to
research tools and current publications. The IRS National
Office Library did not even have some of the more regularly
used tax haven publications. OIO has a library, but, as a
practical matter, it cannot be used by district agents on a
regular basis.

A related problem is the lack of expert legal assistance to CID during the course of a criminal investigation.
Tax haven cases are often more complex and difficult to
develop than domestic cases. The law involving foreign
transactions and reporting requirements is among the most
complex in the Internal Revenue Code. Moreover, criminal
cases often involve violations of nontax statutes, which
can present complicated legal issues.

CID agents are well trained and experienced financial investigators. They are not necessarily experts in the technicalities of the tax law. Accordingly, considering the complex legal issues that arise in the course of a tax haven investigation, it would be useful if CID agents could get legal assistance during an investigation.

It does not appear that special agents have a significant level of legal assistance available to them during an investigation As a general rule, a lawyer is involved only after the investigation is completed, and then only in the course of review of a prosecution recommendation by the District Counsel, Department of Justice's Tax Division, or the U.S. Attorney. As a result, some cases are declined during the review process because of a legal flaw that might have been corrected had an attorney assisted during an investigation. Alternative approaches could have been recommended, or the case dropped before significant resources were expended.

IRS does have a procedure that permits CID to pre-refer cases to District Counsel during an investigation. However, it is rarely used. There are a number of reasons for this. With respect to tax havens, a primary reason is that CID agents believe district counsel attorneys rarely have the expertise to help with the complicated international and criminal issues.

4. Simultaneous and Industrywide Examinations

The Simultaneous Examination Program has become an important focus of the IEP. Basically, the program is a coordinated exchange of information between the U.S. and one of its treaty partners with respect to designated taxpayers. The selection criteria and procedures for each country with which we have a program are set forth in a manual supplement. One of the stated objectives of the program is to improve procedures for exchanging information to be used in examinations of multinational companies which have intragroup transactions that may involve tax havens.

The chief advantage of the program is that it allows each country to see a transaction from both sides. For example, if a foreign company is exporting goods from France to a tax haven and then selling from the tax haven to the U.S., the IRS, under the simultaneous program, can get from France information regarding the sales price. Without the simultaneous program, it is often difficult to get this kind of information in a timely manner. The program does appear to have limits. The tax years under audit must be the same in each country, and as a practical matter, the

taxpayer must have significant international transactions of
interest to both countries. The program, by its nature, is
most useful for cases involving larger companies or cases
involving many taxpayers (such as a tax shelter case). The
program can only be used with treaty partners, and IRS will
probably not be able to arrange programs with all of them.

5. Chief Counsel

International expertise in the Chief Counsel's Office
is diffused among a number of divisions and is not available to the field on a routine basis. While there is specialized international expertise in the National Office, there
is little in the Regional and District Counsel offices.
Field agents often complain that they cannot get expert
legal assistance in tax haven cases. There is no formal
coordination between the international functions in the
various Chief Counsel divisions.

Some of the most difficult tax haven issues involve
international information gathering. However, there is little
international information gathering expertise in Chief Counsel
offices. Today, the Chief Counsel experts are in OIO District
Counsel. Its primary function is to service OIO, which
takes up most of its time. In addition, it provides assistance
to the field upon request. However, they do not get many requests
and we have found that many field personnel are not aware of
the existence of this expertise. The Office does not have the
resources to promote itself.

C. Options

Described below are numerous options that might be
considered for changes in IRS administrative practices and
training to better deal with tax haven related problems. As
with other areas addressed in this report, it is often
difficult to separate tax haven issues from other international
issues. Accordingly, some of the options presented below
should be considered for international issues in general.

1. Improve Coordination With Respect to Tax Haven Issues Specifically and International Issues in General

Improved coordination with respect to tax haven transactions
is needed within the IRS and in the Office of the Assistant
Commissioner (Compliance) in particular. In fact, better
coordination of international issues in general appears
warranted. Furthermore, more focused attention on tax
havens is needed.

The decentralization of the IRS makes coordination particularly difficult. With respect to tax havens, there is a threshold problem that there is no centralized group to gather information. Consideration should be given to creating a unit in the National Office that would coordinate Examination and OIO programs involving tax havens, keep abreast of current tax haven planning and information, and most importantly, disseminate this information to field personnel. The information dissemination function and coordination function should also include CID. This group could make materials available to Examination and CID, provide a certain level of expertise to the field, and keep apprised of developments in the area. Members of the group could attend seminars and prepare reports that would be made available to the agents. Materials gathered at seminars could likewise be disseminated to the field. Further, the group could coordinate with programs, such as the tax shelter program, which include cases that involve significant tax haven issues. The group might also coordinate with other agencies concerned with tax havens.

Creating such a group would, however, further fragment the international area. The Assistant Commissioner (Compliance) should study ways in which coordination among the various compliance functions dealing with tax haven issues can be improved. The goal should be to have one person in the Assistant Commissioner's office who would be aware of the international issues in Compliance, and who would be familiar with tax treaties and the foreign information gathering activities of the IRS. This person might have personnel who would concentrate on monitoring important international issues, gathering information, and providing guidance and assistance to the field. Providing a central focus would also improve coordination with other Assistant Commissioners,[3] Chief Counsel and Treasury's Office of International Tax Counsel.

Consideration should be given to appointing an offshore coordinator in CID. This person could disseminate tax haven information to the field, and could act as a liaison with other groups within IRS, Chief Counsel and other government agencies with respect to tax haven matters.

---

[3] The Assistant Commissioner (Compliance), for example, is the Competent Authority for treaty interpretation, but the Assistant Commissioner (Technical) must concur in interpretations.

OIO might also explore means of improving communications with the field and Justice's Tax Division. Any study by the Assistant Commissioner to determine ways in which coordination can be improved might also focus on means for improving coordination between the overseas information gathering functions of the IRS and the field. Seeking broad experience, as well as foreign language skills in appropriate cases, might be useful.

As described above, while there appears to be adequate coordination with respect to individual cases and gathering information in individual cases, we see inadequate coordination with respect to tax haven issues at a more strategic level. It was our sense from visiting and discussing problems with personnel in other agencies that it would be useful to arrange for some meetings at a managerial level to determine what kind of information sharing could be done. In some respects this is happening with the ad hoc group on narcotics. However, a high level group, focusing on more than narcotics, might be worthwhile.

2. Increase Coverage of Tax Haven Cases

It is clear that the use of tax havens by U.S. taxpayers is significant and is growing. There are large numbers of cases with tax haven issues under audit in the general program. Very few agents in the general program, however, have the expertise to deal with complicated and unique tax haven cases. The IEP contains Examination's international experts, but they focus primarily on large cases. As a consequence, the failure to take on smaller cases has prevented the development of a body of expertise in the international trust, partnership and shelter area in the field. As a result, some tax haven cases are not being adequately developed because most regular agents do not have the training or experience to deal with them. Accordingly, taxpayers can abuse the system with a good chance of success.

The IEP could be expanded to enable it to give more assistance in smaller cases, including those of individuals engaged in shelter or trust transactions involving tax havens. Increased coverage would require that additional agents be assigned to the international program. A decision must be made by managment as to whether such an expansion is justified if it is at the expense of audit coverage elsewhere. Additional agents should be specifically allocated to auditing individuals and smaller companies. This would help to insure that smaller international cases receive adequate attention.

If the IEP is expanded, consideration should be given to mandatory requirements for selecting or referring for audit or assistance individual, partnership and fiduciary returns indicating international transactions involving tax havens. Because some of the more elusive schemes involve non-filers or returns which appear to lack audit potential, it will often be necessary to identify the schemes and the promoters in order to identify the tax returns.

3. Expand Training of International Examiners to Include Noncorporate Issues and Expand Training of Agents in the General Program

Because the International Examiners generally handle large cases involving multinational corporations, they get little exposure to trust or partnership issues. Their training does not cover these issues. If it were decided to expand the IEP as suggested above, then training should include partnerships and trusts.

At times, it appears that agents are not thoroughly familiar with the problems faced by taxpayers in complying with requests for information. Misunderstandings and unnecessary confrontation can result. In addition, today most training is done by the IRS's own agents who, because they are dealing with prior years' tax returns, may not be completely aware of the most recent developments.

To correct this situation, arrangements could be made to hold short training sessions conducted by outside persons. Outside experts could give agents valuable insight into the methods businesses follows in operating. For example, the Federal Bureau of Investigation has a program under which financial experts from the Wharton School of Business teach courses in international banking. They have found this extremely useful in helping their agents to deal with bank fraud cases.

Tax haven awareness training, as well as some general international training, should be given to agents in the general program. Today, many agents in the regular program are not aware of tax haven problems. They do not realize, for example, that transactions involving the Turks and Caicos Islands or Belize are potentially questionable. General training does not make them aware of these kinds of issues, nor does it make them familiar with foreign trusts, foreign bank accounts or other foreign transactions.

233

It would appear that the level of international activities in the general program is high enough that some awareness training, as well as some basic training, could be provided. We would suggest that any awareness training and general international training describe the IEP and OIO, and the referral procedures to each. We found significant confusion among agents as to the distinction between the two programs.

Furthermore, training could give some guidance on dealing with dilatory tactics of taxpayers. Some taxpayers employ delaying tactics when dealing with an IRS agent, particularly where tax haven issues are involved. It is not clear how widespread this problem is, but it clearly exists. In many cases agents are not prepared to deal with these tactics. Agents should be schooled in the basic principle that if the taxpayer fails to corroborate a deduction, the deduction can be denied without the IRS having to go through unreasonable attempts to obtain records. Techniques for setting up §482 adjustments and for denying deemed paid credits where adequate information is not made available could also be taught.

4. Provide Additional Technical and Legal Expertise to the Field

There is clearly a need to provide the field with additional technical expertise. Establishing a tax haven coordinator or group within Compliance might help as might appointing an offshore expert in CID.

Another option that should be considered is to make legal assistance available to agents, particularly CID agents, during the course of an investigation. While adoption of this option would require expenditure of resources, this guidance might replace District Counsel post-investigation review in offshore cases, and thus save the attorney time expended in performing that review. In addition, it would enable District Counsel attorneys to gain much needed experience in both international and criminal issues.

5. Expansion of the Simultaneous Examination Program and the Industrywide Exchange of Information Programs

The Simultaneous Examination Program has already proved useful in dealing with tax haven related cases. It has the potential to be one of the most useful programs for auditing tax haven cases. At the same time, however, it also has the potential to be costly from the point of view of National Office management time. The industrywide program appears to be developing useful knowledge concerning the tax haven operation of a few industries. Consideration should be given to expanding these programs, both by adding additional treaty partners, and by increasing the number of cases under simultaneous examination. This expansion must be coupled, however, with careful monitoring to insure that the program does not grow beyond a useful level, that the best cases are being identified, and that the U.S. is getting its share of the benefits.

6. Chief Counsel

Consideration should be given to designating a National Office attorney as the international evidence gathering expert for Chief Counsel.

As described in Chapter IX, international information gathering is complicated, time consuming and presents unique legal issues. The necessary expertise can only be acquired by seeing a large number of problems. A person who is the focal point for all Chief Counsel information gathering problems would eventually develop that expertise.

This expertise could best be developed and made available to the field by designating one National Office Chief Counsel lawyer as the internal information gathering expert. This person's primary function would be to give guidance to field personnel with international information gathering problems. He could visit district offices in order to make them aware of the availability of his services. In the alternative, this function could be left in OIO District Counsel, but with additional resources so that they could devote more time to educating other district counsel and the field as to the availability of their expertise and to following up on cases to further develop the expertise.

An advantage to keeping the function in OIO District Counsel is that a number of attorneys, including a career-oriented District Counsel, would gain expertise. There is less chance that the expertise would be lost if one attorney left an office. On the other hand, a National Office person would be able to focus more clearly on providing a service to the field, because that would be his sole function. The OIO District Counsel office also services OIO and the same focus is accordingly not as easy to develop.

The Justice Department has, in its Criminal Division, an Office of International Affairs that provides such expertise to that department. Their Tax Division has recently designated one of its attorneys as its international information gathering expert. A Chief Counsel expert could develop contacts in that and other Federal offices concerned with similar problems.

Further, consideration should be given to designating one attorney in each of certain key districts as the international expert for the region or for a number of districts. An international expert could assist agents in Examination and CID when they are faced with difficult technical issues or with international information gathering problems. These attorneys might also be available to advise or assist Chief Counsel attorneys litigating complicated international cases.

Capital Preservation Through Global Investing

Investing globally is one of the most successful ways to accomplish capital preservation and growth. In books such as *The Complete Guide to Tax Havens* and *The Conservative Wealthbuilder: Capital Preservation Through Global Investing*, Adam Starchild reveals how you can create an ultimate global portfolio of investments to hedge against inflation, taxes, confiscations, market, fluctuations, currency devaluations, economic and political turmoil...

Starchild reveals the little-known investment secrets that he has been giving to his clients for the past few decades. His recommendations are not high-flying investment tips, but rather solid, conservative recommendations that over time will help build a healthy nest-egg for you.

You will learn how to build a secret stash of cash that:

- You can access at any time
- Is tax-free and seizure proof
- Pays competitive dividends and interest
- And has no government reporting requirements (even for Americans)

In fact, if you had put $ 10,000 each year into this investment or the last twenty years you would have $590,697 today!

You will also discover:

- How to accumulate income tax-free
- Why offshore mutual funds should form a vital part of your global portfolio
- How to invest in gold, silver and platinum and the investor potential of these precious metals
- Why Switzerland should play an essential part in any global nest-egg strategy
- How and where to best form an offshore trust in order to provide tax and creditor protection for your investments
- How to invest tax-free in the United States

Everything you need to get yourself started on a global path to a secure fortune is in The Conservative Wealthbuilder. Starchild's techniques have been used by many of the world's wealthiest people for decades, including presidents, kings, Arab sheiks... And now for the first time they are available to you. They have been tested and proven over time. You will not find a safer, surer path to financial security than that mapped out for you in this unique work!

Just published (ISBN 0894990500), *The Conservative Wealthbuilder* is available through major bookstores and online booksellers. Also recently published (ISBN 1893713105) *The Complete Guide to Tax Havens* provides a wealth of information on forming offshore corporations and trusts.

The following sections are excerpts from *The Conservative Wealthbuilder* and other books by Adam Starchild:

Investing for the Offshore Entity

Investing for the offshore entity is just as important as creating the corporation or trust in the first place. Failure to invest the corpus and reinvest the income is one of the surest ways to squander the benefits that come from creation of an offshore corporation or trust. Astute choices in investment can lead to the realization of personal financial goals and, potentially, financial freedom. A problem often arises when one considers where to invest his money because there are so many options. Selecting the wrong ones can, at best, hinder the achievement of financial goals, and, at the worst, result in financial ruin. It is important to bear in mind that the investing is as important as the creation and structuring of the offshore entity.

Asset Allocation — The Key To Successful Investing

One of the newest forms of investments in America is called asset allocation. Basically what it means is that one investment is "allocated" to a number of different types of investments by a professional investment allocator. The reason for this allocation is that no one type of investment is the best in all investment climates, and no one type of investment is usually appropriate for all of one person's investment money.

By using an asset allocation program, a person can invest a large amount of his principal in one place, gaining ease of tracking the investment, while attaining the advantage of having a number of different investments to serve his different investment objectives.

The asset allocator performs the service for the investor of allocating varying amounts of a total investment into different areas of investing, such as income stocks, growth stocks, small capitalization stocks, etc., and a variety of fixed income securities.

For modest to medium-sized investments, one method of attaining even more diversification of investments, and expertise in the actual details of the investments, is to allocate the investment among various top-rated mutual funds. As is well known, mutual funds can perform a number of important tasks for the investor. Diversification among a large number of stocks is possible for even a relatively small sum of money. Expertise is available on any type of investment at a relatively low price. Last, there is great liquidity with ease of purchasing and selling.

The actual allocation into different mutual funds will depend upon three principal criteria:

(1) What is the risk to reward profile of the individual investor,
(2) What is the need of the investor for predictable current income as opposed to the desire for capital gains, and

(3) What is the state of the economic and investment cycles at the particular moment in time.

The first and most important criteria are clearly the needs of the investor. These outweigh any thoughts of where any market may be going or where an allocator believes that the most money can be made. The first need which needs to be addressed is the risk which the investor is prepared to accept. All investment involves some degree of risk, but that risk can rage from the minor risk of how inflation can impact an investment in the next 90 days, to the risk of a high flying initial public offering in a company which may have no earnings and no prospect for earnings in the foreseeable future.

The amount of risk which is appropriate for an individual investor depends upon both the investors actual economic situation and his psychological attitudes towards risk of loss. Human temperament plays a very large role in determining risk tolerance. For example, if a person remembers a period of his or her past where they did not have enough money to make ends meet, they may be very adverse to taking any risk at all. Their attitude may be, "We worked hard for that money, and we don't want to lose it."

Others may have almost the opposite approach. They may never have known deprivation, and may have earned a good income all their life. Their attitude may be that they can live very well on their current earnings, and so any savings can be used to speculate. If the speculation turns out to be successful, that will be great and they can raise their standard of living even further. But if the speculation doesn't work out, that's OK too because they will simply continue living as they have.

Thus a good investment allocator will first determine what the needs of his clients are with respect to risk. One method is to determine first how much money is needed to maintain the current standard of living of the investor, and if he or she is not yet retired, how much of the investment will be needed when they do retire. Whatever amount is needed for these purposes is then designated as income producing principal and is invested accordingly into low-risk, high-yielding investments.

The balance can then be invested according to the investor's wishes into areas which can offer the promise of large capital gains in the future. This is the risk portion of the principal, and care must be taken so that the allocator and the investor agree on what amount of risk is to be taken.

The third and equally important task of allocating is to attempt to maximize the return to the investor from the changes in the economic cycle. When business has been in a slump and starts to turn up with both interest rates and inflation low, the largest profits are typically made in the stock market. But as the economy continues to expand, interest rates will rise and so will inflation. These factors make the prognosis for the economy less rosy, and the stock market may start to gyrate, and then fall. Perhaps gently at first and then more rapidly. So the stock market is definitely not the place to be.

At the same time that the stock market is suffering from inflation, the price of hard assets such as gold, oil, and real estate could well be rising rapidly. It is in these areas that fortunes are made during inflationary periods in the economy.

And then as the economy finally begins to cool down due to the effect of high interest rates, interest rates will begin to fall nd the big money may be made by investing in long-term non-callable bonds.

Thus a good allocator must keep in mind the needs of the individual investor and the current status of the economy. And of course he must have an intimate familiarity with specific investments which are available to investors. Whether they be stocks, bonds, or fixed income securities, the allocator must know which are appropriate for the investor and which will likely do well in the present stage of the economy.

As with options in the preceeding chapter, the expertise of Max G. Ansbacher is once again quite useful. His credentials in the stock market are equally impressive. The second book he wrote is titled How to Profit from the Coming Bull Market and it was published in the summer of 1981 near the bottom of the long bear market which had actually begun in 1973.

This book explained how and why a strong bull market was about to start on Wall Street. At the time it was published the book was largely ignored by a public which had grown cynical about a stock market which seemed to do nothing but go sideways or down, year after year.

But just one year after Mr. Ansbacher's book was published, the market suddenly took off like a rocket in August 1982, igniting one of its greatest bull markets ever and establishing Mr. Ansbacher's reputation as an insightful student of the stock market.

We recently asked Mr. Ansbacher what his philosophy was concerning asset allocation. He replied, "Asset allocation is probably the most important single aspect of any investment program. And yet what is so strange about it is that it is often not even considered by investors. Some people will have most of their money in the stock market most of the time, unaware of the large risks which the market sometimes contains. Others believe in bonds, and continue to invest most or all of their money there, apparently unaware that in the 1970's and early 1980's the bond market was the biggest money loser of any investment. I would say that asset allocation is not just important, it is the key to successful investing."

Mr. Ansbacher went follows a deliberatly planned, carefully crafted strategy when handling an asset allocation account for a client. "The first thing I do is to talk to the client in whatever depth is necessary to determine the proper risk profile for the client. This depends upon his current financial situation and what he foresees for his future situation as well as his psychological feelings towards money and the potential loss of money. The second thing I do is to make an outline of the client's need for current income. This naturally has a great deal of influence on how we can invest the funds."

"Only after this has been done, do I then discuss with the client where I think the financial markets are heading and where the best returns are likely to be made in the future. The first step in actually making the investments are to decide upon the proportion of money going into each class of investments. The second part is to select the actual investments. For a number of reasons, I select from among the thousands of mutual funds which are available in the U.S. They range all the way from bond to preferred stocks, to common stocks of all types. There is usually a time and a place for almost all of them, but we try to pick the best one for that particular client at that particular time in the client's life, and in the life of the markets."

Mr. Ansbacher explained that his minimum investment is $100,000, and that he works with some of the biggest mutual fund organizations in the U.S., including Fidelity, Dreyfus and other mutual fund management firms. He does not bill his clients for a fee or commission for the work he does, because his compensation is paid to him by the mutual funds.

We have always believed that to be a good asset allocator is one of the most difficult tasks in the investment world, because it requires so many different considerations. To see just what kind of factors Mr. Ansbacher considers we asked him how he would go about planning an asset allocation program we asked him about a potential (though fictitious) client: a 50-year-old German married man who earns the equivalent of $200,000 a year and has a well-funded pension plan with his company. He is in good health and plans to retire at about the age of 65. We asked Mr. Ansbacher to assume that this man comes to him with $300,000 to invest. Here is how Mr. Ansbacher went about making his asset allocation process.

Mr. Ansbacher's recommendation? "The first question I have is about the amount of $300,000. Since he has a pension plan with his company, it is obviously not pension money. It is also a rather large amount for a person earning $200,000 to want to invest in the U.S. Is it inherited money? Does his wife earn money? Is this his life savings? Did he make a successful investment? The reason I ask this question is that it is very important to know if the money is replaceable. If it is inherited, will there be more to follow, or is this all? First I would want to know whether there will be more money coming in or not."

"Second, I would want to know more about his potential future obligations. Do he or his wife having living parents or other relatives who may need financial support in the future? How much support, if any, does he expect that his children will need in the future? Does he have disability insurance or a company plan in case he becomes disabled before he retires? Is there some specific financial goal that he has, such as acquiring a vacation home, yacht or other item which will require a substantial amount of ready cash. All these factors related to the amount of risk which I would want to take."

"The next set of considerations center around his financial situation now. Since he lives in Germany, this means that he pays a high tax on income such as dividends and interest, but pays no capital gains tax. Right away that sways me into investments which are likely to have high capital gains. I would want to know whether the $200,000 he earns covers all of his current expenses, or whether his current standard of living is so high that he needs extra income each year."

"Once we have the answers to these questions, we can begin to solve the problem of how best to allocate this investment. If there are no likely financial needs coming up in the future, and if at the time of the investment I decide that the stock market is not over priced or likely to decline for other reasons, I would place most of the money into various stock funds. I am particularly fond of funds which use value investing, which means that they pick stocks based upon how large an amount of earnings one gets for each dollar invested. This is another way of saying that they seek out stocks with high quality and low price/earnings ratios."

"The reason I like value investing is that many studies have shown that low price/earnings stocks outperform other stocks in normal markets. And in down markets heir inherent value keeps them from falling as far as others. The second group of stocks I would pick would be senior growth stocks. This means stocks which grow year after year because they are gaining market share, or because they are in a solid growth industry. Examples of this are some pharmaceutical companies which are constantly creating new and better drugs, or highly efficient national retail chains which are constantly gaining market share over local competitors."

"One advantage which growth stocks have for this particular client is that they usually don't pay a very large dividend, which fits right in which his local tax structure. Depending upon the wishes of the client, we would consider some gold stocks as a hedge against inflation. And we might add some mutual funds which specialize in large capitalization companies, because these are the tried and proven winners among all the competition in the economy, and often outperform other stocks when the economy softens."

"I would also place a portion of the assets into a short or medium term bond fund for three reasons:

(1) This could be a source of money in case an emergency arose which required a withdrawal from the fund,
(2) It is a reserve in case some outstanding bargains come up for investment, and
(3) It is a hedge against a downturn in the stock market."

Of course the actual percentage allocations would be discussed with the client. The actual funds selected would depend upon their performance records at the time of the investment. And in general, much of the allocation would depend upon the state of the economy at the time of the investment."

Good advice. From a man well-qualified to give it.

Investing in Options

Another vehicle to consider investing your money is in options. Specifically, trading options on stocks or on a stock index (such as the Standard & Poor's 500 Index). This is route is particularly appealing to foreigners, since the gain or loss from trading in options is a capital gain, and any profits made by a foreigner from trading in such options are free from any tax imposed by the United States.

But, as many investors already know, options are notoriously speculative and most people who try trading in them wind up losing money. Therefore, in order to take advantage of this tax benefit, it is first imperative to find a method of trading options which has a good probability of actually making money.

Almost any method of trading options which has the chance of making an above average return also carries a commensurate high degree of risk. But some practitioners of the arcane art of options trading do manage to do better than others over the years. One such person who has done very well for his clients is Max G. Ansbacher, Chairman of Ansbacher Investment Management, Inc., located in the prestigious Rockefeller Center complex in New York City.

Mr. Ansbacher has a long and distinguished involvement with options. In fact, he is the author of the first book published on the modern form of options, titled The New Options Market, Revised and Enlarged Edition, first published in 1975. Today, he manages accounts for investors in both the U.S. and overseas.

What sets Mr. Ansbacher apart from many others is that he has an excellent record of bringing in above average profits for his clients. Since most people who buy options seem to lose money, we asked Mr. Ansbacher what the key was to his success. He replied, "Yes, I agree that most people who buy options do seem to lose money. But what many people don't realize is that the money which the options buyers lose, doesn't disappear from the face of the earth. Rather it becomes the profits of the options sellers. And therefore, I concentrate in selling options."

What Mr. Ansbacher was saying is that options trading is actually a zero sum game when one looks at the total overall economic effect. This means that buying and selling options has no overall impact on the economy. It neither creates any money or lose any (except transaction costs). If the sellers make money, the buyers lose money. And if the buyers make money, then the sellers must lose money.

Since the options buyers tend to be the ones who lose money, it therefore must be true that the options sellers are the ones who make money over the long run. "The options buyers tend to be less sophisticated than the sellers," Mr. Ansbacher explained. "They don't always carefully assess the chances that their stocks will really go up enough to make money when they buy a call. Similarly, if people think a stock or a stock market is going to go down, they often over estimate how much it is going to go down. They will buy a put which is going to lose money unless the stock makes a really unusually large move within a relatively short period of time. These are the options I sell."

Of course there is not an investment program yet invented which makes money on every single trade, and option selling is no exception. Mr. Ansbacher said, "Certainly there are times when we have losses, but we believe that the probability lies with the sellers. And so we usually find that every loss is matched by many more winners."

If you do become involved in selling options, the best advise is: proceed with caution! Never forget that the risk factor is high. How does a veteran like Mr. Ansbacher control this risk? He said that the first defense was to control the number of options which he sells. "I usually sell only about one fifth the number of options which margin rules permit me to do. The second line of defense is that I use stop loss orders, which in most instances will automatically get me out of the options before the losses rise to a point which I consider unacceptable."

He continued, "The most interesting line of defense and the most important from the point of view of making money, is that I sell out-of-the-money options. This means that I sell options which have a strike price which is a distance away from the current price of the underlying security." We should point out that a strike price is the level at which an option becomes effective.

What Mr. Ansbacher means is that if a stock is 100, for example, he will not sell the 100 strike price call, because it is tool likely that the stock will go above 100 and he might lose money. Instead, he might sell the call with a strike price of 120. The stock would have to be above 120 at the option's expiration for the seller of the option to sustain a loss. Obviously it is less likely that a stock will go up 20 points than it will merely go up a few points. So, by selling out-of-the-money options, Mr. Ansbacher is able to shift the probabilities in his favor.

Another major decision which an options trader has to make is whether to be trading calls, which go up in price when a stock goes up, or puts which go up in price when the stock goes down. Mr. Ansbacher said that he makes this decision based upon a number of factors, including his long experience in the field. "One of the factors I rely upon, is my own Ansbacher Index. This Index tells me whether the puts or the calls are higher priced. Since I am selling these options, I will generally choose to sell the ones which are higher priced. I believe the Index also gives an indication of which way the stock market is likely to go in the intermediate future." Thus, Mr. Ansbacher can sell options on the stock market which will be profitable for his clients if the market moves as The Ansbacher Index indicates it is likely to do.

The minimum account which Mr. Ansbacher accepts is US$100,000, and he accepts accounts from people residing anywhere in the world. Depending upon the type of account, the investor will receive monthly or quarterly statements giving the exact value of theaccount.

For more information contact:

Ansbacher Investment Management, Inc.
Attn: New Clients Information
45 Rockefeller Plaza, 20th Floor
New York NY 10111
telephone: (212) 332-3280
fax: (212) 332-3283; Attn: New Clients Information

Swiss Financial Experts

Swiss investment managers are experienced in working with investors from around the world. Most are fluent in English and have substantial experience in managing various types of investments. They are comfortable managing an investor's entire portfolio if he wishes; however, for investors who prefer to make their own financial decisions, Swiss advisers are happy to offer their expertise to the degree it is required. They can help you manage your investments, or manage them for you - whichever arrangement makes you feel more comfortable. For the entrepreneur who devotes much of his energy to building his venture, the efficiency and competence of Swiss investment managers can be a major attraction.

A fine example of a Swiss money management company is JML Swiss Investment Counselors. Founded by Jurg M. Lattman, who has been providing expert financial advice to investment professionals, bankers, economists, and private investors around the world since 1973, JML experts monitor global economic indicators and trends and provide their clients with some of the best financial advice available anywhere. They make it a simple matter to invest in Swiss annuities as well as take advantage of other global investment options.

One of the leaders in Swiss financial management is JML Swiss Investment Counsellors, a firm which offers a unique style of financial management. Clients can customize and control their own portfolios and still receive comprehensive management advice from some of the world's best experts on financial matters.

Recognizing that investors have differing goals, time frames, and tolerance for risk, JML's managers work with their individual clients to help them target their unique objectives. This naturally requires continued surveillance and analysis of worldwide economic trends, political events, financial markets, currencies, and other factors which could make some investments particularly attractive and others most unfavorable. Few individuals have the time or expertise to undertake this kind of evaluation themselves.

In any event, JML clumps the various opportunities that are available to investors into five separate categories for consideration by its Personal Portfolio Management Program clients:

Cash Equivalents. Principal and interest are guaranteed for finite terms are provided.

- Blue Chips. The investment portfolio consists of high-quality securities purchased for long-term capital appreciation potential.

- Trading. The portfolio consists of securities which are bought and sold for short-term capital appreciation.

- Trends. Often referred to a cyclical portfolios, securities are selected on the basis of economic forecasts by industry, sector, or country. The investor normally needs to wait about six years to realize significant annual returns.

- Visions. The most speculative of the five categories, investments are selected from opportunities in emerging markets and new technologies. It may take ten or more years to realize larger annual yields.
  For more information on JML write:

JML Jurg M. Lattmann AG
Swiss Investment Counsellors
Germaniastrasse 55, Dept. 212
CH-8033 Zurich, Switzerland
telephone: +41 1 368 8233
Fax: +41 1 368 8299; marking the fax "Attn: Dept. 212"

While there are many excellent Swiss investment financial managers, another one of particular note is the management firm of Weber Hartmann Vrijhof & Partners. Offering management services for the portfolios of both individuals and companies, the firm excels at providing personal attention to its clients. Weber Hartmann Vrijhof & Partners was established in 1992 by Hans Weber, Robert Vrijhof, and Adrian Hartmann. The three men have substantial experience in finance and investment. Weber managed Foreign Commerce Bank (FOCOBANK) in Switzerland for nearly 30 years as its president and CEO, Vrijhof was a former vice-president and head of FOCOBANK'S portfolio management group, and Hartmann was head of FOCOBANK'S North American subsidiary in Vancouver. Weber Hartmann Vrijhof & Partners offers specialized investment services designed to meet the individual needs of their clients.

The minimum opening portfolio to be managed by this firm is $250,000 or equivalent. The management team here normally recommends that a portion of the portfolio be invested in hard currencies other than the U.S. dollar including the Swiss franc, French franc, German mark, and Dutch guilder. Respected for their conservative approach to portfolio management, the partners assist clients with opening a custodial account at one of the major private Swiss banks, so that all client securities are held by the bank, not the investment manager.

A large percentage of their clients are based in the United States. One of their main goals has always been to get a certain portion of their clients' wealth out of the U.S. dollar and into European hard currencies such as Swiss francs, Deutschmarks, and Dutch guilders, and then build a portfolio with a mix of bonds and shares.

If you wish to learn more about the services the firm offers, contact them at:

Weber Hartmann Vrijhof & Partners, Ltd.
Attn: New Clients Department
Zurichstrasses 110B
CH-8134 Adilswil
Switzerland
Tel: +41 1 709-11-15
Fax: +41 1 709-11-13, please mark fax "Attn: New Clients Department"

Even though many investors recognize that Switzerland is a center of finance and investment, they do not realize the vast scope of the investment options offered by Swiss financial institutions and companies. Switzerland is a prime spot for investment for numerous reasons, most importantly for the strength of its currency, security of its financial system, and steady returns on investment.

Dunn & Hargitt: Offshore Managed Commodities Accounts

An offshore managed commodities account is typical of the type of investment that is available to an offshore corporation or trust, but is not available to Americans.

The Dunn & Hargitt International Group, founded in 1961, has specialized in doing research for developing Portfolio Management Programs that have the potential of providing investors with a high return on their capital by investing in a diversified portfolio trading in the commodity, currency, precious metals, and financial futures markets in the United States and throughout the world.

The Dunn & Hargitt group offers investors the possibility of participating in several of the different pools that are managed by them by investing through the investment programs that are offered by their affiliate, Winchester Life in Gibraltar, but which are actually managed by The Dunn & Hargitt International Group.

At the time of publication they are offering three possible investment alternatives, including The Winchester Life Umbrella Account (which allows 100% of a client's money to be invested in a diversified futures portfolio), The Winchester Life 100% Guaranteed Investment Account (in which Lloyds Bank acts as custodian trustee and US Government Zero Coupon Treasury Bonds are set aside to guarantee the client's capital), and The Winchester Life 150%

Guaranteed Investment Account (which is a similar program, but guaranteeing that the client will receive at least 150% of the value deposited with a maturity date at least ten years in the future).

The average net return for the 150% Guaranteed Investment Account over the last six years would have been 22% a year. The average net return on the 100% Guaranteed Investment Account over the last six years would have been 27% a year. The average annual net return for The Winchester Life Umbrella Account over the last twelve years would have been 35% a year.

The minimum accounts accepted are $20,000 for The Winchester Life Umbrella Account, $20,000 for The Winchester Life 100% Guaranteed Account, and $50,000 for The Winchester Life 150% Guaranteed Account.

Although commodities are a speculative form of investment, investors everywhere are diversifying part of their portfolios to take part in the considerable potential profit opportunities that are available in the commodity, currency, precious metals and financial futures markets. The programs devised by the Dunn & Hargitt International Group will make profits if significant trends develop in either direction; i.e. up or down. This does not mean that short term results are always profitable, however the Dunn & Hargitt proven trading systems can provide above average returns over the longer term. Their objective is to make a profit for their clients of between 20% and 40% per annum and their computer trading systems are geared to this level of performance.

For more information, contact:

The Dunn & Hargitt International Group
Department S-697
P.O. Box 3186
Road Town, Tortola
British Virgin Islands

The structure of the Dunn & Hargitt Group has been established so that no taxes are withheld from the client's investment on the international commodity, currency, precious metals and financial futures markets. Because of this they can only manage money for investors who are neither citizens nor residents of the United States, United Kingdom, or Belgium, and they will not mail their brochures to those countries.

The Dunn & Hargitt International Group offers complete confidentiality to all of its clients, and will not reveal any information on a client or on its accounts to any third parties.

Sources of Help in Forming Offshore Entities

Skye Fiduciary Services Limited

Skye Fiduciary Services Limited, based in the Isle of Man, are specialist consultants, designers and trustees and managers of offshore and international fiduciary structures.

They were established in 1991 by Charles Cain to provide specialist consultancy and management services in respect of offshore fiduciary structures, specializing in clients from or connected to the USA. The beginnings of Skye Fiduciary Services Limited go back over twenty

years. In 1972, their Executive Chairman, Charles Cain, after some years working in international banking in East Africa and the United Kingdom, returned to his native country as the managing director of a merchant bank. Three years later he resigned to start his own business, which became, by 1989, the largest corporate and trust management business in the Isle of Man. In 1989, however, as a consequence of an illness, he sold out to a large financial services group.

In 1991, fully recovered, he established Skye Fiduciary Services Limited.

From its executive office in the Isle of Man, Skye Fiduciary Services Limited provides a design and management service relating to offshore companies and trusts.

Unlike many firms that simply provide offshore corporations, one of Sky's major functions is to provide trade management services. These include:

- arranging and supervising appropriate banking and trade finance facilities and services.
- trade documentation
- exchange control planning
- double tax treaty planning.
- administration of trading entities
- arranging bank Letters of Credit and other financial instruments
- arranging leasing, invoice discounting and credit factoring
- arranging tax efficient vehicles for transferring royalties and other income flows derived from intellectual property rights.
- offshore joint venture vehicles and holding structures for US persons
- international trading structures.

For more information contact:

> Skye Fiduciary Services Limited
> Attn: New Clients Information
> 2 Water Street
> Ramsey, Isle of Man 1M8 1JP
> Great Britain
> Telephone: +44 1624 816117
> Fax: +44 1624 816645; attn: New Clients Information

ICS Trust (Asia) Limited

The other firm I can personally give my highest recommendation to is ICS Trust (Asia) Limited, based in Hong Kong.

The handover of the former British Crown Colony of Hong Kong to China is complete, and it is now called the Hong Kong Special Administrative Region, generally abbreviated to Hong Kong S.A.R., even on official documents.

As more than one local businessman has put it, "now that the politicians and journalists are gone (from covering the handover), we can get down to business." This attitude is typical of Hong Kong, still a true capitalist center. In fact, many of the wealthy who left to obtain second citizenships in Canada, Australia, and elsewhere, have now returned home to continue building their fortunes.

Offshore re-invoicing can be a very useful tool for exporters as well as importers, since it allows for the accumulation of tax-free profits in an offshore environment.

Through re-invoicing, an offshore corporation is established as an international intermediary between importers and their suppliers or between exporters and their customers. The offshore corporation can thus either 1) buy products, on behalf of the importer, at the negotiated price level and then sell, or re-invoice, these same products to the importer at a higher price, thereby accumulating profits offshore where there is no tax liability and significantly reducing profits in the country of destination where there is tax liability, or 2) buy products at discount prices from the exporter, thereby creating a very small profit in the exporting country with tax liability and sell, or re-invoice, these same products at market value prices to overseas buyers, thereby accumulating profits offshore where there is no tax liability.

In order to be profitable, offshore re-invoicing operations need to be situated in an environment where import-export transactions are either tax-free or low tax (in relation to the onshore portion of the operation).

Once the offshore company has been established, the management corporation needs to acquire the services of a post office box, a telex, a telephone, and a facsimile for its use. When all this is in place, the management company can begin re-invoicing. An offshore service provider can arrange these services.

The merchandise can be sent directly to the exporter's client or to the importer. The only functions performed in the offshore haven are the preparation and dispatch of the new invoice and the management of the funds in the way instructed by the client and complying with local regulations.

The major advantage of Hong Kong is simply that it is a real business center, not just a tax haven. One of the consequences of that is the ability to add value to services that are provided in only skeleton form in other tax havens. The reinvoicing business is a prime example. Most tax haven jurisdictions host a number of trading companies that do nothing more than reinvoicing. But one Hong Kong firm has now developed this traditional service into a "real" business mode, with an ability to arrange local trade financing. This is a healthy step away from traditional tax havenry into a true offshore business center.

ICS Trust Company Limited is part of the ICS International group of companies headquartered in Hong Kong. This highly successful entrepreneurial group was started by Elizabeth L. Thomson. Elizabeth describes herself as "a lawyer by profession" (2 law degrees, a member of 4 Law Societies internationally), "an entrepreneur by choice"! She has helped innumerable people start new enterprises in many parts of the globe and is well known in Hong Kong for her work with women entrepreneurs.

With a staff of 40 at ICS, every aspect of your business is covered from deciding to incorporate, to obtaining financing from the bank, to managing your paper work including Letters of Credit, to investing your hard earned profits! ICS is truly a "one stop shop" for entrepreneurs.

Their clients range from multinational companies for whom they run Direct Import Programs worth millions of dollars to individuals who seek tax sheltering and estate planning on an international scale. As an entrepreneurial group, they attract many entrepreneurs as clients business people who have grown their business to a level of maturity and profits that requires expansion into Asia for many diverse reasons.

Instead of just a paper thin traditional tax haven reinvoicing company, with ICS you can develop a real business in Hong Kong. With their extensive banking contacts, ICS professionals will "shop" for the best letter of credit facilities that Hong Kong's competitive banking scene can offer, likely better facilities than you can find at home. Depending upon the client, ICS can often arrange letter of credit banking facilities for clients with either a low or zero margin deposit, usually required by the opening bank. By freeing up your collateral and capital, they provide you with more purchasing power to increase sales and gain higher profits.

Most of these reinvoicing transactions are usually effected such that they are tax free in Hong Kong. There is no withholding tax on dividends so it is often possible to engage in international trade through a HK company and obtain dividends from that company tax free.

ICS will also work with international banks and factors in Hong Kong and overseas to arrange financing, secured primarily on the strength of purchase orders from your clients. Working with banks, factories, shipping companies and freight forwarders, ICS will structure a transaction to increase the likelihood of obtaining flexible, low cost facilities.

The goods do not need to go through HK for us to use a HK vehicle to pass title. Most of their clients ship from a third country direct to their own country.

Although the traditional Hong Kong focus is on firms who trade in goods, it is also possible to use these structures in cases where services are to be provided from overseas. For example, a firm could contract out a study to a company in Hong Kong. This Hong Kong company could then sub-contract out the work to a third party firm and the profit kept in Hong Kong, tax free.

If you import goods from Asia for sale to large chains, ICS can help you expand your credit facilities and increase your domestic sales by establishing and running a Direct Import Program for you. Combined with their international trade finance capabilities, the Direct Import Program is a powerful tool for generating more profits.

The primary goal of the Direct Import Program is to maximize your profits by making your customers perceive that they are buying "direct." This is achieved by:

- setting up a subsidiary company in Hong Kong
- getting your buyers to open their L/C or orders to this subsidiary
- liaising with suppliers to ensure goods are to specification.

The Direct Import Program works because of two powerful reasons:

- The trend in the retail industry is for buyers to "buy direct" from the Orient. Having a subsidiary in Hong Kong which receives orders or L/Cs greatly enhances this perception.
- Large retail chains often can obtain freight and insurance at significant savings because of their economies of scale. Selling FOB Asia can often result in a lower selling price for the importer but with the same profit.

ICS will set up and manage the subsidiary company for you, and prepare financing proposals for presentation to local banks. When everything is complete, goods are shipped directly from the Asian factory to the customer. The fact that you are now seen as an Asian supplier (and not the middleman) is often an important factor that clinches the deal. The added prestige of a Hong Kong office makes the customer think he or she is buying "direct" and therefore receiving the lowest price.

To get started, you should contact ICS with as much detail as possible about your business and its trading activities.

For further information, contact:

Mr. Kishore K. Sakhrani
Director
ICS Trust (Asia) Limited
8th Floor, Henley Building
Five Queens's Road, Central
Hong Kong
Telephone: +852-2854-4544
Fax: +852-2543-5555

Britannia Corporate Management Limited

A consulting business specializing in the formation of offshore corporations and trusts is Britannia Corporate Management Limited, located in the Cayman Islands. Its president, Gary F. Oakley, is a Canadian with 17 years of Cayman Islands residency. Britannia is licensed to manage investment holding and trading companies, real estate holding companies, patent holding companies, and insurance holding companies. It is licensed to incorporate and manage corporations registered in the Cayman Islands. As such, the firm can service as the registered office of a corporation, provide its secretary, officers and directors, or undertake any day-to-day functions that may be required. More information can be obtained by writing the following:

Britannia Corporate Management Limited
Attn: New Clients Information
P. O. Box 1968
Whitewall Estates, Grand Cayman
Cayman Islands

Britannia can be reached by fax at +1 345 949 0716, marking your fax to "New Clients Information."

You will be well-advised and well-serviced in the hands of any of these fine companies.

About the Author

Over the past 25 years, Adam Starchild has been the author of over two dozen books, and hundreds of magazine articles, primarily on business and finance. His articles have appeared in a wide range of publications around the world — including Business Credit, Euromoney, Finance, The Financial Planner, International Living, Offshore Financial Review, Reason, Tax Planning International, The Bull & Bear, Trust & Estates, and many more.

Now semi-retired, he was the president of an international consulting group specializing in banking, finance and the development of new businesses, and director of a trust company.

Although this formidable testimony to expertise in his field, plus his current preoccupation with other books-in-progress, would not seem to leave time for a well-rounded existence, Starchild has won two Presidential Sports Awards and written several cookbooks, and is currently involved in a number of personal charitable projects.

His personal website is at http://www.adamstarchild.com/

Offshore Asset Protection and Tax Deferral with Portfolio Bonds

A relatively new and little-known strategy for the wealthier investor is the offshore portfolio bond (also known as the private portfolio bond, offshore insurance bond, and similar names). This investment device combines the banking and insurance: It is a professionally managed offshore account with the benefits of both a traditional offshore trust and an offshore insurance investment. For U.S. investors with large retirement accounts, the portfolio bond can be used with a rollover account so that the portfolio bond becomes part of the retirement account, opening up a number of additional opportunities. (The minimum investment in a portfolio bond is generally 250,000 Swiss francs.)

The portfolio bond can be considered as a simple holding structure, eliminating the need for complex holding companies and trusts, and without the reporting requirements those entities require. Usually the portfolio bond is domiciled in an offshore tax haven, through which the investor (or his/her selected bank or adviser) can direct the insurance company to invest in a wide range of investment vehicles such as shares, unit trusts, cash deposits, bonds etc.

The investor enters into a contract in his name with an offshore insurance company. The offshore portfolio bond is an insurance policy or an annuity policy, not a securities account or bank account, so it does not have to be reported as an offshore account. The value is precisely the amount invested and the money grows as it is managed. The investor can select one or several money managers - either banks or independent investment advisors.

There are the usual benefits of confidentiality, individual asset allocation and strategy. But there are also unique benefits to this form of investment.

For estate planning purposes, the portfolio bond allows distributions separate from the ordinary probated estate, and allows the designation of any beneficiary (although there may be restriction is the investor is domiciled in a country that has some compulsory provisions as to legal heirs. Upon death the insurance company will transfer the money to the beneficiaries within a few days after receipt of the death certificate. Because it is an insurance policy, no power of attorney, no last will and no certificate of inheritance are required. The beneficiaries get immediate access to the money and it will be paid out according to the original directions, such as a lump sum or annual payments.

Properly structured and established in the right jurisdictions, portfolio bonds enjoy legal protection from creditors and cannot be seized or be included in any bankruptcy proceeding. The asset protection comes from the insurance part of the portfolio bond.

258

In some jurisdictions the law is very strict and the protection rock solid. If properly structured, the money is protected even if there is a judgment or court order against you. This major advantage is of particular interest to professionals, or anyone who is exposed to possible lawsuits, malpractice cases, nervous creditors or vengeful ex-spouses.

In some jurisdictions an offshore portfolio bond is secret by law. In Liechtenstein, for example, there is an insurance secrecy law analogous to the banking secrecy law in Switzerland. No information is provided to any third party (natural person or legal entity).

Unlike many other offshore investments, portfolio bonds are, in some jurisdictions, completely free of local taxes. No taxes are due if purchased in offshore jurisdictions like Switzerland or Liechtenstein. As far as income, capital gains and estate tax are concerned, the law of the investor's tax domicile is decisive.

In various countries insurance policies enjoy substantial tax benefits if correctly structured. Portfolio bonds offer utmost flexibility and can be tailor-made to fit the legal requirements for tax benefits in the investor's country.

The underlying investments can be freely selected. The portfolio can contain any investment of the investor's choice as long as the value can be established (e.g. non listed stock, real estate and shares of the client's own company etc.).

The portfolio bond provides utmost liquidity. Money can be added and taken out with a few days notice. If the investor has chosen a tax privileged solution, domestic tax law might require the funds to remain within the portfolio bond for a certain period or up to a certain age. But even then it is always possible to borrow against the portfolio bond.

The portfolio bond is a complex area of investment and tax planning, and it is important to work with an expert. A recommended contact in this field is NMG International Financial Services, Ltd., a subsidiary of The NMG Group, which was originally formed as an actuarial consulting and related financial services company in Singapore in 1991. Today, NMG has become the largest provider of financial services consulting in Asia, and has established itself as a market leader in specialist advice on emerging economies. NMG now has consulting operations and representation in 18 cities on six continents.

NMG International Financial Services Ltd. is domiciled in Zurich, Switzerland. It is an independent investment consultancy firm established to satisfy the investment and financial

protection needs of international clients. They do this by selecting outstanding Swiss and international insurance and banking products while offering exceptional advice and service.

In addition to portfolio bonds, they do provide access to Swiss fixed and variable annuities, life insurance, and related products.

Contact:
>   Marc Sola or Maria Amstad
>   NMG International Financial Services Ltd.
>   Suite 5
>   Goethestrasse 22
>   CH-8022 Zurich, Switzerland
>   Telephone: +41-1-266-2141
>   Fax: +41-1-266-2149   Please mark fax "Attention: Suite 5"

or complete their online inquiry form on the Internet at http://www.swissinvesting.com/nmg/

www.ingramcontent.com/pod-product-compliance
Lightning Source LLC
Chambersburg PA
CBHW051207200326
41519CB00025B/7035